W9-DDJ-799

3RD EDITION

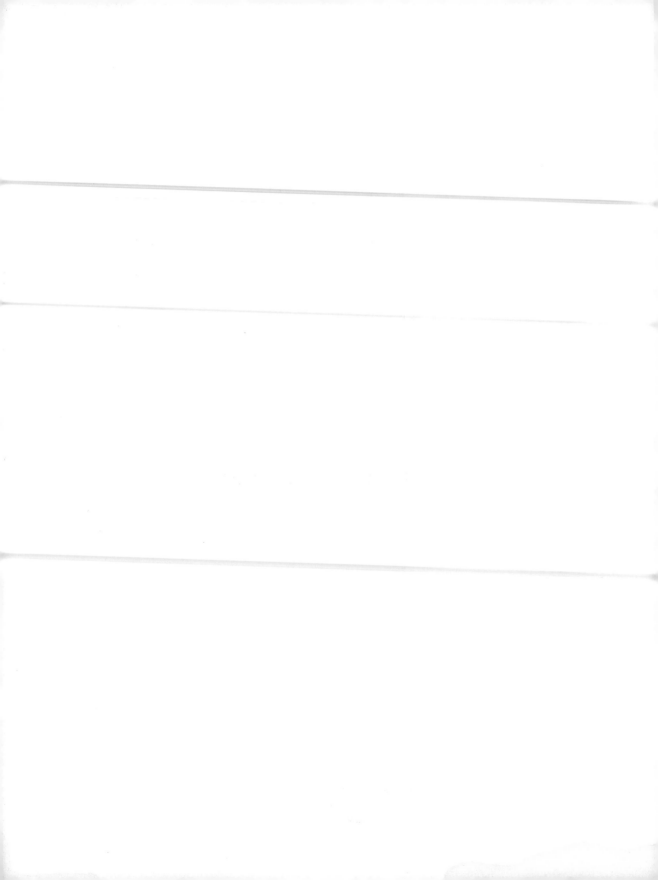

SMASHING WORDPRESS®

BEYOND THE BLOG

3RD EDITION

Thord Daniel Hedengren

WILEY

A John Wiley and Sons, Ltd, Publication

This edition first published 2012
© 2012 John Wiley & Sons, Ltd.

Registered office
John Wiley & Sons Ltd, The Atrium, Southern Gate, Chichester, West Sussex, PO19 8SQ, United Kingdom

For details of our global editorial offices, for customer services, and for information about how to apply for permission to reuse the copyright material in this book please see our website at www.wiley.com.

A catalogue record for this book is available from the British Library.

ISBN 978-1-119-94271-9 (paperback); ISBN 978-1-119-94366-2 (epdf); 978-1-119-94368-6 (emobi); 978-1-119-94367-9 (epub)

Set in 10/12 Minion Pro Regular by Indianapolis Composition Services

Printed in U.S. by Command Web

Who do you dedicate a book on WordPress development to? Your parents? Your pets? Your lovers? Your slightly mentally deficient alter ego who wears tights and that weird interpretation of the WordPress *W*?

None of the above. What do they know about this stuff anyway? Except that weird *W* guy, of course. He's a genius, in his own sense.

I'd like to dedicate this book to the WordPress community, the core team, and all developers out there who are contributing to the ecosystem with themes, plugins, and blog and forum posts. You're all doing something to keep this platform of ours — yes, ours — propelling forward, and this is important. What we're part of here isn't just some web publishing platform thingy to help the major corporations save money. It isn't about creating new blogs, sites, or startups on a budget. It's not even about the accessibility of modern web technology.

This is about being able to express yourself and giving your fellow man the same opportunity. WordPress and open source are as much about free speech and power to the people as anything else. This is what keeps me going, keeps me invested, and keeps me interested in this platform.

So there. This book is dedicated to the possibilities a platform such as WordPress offers for everybody. Use it; speak your mind; make a difference. And have fun while you're at it!

Thord Daniel Hedengren

PUBLISHER'S ACKNOWLEDGMENTS

Some of the people who helped bring this book to market include the following:

Editorial and Production
VP Consumer and Technology Publishing Director: Michelle Leete
Associate Director–Book Content Management: Martin Tribe
Associate Publisher: Chris Webb
Assistant Editor: Ellie Scott
Development Editor: Dana Lesh
Copy Editor: Dana Lesh
Technical Editor: Justin Tadlock
Editorial Manager: Jodi Jensen
Senior Project Editor: Sara Shlaer
Editorial Assistant: Leslie Saxman

Marketing
Associate Marketing Director: Louise Breinholt
Senior Marketing Executive: Kate Parrett

Composition Services
Compositor: Indianapolis Composition Services
Proofreader: Susan Hobbs
Indexer: Potomac Indexing, LLC

ABOUT THE AUTHOR

Thord Daniel Hedengren is addicted to words, which led him to launch his first online newsletter in 1996. It all went downhill from there, with dozens of sites and a career as an editor and freelancer in Sweden and abroad.

Going international all started with a blog post, which led to a book deal with Wiley, which in turn resulted in the *Smashing WordPress: Beyond the Blog* book and its follow-up *Smashing WordPress Themes: Making WordPress Beautiful,* and an even stronger voice in the WordPress community. You're holding the third edition of the critically acclaimed *Smashing WordPress: Beyond the Blog* in your hands right now. This is really just the beginning because that word obsession keeps Thord spewing out new stuff.

When not obsessed with words, Thord and friends are building cool websites using Word-Press at his web design firm Odd Alice. He also edits magazines and writes freelance articles for both print and web publications, in both Swedish and English. You can follow everything Thord on http://tdh.me.

Thord lives in the land of kings, Sweden.

CONTENTS

INTRODUCTION

Writing a book about WordPress isn't the easiest endeavor that you could tackle. When my editor and I first started discussing this project, the idea was to create something that not only acts as an introduction to web developers and professionals who want to utilize the power of the WordPress platform, but also sparks the minds to create things beyond the obvious.

Or go *beyond the blog*, as it were, which is also the subtitle of this book. That subtitle still stands, as this book reaches its third edition.

The whole point is really to prove that WordPress is so much more than a blog-publishing platform. You can build just about anything with it, and you should as well if you like fast deployments and great flexibility. It is not always the perfect choice, but it should definitely be considered at all times. The ease with which you can both build and use this platform is a selling point, just as is the living community that can back you up when you run into problems and the fact that this is open source at its finest.

Although I think that anyone with some knowledge of HTML, CSS, and PHP can learn WordPress from this book, it is important to remember that this is not a beginner's book. I start at a pretty high pace to make sure that even professionals get the fundamentals right. It is so easy to stick to familiar territory and do things the way they've always been done, instead of learning to do them right. And although having the basics in here will help anyone get started with WordPress, you really should know some HTML and CSS and have at least a grasp of what PHP is and does. If those are alien concepts to you, I urge you to read up on them first.

That being said, *Smashing WordPress: Beyond the Blog* is indeed written with the idea that anyone with the suitable background can learn WordPress using this book, as well as take the platform beyond the obvious. When you're done with this book, you'll be ready to build just about anything using WordPress.

To convey this message, *Smashing WordPress: Beyond the Blog* is divided into four parts.

PART I: GETTING STARTED WITH WORDPRESS

The first part tackles the WordPress essentials, from install to what actually makes the system tick. It gives you everything you need to get started with WordPress, albeit at a slightly quicker pace than traditional beginner books. However, coverage doesn't stop there because there are a lot of things you should be aware of when getting started with WordPress, such as security measures, moving the install, and so on. The idea is to not only help beginners get started, but also enlighten current users to the problems and options available.

PART II: DESIGNING AND DEVELOPING WORDPRESS THEMES

WordPress themes are what the user sees; they are the skin of your site and control how the content is presented. When you work with a site running on WordPress, you'll spend a lot of time altering the theme files to get WordPress to do what you want. This second part not only introduces the technical features of themes, but also gives you the required knowledge to start building your own.

PART III: USING PLUGINS WITH WORDPRESS

The third part is all about developing WordPress plugins. The fact that you can extend WordPress with plugins means that there really is no limit to what you can do with the platform. If you can make it work in PHP, you can run it in WordPress, more or less. This also means that this part of the book is highly conceptual, dealing with the basic communication between your plugin (which in fact is your PHP code) and WordPress itself.

PART IV: ADDITIONAL FEATURES AND FUNCTIONALITY

The fourth part is all about using WordPress for purposes other than blogging. Here you look at how WordPress can be used as a CMS to power more traditional websites, and you build a couple of sites from the ground up to prove that the platform can indeed do other things than just run bloggish websites.

This part is all about making you think differently about WordPress. The goal is to do away with all your thoughts about WordPress as only a blogging platform. This is a publishing platform — nothing else.

In this part, you'll also find a selection of nifty tricks and techniques that you can use to further enhance your site. A lot of the things you might need in your WordPress projects have been done already, and this part gives you a little peek into that.

PART V: APPENDIXES

In the appendixes, you'll find a selection of plugins and themes that can make your life easier. The idea here is to provide you with some tools that will make building great WordPress sites a little easier. Because there are so many options out there in terms of plugins and themes — which is a good thing, mind you! — this is meant as a time-saving shortcut and not a complete listing of everything that is great. Hopefully, you'll find what you're looking for here, or at least get an inkling as to what you should be looking for.

START THINKING AND GET PUBLISHING!

Smashing WordPress: Beyond the Blog was written with the web developer in mind, but anyone who has fiddled a little bit with HTML, CSS, PHP, and WordPress can benefit from this book. It is truly a breeze to get started in WordPress, and WordPress is all you'll need to begin rolling out your projects. After that, you'll have to get your hands dirty, modifying or building themes and creating the necessary plugins to build the site you've envisioned.

In other words, start thinking and get publishing with WordPress, whether you're building the next Engadget or *Wired,* or something entirely different.

1

THE ANATOMY OF A WORDPRESS INSTALL

INSTALLING WORDPRESS IS neither difficult nor time-consuming, and the instructions available on WordPress.org are more than adequate to guide you through the basic install. With the extra knowledge that you'll get in this chapter, however, you can supercharge your WordPress setup with themes and plugins. WordPress is the bricks and mortar of the site, but themes and plugins are what make it really tick.

Remember that "WordPress" in this book refers to the standalone version of Word-Press available for free from http://wordpress.org. Don't get this mixed up with Automattic's hosted version on http://wordpress.com. This book is all about the main version available from wordpress.org, with more specifically version 3.3 in mind.

THE BASIC INSTALL

Installing WordPress is a breeze; the PR talk about a "five-minute install" is right on target. In fact, the only reason that the install should take even that long is the fact that uploading the files sometimes takes time due to slow Internet connections or sluggish web hosts. Most likely, you'll already have a fair amount of experience with basic WordPress installs, so I'll be brief on this matter.

First, make sure that your system meets the minimum requirements. The most recent set of requirements can be found at http://wordpress.org/about/requirements. If your host supports PHP 5.2.4 or higher and runs MySQL 5.0 or higher, you'll be fine. However, you should make sure that your host has `mod_rewrite` installed because that will be needed for prettier links.

There are two ways to install WordPress: the guided way and the manual way.

A third installation method is the one-click install offered by some web hosts. One-click installs are briefly described later in this chapter. There's also a fourth option for installing WordPress using Subversion or Git, but I'll skip that in this book.

THE GUIDED INSTALLATION METHOD

WordPress is one of the easiest open source publishing systems out there to get up and running. Just download the most recent version of WordPress (from http://wordpress.org/download), extract the archive file (usually you're grabbing a zip file), and then upload the files within the wordpress folder to the place where you want to install WordPress, using FTP. For example, if you want to install WordPress on `mysite.com`, you just upload the files to the root folder for `mysite.com`.

Point your web browser to the install directory (which would be `http://mysite.com` in this example) and provide the requested information, as shown in Figure 1-1. You'll need your database name, username, and password, and possibly also the address to the database server if you or your host have an external address. Your host will supply this, along with everything you need to actually set up your database. This might involve a web interface such as cPanel or phpMyAdmin or the use of SSH or your software of choice. Consult your host for more information on how you work with MySQL and set up databases.

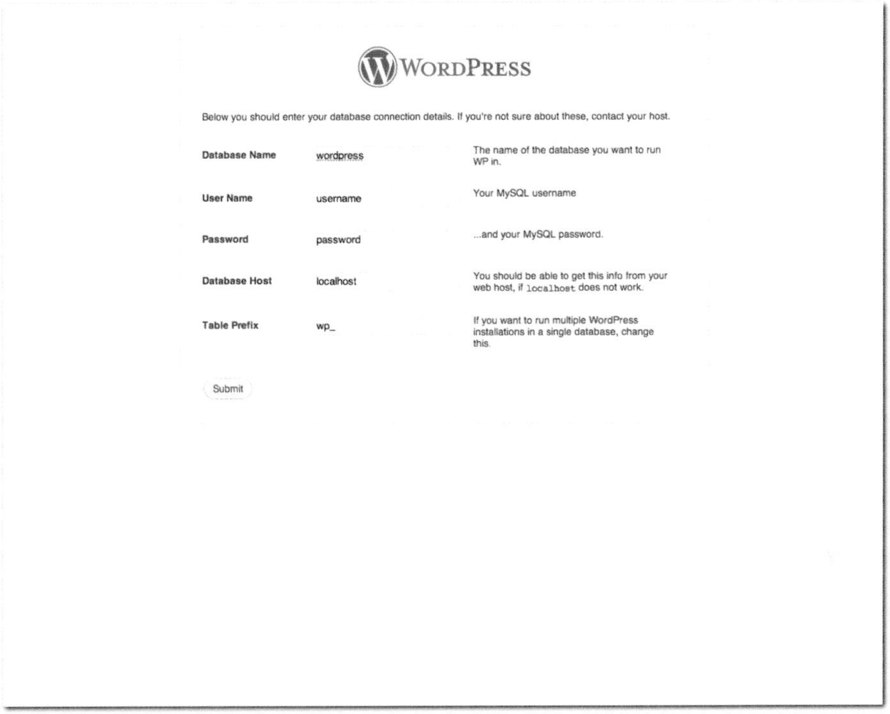

Figure 1-1: The install interface.

Click Submit to get to the site setup, shown in Figure 1-2. On this screen, fill out the name of the site, the admin account credentials you would like, and so on. Make sure that you use a working e-mail address and keep track of your password. After you have entered all the requested information, click the Install WordPress button. You're just about done. Log in — and there you have it: WordPress is up and running!

The guided install doesn't provide options to make WordPress run in any language other than the default, English. If you want your installation to run in a language other than English, consult the manual install procedure detailed in the following subsection.

Figure 1-2: Fill out the details.

THE MANUAL INSTALLATION METHOD

For a manual install, you'll need the following:

- The most recent version of WordPress (available from http://wordpress.org/download).
- A MySQL database as a user who has write privileges. (Ask your host if you don't know how to set this up.)
- Your favorite FTP program.

To install, unzip your WordPress download and upload the contents of the wordpress folder to your destination of choice on your server. Then open the wp-config-sample.php file and find the database parts where you fill out the database name and the username and password with write privileges. This is what wp-config-sample.php looks like:

```
// ** MySQL settings - You can get this info from your web host ** //
/** The name of the database for WordPress */
define('DB_NAME', 'database_name_here');

/** MySQL database username */
define('DB_USER', 'username_here');

/** MySQL database password */
```

```
define('DB_PASSWORD', 'password_here');

/** MySQL hostname */
define('DB_HOST', 'localhost');

/** Database Charset to use in creating database tables. */
define('DB_CHARSET', 'utf8');

/** The Database Collate type. Don't change this if in doubt. */
define('DB_COLLATE', '');
```

Next, still in wp-config-sample.php, find the section that deals with secret keys. This part starts with commented information text titled "Authentication Unique Keys" and is followed by four lines (as of this writing) where you'll enter the secret keys. This is a security function to make your install more secure and less prone to hacking. You'll need to add these keys only once, and although they can be entered manually and can be whatever you like, there is an online generator courtesy of WordPress.org that gives you random strings with each load. Just copy the link (https://api.wordpress.org/secret-key/1.1/salt) to the generator from your wp-config-sample.php file and open it in your favorite web browser. You'll get a page containing code looking something like Figure 1-3.

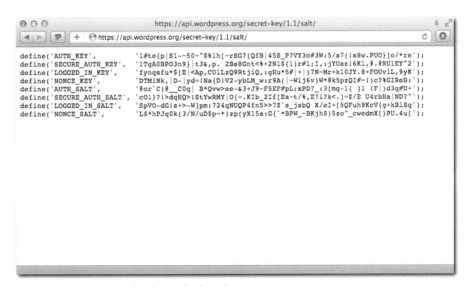

Figure 1-3: Your random key, ready to be copied and pasted.

Copy the contents from the generator page and replace the following code in wp-config-sample.php with them:

```
define('AUTH_KEY',          'put your unique phrase here');
define('SECURE_AUTH_KEY',   'put your unique phrase here');
define('LOGGED_IN_KEY',     'put your unique phrase here');
define('NONCE_KEY',         'put your unique phrase here');
define('AUTH_SALT',         'put your unique phrase here');
```

```
define('SECURE_AUTH_SALT', 'put your unique phrase here');
define('LOGGED_IN_SALT',   'put your unique phrase here');
define('NONCE_SALT',       'put your unique phrase here');
```

By replacing the code with the lines from the generated page, you've made your install a little bit more secure from those nasty hackers.

The last thing you may want to change in wp-config-sample.php is the language. WordPress is in English (U.S. English, to be exact) by default. To change the language, you'll need to upload a language file to your wp-content/languages/ folder. The language files are in the .mo format; you can find most of them at http://codex.wordpress.org/WordPress_in_Your_Language. You also need to alter the following little snippet in wp-config-sample.php to let WordPress know what language you want:

```
define('WPLANG', '');
```

You need to add the language code: This is the same as the language file, without the file extension. So if you want your install in Swedish (the language of kings), you'd download the sv_SE.mo file, upload it to wp-content/languages/, and then pass the language to the WPLANG function, like this:

```
define('WPLANG', 'sv_SE');
```

This won't necessarily display any themes or plugins you use in your language of choice, but WordPress and its core functionality will be, as will any code that supports it. (You'll learn about localization of themes and plugins in Chapter 6.)

That's it! Rename wp-config-sample.php to wp-config.php and point your web browser to your install location. You will see a link that initiates the install procedure, in which you'll fill in the blog title and the admin user's e-mail address and choose whether or not the blog should be open to search engines for indexing. (Most likely this will be the case, but if you want to fiddle with it first, disable it; you can enable it in Settings later.) After this, you'll get an admin username, a random password (save that!), and, hopefully, a success message, along with a link to the blog.

Not very complicated, right?

USING AN EXTERNAL DATABASE SERVER

One of the most common causes of a failed WordPress install is that the MySQL database is located on a separate server. If you're getting database connection errors and you're quite sure that both the username and password for the database user are correct, along with the full write capabilities, then this is most likely the problem.

To fix this, just find this code snippet in wp-config.php (or wp-config-sample.php if you haven't renamed it yet) and change localhost to your database server:

```
define('DB_HOST', 'localhost');
```

What the MySQL server may be called depends on your host. It may be `mysql67.the superhost.com` or something entirely different. Just swap `localhost` with this and try running the install script again. If you need to pass a specific port, that is usually done by adding a colon and then the port number.

Naturally, if you can't find your database server address, you should contact your web host and ask for details.

OTHER DATABASE SETTINGS

You may want to consider some more database options before installing WordPress. (Probably not, but still, they warrant mention.)

First, you may want to change the database character set and collation. These options tell WordPress what character language the database is in, and it should almost always be UTF-8. This is also the default setting in wp-config-sample.php; hence, you won't need to fiddle with it unless you have a special need to do so. If you do, however, this is what you're looking for:

```
define('DB_CHARSET', 'utf8');
```

That's the character set, with UTF-8 (obviously spelled out as `utf8` in code) as the default. Most likely, you won't (and shouldn't) change this, but there might be situations when you need to, so keep this in mind for reference.

The collation, which is basically the sort order of the character set that WordPress will apply to the MySQL database in the install phase, can be changed in this line:

```
define('DB_COLLATE', '');
```

It is empty here, which means that it will pass the character set in `DB_CHARSET` as the collation. By default, that is UTF-8, but if you need this to be something specific, you can add it like this:

```
define('DB_COLLATE', 'character_set_of_choice');
```

USEFUL WP-CONFIG.PHP FEATURES

The previous changes and settings might be the most commonly used parts of wp-config.php, but there are other things you can do. Beginners beware here because wp-config.php is no playground. If you fiddle too much with this file and make a mistake somewhere, you can take down your entire site. If you do intend to play with wp-config.php, do it in a test install until you know for sure what you're doing.

With that said, there are some useful things you can do with wp-config.php. One of these is overriding the site URL and WordPress path usually set in the database (in the wp_options table) using the General Settings page. You can use WP_SITEURL to set the site's URL directly in wp-config.php if you like:

```
define('WP_SITEURL', 'http://mydomain.com/blog/');
```

Likewise, if you want to define the path to the WordPress install, you can do that directly in wp-config.php as well, using WP_HOME:

```
define('WP_HOME', 'http://mydomain.com/wp/');
```

Both these techniques will override the settings within the WordPress admin interface, as will WP_CONTENT_URL. As the name hints, this will define where the wp-content folder is located, making it possible to move it someplace else:

```
define('WP_CONTENT_URL', 'http://mydomain.com/files/wp-content');
```

Notice the lack of the trailing slash in the path to the wp-content folder. There are similar possibilities for the plugin directory; you'll soon note that most of these path settings work the same way. Naturally, you can use PHP or the server settings themselves to point these to the correct place dynamically, but I'll not delve further into that.

Post revisions are saved versions of posts and pages. You can disable them if you like:

```
define('WP_POST_REVISIONS', false );
```

Should you want to keep them around but just save up to five revisions, for example, you just change false to a number:

```
define('WP_POST_REVISIONS', 5 );
```

WordPress autosaves posts and pages within the admin interface. By default, the autosaves occur every 60 seconds, but you can change the frequency of these autosaves to whatever you like, such as to every 180th second:

```
define('AUTOSAVE_INTERVAL', 180 );
```

WP_DEBUG is a great tool to use when you need to see what went wrong. It is the way to view database errors and get warnings about using deprecated (no longer supported) functions or files:

```
define('WP_DEBUG', true);
```

Setting WP_DEBUG to false is just like not using it at all, meaning that errors that don't have any direct impact on your site will be suppressed.

If you want to enable network support, more commonly referred to as *multisite,* you do that in wp-config.php as well:

```
define('WP_ALLOW_MULTISITE', true);
```

This opens up the necessary settings and features in the WordPress admin interface. I'll get to that later in this book, so pay it no more heed than this for now. For even more tricks and settings available to the wp-config.php file, consult the Codex page at http://codex.wordpress.org/Editing_wp-config.php. Here you'll also find instructions on how to log errors on a live site, using `WP_DEBUG_DISPLAY` and `WP_DEBUG_LOG` to make sure that your error messages aren't shown to all the visitors but rather saved to a log file.

A FEW WORDS ON INSTALLERS

Some web hosts offer installers that will get your WordPress install up and running with just a click from within the web host admin interface. The most popular of these one-click installers is probably Fantastico. At first, a single-click install sounds like a really good idea because you don't have to fiddle with config files or anything; it'll just slap the blog up there, and you can get started.

However, take a moment to do some research before going down this route. The most important aspect to consider is what version of WordPress the installer is actually setting up. Old versions shouldn't be allowed because they are outdated and, at worst, a security hazard. After all, with every WordPress release, several security holes are jammed shut, so it is not just about releasing funky new features for your favorite blogging platform.

Installers such as Fantastico are great and can save time if they do install the most up-to-date version. If you find one that does use the latest version, you should still do a little investigating to make sure that other users haven't reported any serious problems. If the coast is clear and you really don't want to do the five-minute manual install, then by all means go for it.

After having installed WordPress using an installer, you should use the built-in upgrade feature or perform upgrades manually using FTP should your host not support the automatic one. Make sure that the installer doesn't do something strange with the install that stops you from doing this: You don't want to be tied to the installer script for updates.

MOVING THE WORDPRESS INSTALL TO A DIFFERENT DIRECTORY

Sometimes you want to put your WordPress install in its own folder. This will help avoid clutter in your web hosting environment by removing all those WordPress files and folders from the root of your domain, and it will make it easier to manage your various web endeavors. Suppose you want to add other web software installs; you may have a hard time finding the files you need if they're all mixed in together (although it helps that everything WordPress at this level is named *wp-something*). It just gets messy if you want to do anything other than just use WordPress.

Installing to a subfolder is the same as installing to the root of a domain, so I won't go into that. The idea is to have the WordPress install in a subfolder but have the blog being displayed as if it were in the root folder, while keeping the root folder on the server clean. You can either install WordPress to the subfolder directly or install it to the root folder and then move the files to a subfolder. How you decide to tackle it is up to you; both ways are easy.

The following instructions assume that you have already installed WordPress in your root folder and now want to move it to a subfolder. For this example, suppose that you have WordPress installed in the root folder (`domain.com`) and want it to be in a subfolder called wpsystem instead, while keeping the actual site in root. This means that when people visit `http://domain.com`, they'll see your WordPress site, but when you log in and manage it, you'll be working in the wpsystem folder (or `domain.com/wpsystem/wp-admin/`, to be precise).

You should set up permalinks before doing this because you'll want them to work regardless of whether you use a subfolder. The permalink options, shown in Figure 1-4, are found under Settings → Permalinks.

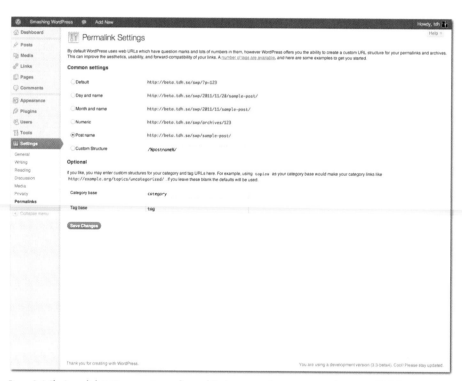

Figure 1-4: The Permalink Settings page is one of several Settings pages where you can tweak your install's behavior.

To move your WordPress install to the new directory, first create the wpsystem folder. Then go to the General Settings page and change the WordPress address URL field to `http://domain.com/wpsystem` to reflect your new folder, and the Blog address URL field to `http://domain.com`, where you want your site to be. Next, click the Update button and move all the WordPress files to their new directory at `http://domain.com/wpsystem`, except for the index.php and .htaccess files, which should be where you want your site to be (`http://domain.com`).

When the files have been moved, open index.php and locate this code snippet:

```
require('./wp-blog-header.php');
```

And replace it with this code snippet:

```
require('./wpsystem/wp-blog-header.php');
```

As you can see, the code now points to the wpsystem folder instead and to the wp-blog-header.php file.

Log in to the WordPress admin interface (which is now on `domain.com/wpsystem/wp-admin/`) and update the permalinks, and there you have it.

HACKING THE DATABASE

Most of the time you needn't worry about the database; WordPress will take care of it for you. There are database changes between versions sometimes, but program updates will take care of everything, and other than keeping a backup of your content, the database can be left to live its own life.

That being said, if something goes wrong, you may need to make some edits in the database to fix it. Common issues are password resets, weird URLs as a result of a failed move, domain name changes, and widget-related issues.

> *A word of caution: Before moving on, you should remember that making alterations in the database is serious stuff. There are no undos here; what is deleted is deleted for good. Even if you know what you're doing, you should always make a fresh backup before altering anything at all. If you don't know your way around a MySQL database and phpMyAdmin, don't mess with the database. You will break things.*

LEARNING WHERE EVERYTHING IS

Finding your way around the WordPress database is pretty easy. It consists of 11 tables, which in turn are full of content. Just browsing the database should answer most of your questions, and you can make any edits on the spot if you know what you're after. Naturally, there is a full database description in the documentation (http://codex.wordpress.org/Database_Description), and you should consult that whenever you need to find something.

The 11 main tables are

- wp_commentmeta: Metadata for comments
- wp_comments: Contains all comments
- wp_links: Contains added links and link data
- wp_options: The blog options
- wp_postmeta: Metadata for the posts
- wp_posts: The actual posts
- wp_terms: Categories and tags
- wp_term_relationships: Associates categories and tags with posts
- wp_term_taxonomy: Descriptions for categories and tags
- wp_usermeta: User metadata
- wp_users: The actual users

All these tables are important, of course, but if you need to fix or change something directly in the database, chances are that it is in wp_options (for blog settings, like URLs and such), wp_posts (for mass editing of your blog posts), or wp_users (for password resets and such).

FIXING ISSUES BY HACKING THE DATABASE

Most of the time, WordPress will behave as expected, and you can stay clear of the database. However, should you get the dreaded blank page when visiting your site, it is probably a widget issue, and a possible solution is to clean out the widgets in the database. The widget data is hiding in the wp_options table. Exactly what you need to do and what the various widgets are called depends on what plugins you have, so tread carefully. Most likely, the data is named in a way that seems logical according to the plugins you use, and with that in mind, you should be able to find what you're looking for. This may sound a bit hazardous, but it is worth giving it a go should you encounter a blank screen on your blog after an upgrade. If you need help, the support forums on WordPress.org are a good resource.

Another issue you may want to resolve in the database is changing or resetting a password for a user. This is best done from the WordPress admin where it is simple enough, but if you for some reason can't access the admin area, the database is the way to go. You can't actually retrieve the password from the database because it is encrypted and all you'll see is gibberish, but you can change it to something else. Just remember that passwords need the MD5 treatment, which can be done through phpMyAdmin or just about any MySQL managing tool you may use. Basically, what you do is type the new password in plain text and choose MD5 for that particular field. You'll end up with a new line of gibberish, which actually says what you typed in the first place. Again, if this sounds scary to you, don't do it without learning more first!

Finally, you may want to mass edit your posts. Maybe you've got a new domain and want to change the source for all images you've used over the years, from `olddomain.com/wp-content/image.jpg` to `newdomain.com/wp-content/image.jpg`, for example.

There are plugins that will help you with this, so you should probably check those out first. If you're comfortable with the database, though, you can run a SQL query to search for all these elements and replace them with the new ones. It could be something like this:

```
UPDATE wp_posts SET post_content = REPLACE (
  post_content,
  'olddomain.com/wp-content/',
  'newdomain.com/wp-content/');
```

This code searches the wp_posts table for any mention of `olddomain.com/wp-content/` and replaces it with `newdomain.com/wp-content/`. That in turn fixes all the image links in the example. Nifty little SQL queries for batch editing can come in handy, but remember: There are no undos here — what's done is done — so make sure that you've made a backup of the database before even considering doing these things.

BACKING UP

Anyone who has lost data in a hard drive crash or similar event knows the importance of backing up, and it goes without saying that this applies to your online content as well. Backing up WordPress is actually a two-step process because your blog consists of both a database (with all the content) and static files (image uploads and other attachments). Then you have your theme, your plugins, and so on that you may or may not have altered but still don't want to lose because doing so would mean that you would have to collate them all over again. In fact, with the inclusion of automatic updates within the admin interface in WordPress (a great feature in itself), backing up these things has become even more important.

The only elements you can lose without causing too much trouble is the core WordPress files. These you can always download again, although you may want to keep a copy of wp-config. php somewhere safe.

Several options are available for your database backup needs. The most obvious one would be to use a web interface such as phpMyAdmin and just download a compressed archive containing the data. This process is described later in this chapter, so I'll let the details be for now. However, you need to remember to do this on a regular basis, and that may be a problem. Also, phpMyAdmin and similar database management interfaces aren't exactly the most user-friendly solutions out there, and most people would rather not mess around with the database more than they truly have to.

Enter the wonderful world of WordPress plugins, where you can get backup solutions that'll automatically e-mail your database's content to you, sync it to an external service, or something similar. There are several plugins available; some preferred ones are listed in Appendix A, "Essential WordPress Plugins," at the end of this book.

That's the database content; now for the static files. This part is very simple: Just keep backing up the wp-content folder. This folder contains all your uploads (images, videos, and other files that are attachments to your blog posts), along with your themes and plugins. In fact, it is the only part in the WordPress install that you should have been fiddling with, not counting the wp-config.php file, the .htaccess file, and possibly the index.php file in the root folder. Backing up wp-content will save all your static files, themes, plugins, and so on, as long as you haven't set up any custom settings that store data outside it.

So how can you back up wp-content? Unfortunately, the simplest backup method, which of course is downloading it using an FTP program, relies on your remembering to do so. Some web hosts have nifty little built-in scripts that can send backups to external storage places, such as Amazon S3 or any FTP server, really. This is a cheap way to make sure that your static data is safe, so you should really look into it and not just rely on remembering to perform an FTP download yourself. In fact, these built-in solutions often manage databases as well, so you can set up a backup of that as well. Better safe than sorry, after all.

The last stand, and final resort should the worst happen to your install, is your web host's own backup solution. There is no way anyone can convince me to trust that my web host, no matter how good it may be, will solve any matter concerning data loss. Some hosts are truly doing what they claim, which may be hourly backups, RAID disks, and other fancy stuff, but even the most well-thought-out solution can malfunction or backfire. Most hosts have some automatic backup solution in place, but what happens if the whole data center is out for some reason, or there's a power outage? You may not think that this could happen today, but if Google can go offline, so can your web host.

In other words, make sure that you have your very own backup solution in place. Hopefully, you'll never have to use it, but if you do, you'll be happy you thought it through from the start.

SWITCHING HOSTS

Sometimes you need to switch web hosts. You may outgrow your host and need more power for your site (congratulations!), or perhaps the quality of service has declined. Whatever the reason, it is not very uncommon that you want to move your site from one host to another. This involves everything from pointing domains to actually moving the files for your site, not to mention the database. I just cover the WordPress parts of the move here, so if you need help moving your domain, e-mail, and stuff like that, by all means contact your new host, who should be able to give you the help you need.

There are several ways of moving to a new server. My preferred method is using the Export/Import functionality found under Tools in WordPress admin.

USING THE EXPORT AND IMPORT TOOLS

Previously, there were a few exporters and importers in WordPress admin, but these have been moved to plugins, so you might be prompted to download and install a plugin. Go ahead and do that if necessary. Also, before moving, make sure that your WordPress install is up to date. Then go to Tools and choose to export the content, as shown in Figure 1-5. You'll get a file containing the data.

Figure 1-5: Exporting data.

Next, install WordPress on your new server. Any decent web host will have alternative URLs to access your content on the server online, without actually having to have your domain pointing to them. When you've got a running WordPress install, delete the automatic pages and posts because these won't be overwritten. You want the install to be clean.

After that, download the wp-content folder from your old server and upload it to your new one. Now you've got all your images, plugins, themes, and so on in place. There is a built-in option in the post importer that will try and download the images from your posts to your new server, but it fails more often than not, so it is better to manage the static files in wp-content manually using your favorite FTP program.

Finally, you're ready to import the exported file from your old server. Go to Tools (see Figure 1-6) and go through the Import Wizard, taking care that your exported file from the old server is up to date. Import it, let the script chew through the content, and then you're all done! Verify that everything is working properly, give yourself a pat on the back, and then redirect your domain to your new server. You may have to edit your new blog's settings because it may have taken URLs from the web host's internal system, so change them to correspond with your blog's domain name. While waiting for the domain to be pointed to your new server, the blog will break, of course, but then again, your old one is still working. You may want to close comments on it, though, because those will be "lost" when the visitor is suddenly pointed to the new server with your new WordPress install, which is based on the content of your old one at the point when you exported the file.

Figure 1-6: WordPress can import from a number of systems, but you want WordPress this time because that's what you exported from.

WHEN EXPORT/IMPORT WON'T WORK

Unfortunately, there are times when the Export/Import way won't work — usually because there is just too much content for PHP to parse in the import. This is possibly due to your host's server settings and is only a problem if you have a big blog.

If this is the case, you'll have to do things a little bit differently. Ideally, you can re-create your environment identically on your new server, with the same database name and the same username and password to manage it. If you can do this, moving will be a breeze. All you have to do is get a dump from the MySQL database using your favorite MySQL admin tool and then import it into the new one. This probably means using phpMyAdmin and the backup instructions from the WordPress Codex (found at http://codex.wordpress.org/Backing_Up_Your_Database). Here's how you do it:

1. Log in to phpMyAdmin and select the database you want to back up.
2. Click the Export tab (shown in Figure 1-7) in the top menu.
3. On the left side, make sure that all the necessary tables are marked. (The Select All link will help.) This would be all of them, unless you have other stuff in the same database as well.

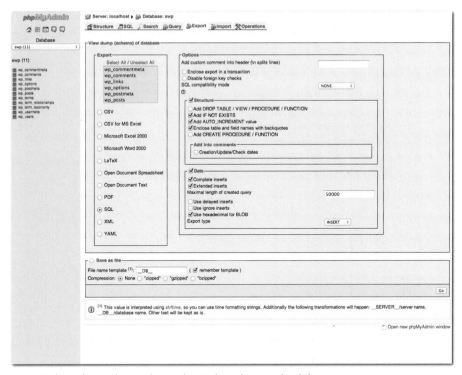

Figure 1-7: phpMyAdmin is a lot more daunting than WordPress, but it gets the job done.

4. On the right side, select the Structure check box and then select Add DROP TABLE, Add AUTO_INCREMENT Value, and Enclose Table and Field Names with Backquotes. Also click the Data check box, but leave the choices within unchecked.

5. Scroll down, click Save As File, and pick the kind of file that you want to download — probably a zipped one.

6. Click the Go button. This will download the database, which you will import on your new server.

7. Importing a dump in phpMyAdmin is even easier. Make sure that you have created a database with the same name, as well as the username and password, as you had on your previous server. This means that you won't have to alter the wp-config.php file.

8. Import the dump to the new database by logging in with your favorite MySQL manager. If this is phpMyAdmin, just select the database and choose the Import tab (which is next to the Export one) at the top. Use the importer to find your downloaded dump and import it.

9. Finally, download your full WordPress install from your old server and upload it in an identical manner to your new one. Again, give it a spin using your web host's temporary addresses and make sure that everything seems to be working. Point the domain to the new server, and when it resolves, everything should be running smoothly.

However, you may not be able to re-create the environment in exactly the same way. If this is the case, just alter wp-config.php accordingly; most likely, it is the database name, username, and password, as well as possibly the need for an external database server, that you'll have to edit.

Moving WordPress from one server to another may seem scary at first, but it isn't as bad as it once was. Sure, if you've got a big blog and aren't comfortable doing stuff in database admin interfaces such as phpMyAdmin, then this may be a bit much. Get help, or give it a go yourself. Just make sure that you have all the backups you could possibly need, and don't mess things up on your old (current) server, but rather on the new one. After all, you can always just create a new database and WordPress install there and give it another go.

HOW TO MAKE YOUR WORDPRESS INSTALL MORE SECURE

There are a few simple things you can do to make your WordPress install more secure, and a few that are pretty much hardcore. The first and foremost task, however, is to keep WordPress up to date. What each new version really does depends, but it could possibly remove security holes, bugs, and other exploits that can make your install vulnerable, and not updating regularly means that you won't get these fixes.

> *You should also make sure that you've got your secret keys set in the wp-config.php file. Those make the install more secure. See the installation process earlier in this chapter in the section "The Basic Install" for more on this. Usually they're set, but if you used an installer, they might not be, so it doesn't hurt to check in wp-config.php and add them if needed.*

USERS AND PASSWORDS

The first thing I do after having installed WordPress is create a new user with admin privileges and log in with that user instead of the previously default "admin" user. Why? Because everyone knows that if there is a user named *admin,* then that account has full admin capabilities. So if you wanted to hack your way into a WordPress install, you'd start by looking for the admin user to try to brute force a login. After you're in via this method, you can do anything you want. So it's worth getting rid of the admin user after you have logged in for the first time and created a proper account because it has fulfilled its purpose.

That being said, deleting the admin user won't guarantee that hackers won't find another user to build their attempts on. If you have user archives on your blog, those will give you away. One solution would be to not display these or any links to an author page (other than ones you've created outside of WordPress's own functionality), but what do you do if you feel you need them? All in all, there are tons of places where usernames could be obtained within an install, and most themes use them in some fashion, which makes it even easier. That being said, there really is no reason to have a user such as admin that everyone will know has administrative rights lying around.

The solution is to be sparse with account credentials. There is no need to have an administrator account for writing or editing posts and pages; an editor's credentials are more than enough. Granted, should an account with editor status be hacked, then it will be bad for your site because the editor can do a lot of things, but at least it is not an administrator account, and that will keep the worst things at bay. And besides, you keep backups, right?

Passwords are another obvious security risk. You've probably been told to use a strong password, to make it long and to use letters, numbers, special characters, and so on. Do that: The more complicated the password is, the harder will it be to crack.

SERVER-SIDE SECURITY STEPS

The MySQL user for your WordPress database, which incidentally shouldn't be shared with any other system, doesn't actually need all write privileges. In fact, you don't need to be able to lock tables or indexes or create temporary tables, references, or routines. In other words, you can limit the capabilities somewhat to make the system more secure.

Some people will also recommend that you add extra logins using Apache's .htaccess. I don't do that myself because those login forms are annoying. Besides, there are plugins that can do the job better. (See Appendix A for more information.)

One step you may want to take is to make sure that there is an empty index.php or index.html file in every folder that doesn't have an index file. This is usually the case by default in WordPress, but it doesn't hurt to check. What this does is make it impossible to browse the folders directly, something that some web hosts support.

You could do the same thing by adding the following code to your .htaccess file if you prefer to disable directory browsing globally:

```
# Disable directory browsing
Options All -Indexes
```

The `-Indexes` prevents directory browsing, so changing it to `+Indexes` would enable it instead.

Another server-side issue is forcing SSL encryption when logging in to the WordPress admin. This means that the traffic sent when you're doing your thing in the admin interface will be a lot harder to sniff out for potential bad guys. It's pretty easy to force SSL; just add this code snippet to your wp-config.php file, above the "That's all, stop editing! Happy blogging" comment:

```
define('FORCE_SSL_ADMIN', true);
```

SSL won't work without support from your host. Some web hosts give you all you need to start this service from within their admin interface, but others will have to activate it for you and may even charge you for it. While I'm on the subject, make sure that you access your host with FTP using a secure connection, such as SFTP. If your host doesn't support a more secure FTP connection, ask them to enable it for you.

Finally, making sure that your files and folders have the appropriate permissions will go a long way. Files should be owned and writable by the user account and be set to 644. Folders should be set to 755. You'll need to be able to use CHMOD or use FTP software that can set file and folder permissions to get these settings right. Ask your host if you're uncertain about these things. You can read more about files, folders, and permissions in the Codex at http://codex. wordpress.org/Changing_File_Permissions.

LOOKING AHEAD

It doesn't matter if this is your first foray into the wonderful world of WordPress or if you're an experienced user and developer. The important thing is that you have the basic installation figured out, have made it secure, and understand the publishing beast that is WordPress. From here on, you'll start building sites and creating plugins to achieve your goals.

Next up is diving into what makes WordPress tick. That means that you'll get to play with the loop, start looking at themes and plugins, and activate that idea machine in the back of the head that comes up with all those cool adaptations. The brilliance of WordPress is that it is very flexible and that you can build so many things with it; just thinking about the possibilities will undoubtedly inspire you.

If you have a WordPress install to play with (preferably something that isn't too public because you may break something), get your sandbox set up and get ready to dive into the WordPress syntax.

2

THE WORDPRESS SYNTAX

NOW THAT YOU'VE got your WordPress install set up, it's time to do something with it. This chapter is all about getting to know more about WordPress. It doesn't go into depth on every file in the system but rather serves as an introduction to how WordPress outputs content. You'll learn about the important template tags as well as

conditional tags and how you can control their output and actions by passing parameters. You also take a look at themes and what they consist of, to help you further grasp how WordPress sites are built.

It's time to get started.

WORDPRESS AND PHP

From here on, it will help if you know a little bit about PHP, as well as HTML and CSS. If these are alien concepts to you, be sure to read up on them at least a bit. A good, albeit a bit technical, place to start is the official specification documents from W3 (www.w3.org) and Zend's PHP 101 course (http://devzone.zend.com/article/627). You don't need to be an expert, but a little knowledge is definitely needed.

WordPress is written in PHP, a popular scripting language offering developers the possibility to build just about anything. If you're even the least bit knowledgeable in PHP, you'll quickly find your way around WordPress and the various functions that it offers on the plugin and theme development end of things. That being said, you don't need any prior PHP experience to do funky stuff with WordPress. Granted, you won't be able to create WordPress plugins without knowing PHP, but you can certainly make things happen with the built-in template tags used in themes, and that will get you a long way. These template and conditional tags help developers create things with WordPress, without having to write brand-new functions for everything.

Does this sound like Greek to you? Don't worry, even if you've never written a *Hello World!* PHP script, you'll be able to build just about anything content-driven with WordPress before you're done with this book.

THE WORDPRESS CODEX

The WordPress Codex (see Figure 2-1), which is the manual in wiki form found on http://codex.wordpress.org, will be very helpful when you start working with the code. You should become familiar with it and add a bookmark to the main page. Whenever you branch out from the examples in the coming chapters, or when you want to know more about a concept, the Codex is where you'll find the information needed to keep moving. Whereas the Codex contains basic information and tutorials, you'll often find yourself returning to a few reference listings, such as the template tags (http://codex.wordpress.org/Template_Tags), which are explained shortly, and the function reference (http://codex.wordpress.org/Function_Reference) for your more advanced needs.

THE WORDPRESS CORE

Any good content management system (CMS) will keep its core files separate from other files so that you don't ruin the code that makes the system work, and WordPress is no exception. For WordPress, the *core* refers to the internal files that make WordPress work. These are the parts of WordPress that you should never touch, as any update to the platform will overwrite your changes. Messing around with WordPress core files can also break theme and plugin functionality, as well as open up your install for malicious use from outsiders. In short, don't touch the WordPress core. The only core file you should ever touch is wp-config.php (see Chapter 1, "The Anatomy of a WordPress Install"), which contains the necessary details for your install.

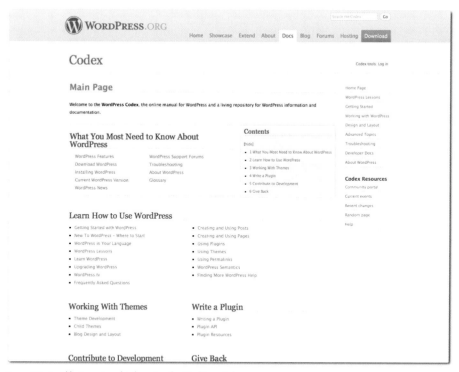

Figure 2-1: You'd better get used to browsing the WordPress Codex.

Outside of the core is the wp-content folder, where you'll drop themes as well as plugins and uploaded files. All these things work on top of WordPress, so there's no risk of ruining the actual system files (unless you've installed malicious code, but that's a completely different matter) when you develop a site. In fact, the whole idea is that the only time you're editing or even doing anything outside of the wp-content folder is when you're installing the system — and possibly when moving the install files to a different folder. Naturally, there is some cool stuff that requires editing the .htaccess file, and you'll come across plugins that want you to do things outside of wp-content. That's fine, of course, although you should be a bit cautious. In short, whenever you're told to edit a file outside of wp-content, beware. Creating new files is one thing; editing existing files is a no-no, wp-config.php and .htaccess excluded.

The whole point, however, is that the WordPress core is untouchable. Don't mess with it unless you really need to, and if you do, you should rethink and rethink again because chances are there's a better solution. Hacking the core is bad, and that's why the wp-content–based theme and plugin structure are so good. All that being said, you can do whatever you want with WordPress as it is open source software. Fork it and create your own publishing platform if you want to. For this book, I'll assume you don't want to do that, but rather just use WordPress, which means that you won't touch the core files. The option is there if you want or need it, though.

THEMES AND TEMPLATE FILES

To put it simply, a *theme* is a skin for your blog. You can choose from many different themes to have WordPress display your content in different designs, as shown by Figures 2-2 and 2-3, which display the same post using two different themes.

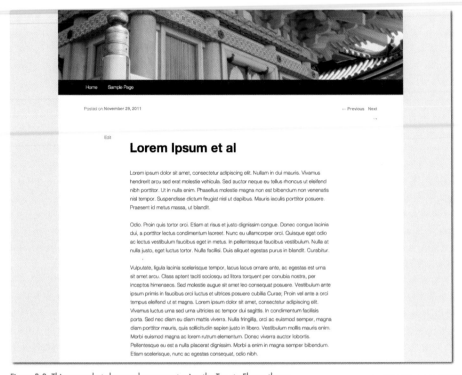

Figure 2-2: This screenshot shows a dummy post using the Twenty Eleven theme.

You can use a really basic theme that simply outputs the content in the default presentation scheme, or you can completely alter the way your site's content is displayed, giving it whatever presentation you like.

A theme must always contain a style sheet file called *style.css*. This file holds your basic style, the theme name, and data. In addition to the style sheet, you'll have a bunch of PHP files, some absolutely necessary and some just good practice to make life easier on you or to make interesting stuff happen. These PHP files are called *template files.* You'll find index.php, which is the main file for listings and search results and the fallback file for situations in which there is no other template file available. Other common template files include sidebar.php, which holds the sidebar content, comments.php for comment functionality, and header.php and footer.php files for your site's header and footer, respectively. You may also have single.php for single post view, page.php for static WordPress pages, and maybe a dedicated template file for search results (search.php), along with your category listings in category.php, and so on. Add any number of page templates that you can apply to WordPress pages, and you get a tiny little glimpse of how versatile WordPress is. Technically, your theme can consist of just a style.css and an index.php file, but most themes have more template files than that.

Figure 2-3: The same post from Figure 2-2, but viewed in the Notes Blog theme.

With your template files, and the WordPress functions as well as plugins and traditional PHP code, you can make your site behave in just about any way imaginable. Don't want the commenting capability at all? Just remove the code! Maybe you want a specific product page to look completely different? Then create a page template and style it any way you like. It goes on and on, and later in the book, you'll see how to build sites that are nothing at all like the common blog.

Just to make things a little more complicated, you can have even more functionality in your themes. The functions.php file can provide plugin-like features to your theme, and just about any template file can contain PHP code that does things beyond WordPress. I haven't even gotten started on *widgets* yet, which are areas where you can drop elements from within the admin interface. There is also the option to keep the loop, which is the code that outputs the main content in your theme, separate from your other template files using loop.php and such. The loop is covered in-depth in Chapter 3, "The Loop."

Figure 2-4 shows the Manage Themes page in the WordPress admin interface. From this page, you can change your theme with a single click or get new themes from the WordPress.org theme repository.

Figure 2-4: The WordPress admin interface makes theme management easy.

The best way to learn about themes is to use them. Install a theme on a test blog, play around, and then take a look at the files it consists of. Don't bother with images and forget about the style sheet as well (it is just a design), but do take a look at index.php and both header.php and footer.php to understand the way themes are built. It's not very complicated: First, you load index.php (or whatever main template file is used; this could also be single.php, category.php, or something else), and then that file will load files such as header.php, footer.php, and possibly sidebar.php, for example.

You'll play with themes later, but for now all you need to know is that it's in the theme's template files that the magic happens. There you'll find the code that outputs the content you've posted using WordPress, and although various themes may look and behave differently, they are just displaying the same thing in different ways, thanks to the template files.

USING THE TEMPLATE TAGS

Although WordPress is written in PHP, it is in fact a framework in itself. You can use PHP to do stuff with your WordPress theme or plugin, but most of the functionality is managed with template tags. If you open a theme file (just about any file with the extension .php, such as index.php or single.php), you'll find a lot of PHP-like functions, such as this one:

```
<?php bloginfo( 'name' ); ?>
```

This is a template tag, and it outputs the blog's name. The PHP part, which consists of `<?php` at the beginning and `;  ?>` at the end, tells WordPress to process whatever's inside it — in this case, the template tag `bloginfo()`. Within the parentheses, you'll find the parameter, passed inside quotation marks. In other words, `'name'` is the parameter in this example (which would output your blog's name).

In the following example, you'll use `get_template_directory_uri()` to get the URI (without a trailing slash, as you can see) for the template folder so that you can reference an image. The following code outputs an image called smashing.gif in a theme file:

```
<img src="<?php get_template_directory_uri(); ?>/smashing.gif" />
```

You'll recognize the `img` HTML tag. `get_template_directory_uri()` outputs the path to the theme's folder. And then you just add the smashing.gif filename to complete the path, and you've got a potentially working image path in your theme. Of course, you would need the image in the theme folder as well.

So template tags are basically PHP functions that can handle parameters to do different things. Some have default values, others don't, and some have more settings for you to play with than others. Most of them will work anywhere in your WordPress theme files, but some need to be within the loop. (The loop is basically the code that outputs the content, such as posts or pages. Loops are examined in the next chapter.)

You'll find a complete listing of template tags in the Codex at http://codex.wordpress.org/Template_Tags. Consult it whenever you need to do something out of the ordinary within your themes or when you want to alter things in an existing theme. Each template tag is described, along with usage and sample code to help you understand it. This is the beauty of WordPress: You can actually copy and paste your way to a different result without knowing any PHP at all.

THE INCLUDE TAGS

There are a couple of template tags that you'll find in just about any theme template file. The *include tags* are simply PHP include functions used to load files, which in turn might output the content of the necessary files within your theme. In other words, they are just a way to make it a bit easier to grab that header, footer, and sidebar:

```
<?php get_header(); ?>
<?php get_footer(); ?>
<?php get_sidebar(); ?>
```

The include tags differ from other template tags in that what you're doing is including other files, rather than adding a specific type of functionality or element. In other words, the include tags include the template files that contain the template tags.

You'll find them in your theme's index.php file, for instance, and they automatically include header.php, footer.php, and sidebar.php, respectively, where the tags are placed. These three tags actually supports alternative headers, footers, and sidebars by adding a string to the tag, like this:

```php
<?php get_sidebar( 'left' ); ?>
```

This would include sidebar-left.php rather than the default sidebar.php, so you'd need to create that file, of course. Should sidebar-left.php not be present, `get_sidebar()` will revert to sidebar.php. The same principle goes for `get_header()` and `get_footer()`.

You might also find the `get_template_part()` include tag, fetching the loop from its own template file, like so:

```php
<?php get_template_part( 'loop', 'index' ); ?>
```

The first parameter, `loop`, tells WordPress that it is supposed to get a loop template. The second parameter tells WordPress to look for a loop template called *loop-index.php*. If the second parameter had been `page` instead of `index`, WordPress would have looked for loop-page.php instead. Should loop-index.php not be found, WordPress will default to loop.php. I'll dig into this in Chapter 3. The same logic will work for other parameters as well, so it doesn't have to be `loop`.

Should you want to include other files such as an alternative template for your content, for example, you can use `get_template_part()` for that as well:

```php
<?php get_template_part( 'content' ); ?>
```

Just remember that `get_template_part()` is meant for including template parts, nothing else. Should you for any reason want to use a traditional PHP include, you would combine it with `get_template_directory()`, which is something that you shouldn't do within themes.

Finally, there's an include tag for the comments, which any good theme has in comments.php. Should there be no comments.php file, WordPress will include one from wp-includes/theme-compat/comments.php instead, which is a fallback file that the system provides. Just put the `comments_template()` tag where you want comment functionality and remove it where you don't think you need it:

```php
<?php comments_template(); ?>
```

If you want to, you can load an alternative file for comments by passing a parameter to `comments_template()`. You can also choose to separate comments by type (true or false), which would mean that regular comments and pingbacks would be separated if set to true. You can read more about `comments_template()` in the Codex at http://codex.wordpress.org/Function_Reference/comments_template.

PASSING MULTIPLE PARAMETERS TO A TEMPLATE TAG

Outputting content with template tags is easy enough. Some won't take parameters at all, and others, like `bloginfo()`, will just take one. Others, however, will take several parameters.

Two really useful template tags for bloggers are `edit_post_link()` and `edit_comment_link()`. They basically do the same thing, which is to add an edit link to posts or comments so that you (when logged in as a user having the necessary credentials) can fix errors quickly by clicking the edit link: This will take you to the admin interface where you can correct your error or censor that particularly nasty (but most likely valid) comment. These tags are especially handy if you have disabled the top admin bar.

To use these tags, put them in your theme's file along with the posts/comments. Both tags work the same way. The tags need to be within the loop, which is discussed in the next chapter, but for now, all you need to know is that `edit_post_link()` goes with the code that outputs the posts, and similarly, `edit_comment_link()` goes with the code that outputs the comments.

For example, this is how `edit_post_link()` looks when passing its default parameters:

```
<?php edit_post_link(); ?>
```

If you put that code in your theme, you'll get a link that says "Edit This" wherever you put the code, and that's it. Suppose you want this link to show up on its own row, say "Admin" before the actual link, and say "Edit this post" rather than the "Edit This" default. Simple — just use this instead:

```
<?php edit_post_link( 'Edit this post', '<p>Admin: ', '</p>' ); ?>
```

`edit_post_link()` supports four parameters. The first one is the link text, `'Edit this post'` in this case, and the second is what goes before the link. Remember, you wanted a separate paragraph for the edit link, and you wanted it to say "Admin" in front, so here's `'<p>Admin: '`. (Note the blank space after the text to make some room in front of the link.) The third parameter is what goes after the link, which is just `'</p>'` because you need to close the `<p>` tag. Finally, the fourth parameter is `$id`, which would be the post ID, and is omitted here.

In other words, `edit_post_link()` can handle four parameters, and they are passed, in this sense, to speak a little PHP:

```
<?php edit_post_link( $link, $before, $after, $id ); ?>
```

Remember, parameters are usually passed within quotation marks and separated with commas and a space to make them more readable.

Not all that complicated, right? All you need to know is which parameters there are to pass and in what order they need to be. The order is important: Without the correct order, you might get the wrong text linked and would definitely break your design, or at least the validation of the site.

FUNCTION AND QUERY-STRING STYLE ARGUMENTS

Now look at something a bit more complicated:

```
<?php wp_tag_cloud(); ?>
```

This template tag will output a tag cloud displaying at most 45 tags, with the smallest one at the font size of 8 pt (points), and the largest at 22 pt. They are displayed in a flat listing and sorted by name, in ascending order. You know this because these are the default values, and there are a lot of them, as you can see in Table 2-1. In fact, wp_tag_cloud() can pass 14 arguments to a parameter.

Table 2-1: Default Tag-Cloud Parameters

Parameter	Description	Default Value
smallest	Smallest tag size	8
largest	Largest tag size	22
unit	What font size unit is used	pt
number	How many tags to display at most	45
format	How to display the tags	flat
separator	What goes between the tags	whitespace
orderby	How to order the tags	name
order	How to sort the tags	ASC
exclude	What tags to exclude	none
include	What tags to include	all
link	Should links be edit or view	view
taxonomy	The basis for the tag cloud	post_tag
topic_count_text_callback	Lets you create a custom tooltip for links	default_topic_count_text
echo	Whether to show the tag cloud or return it	true

If you compare these values to the description of the default output of wp_tag_cloud(), you'll see that they are passed without your needing to pass any arguments manually.

Now try altering the tag by changing some arguments within this parameter. There are two ways to pass arguments to the `wp_tag_cloud()` parameter: function or query-string style. If you've been using WordPress for a while, you have no doubt seen them both. Function style is the preferred method today, but you'll run into query-string style as well.

First, pass one argument to the parameter for `wp_tag_cloud()` using query-string style:

```php
<?php wp_tag_cloud( 'unit=px' ); ?>
```

This is easy enough to understand; you've just set `unit` to `px`, an argument you learned about in Table 2-1 (or through the Codex at http://codex.wordpress.org/Function_Reference/wp_tag_cloud). When passing one, or even a few parameters, the query-string style makes sense at first glance. If you want to pass more parameters, just add an ampersand (`&`) between them, within the parameter, with no spaces. Change the tag order to `count` rather than `name`:

```php
<?php wp_tag_cloud( 'unit=px&orderby=count' ); ?>
```

Simple enough, right? Now switch to the preferred function method instead and bear with me on this because the reason will become apparent in a little bit. First, the preceding example, using function style, would mean that you save the arguments in an array and then pass that to `wp_tag_cloud()` instead, like this:

```php
<?php
    // The arguments
    $args = array(
        'unit' => 'px',
        'orderby' => 'count'
    );
    // Pass the arguments
    wp_tag_cloud( $args );
?>
```

The same arguments as before are stored in the array, which goes in `$args`, which in turn is used as the parameter for `wp_tag_cloud()`. Simple as that.

You can add even more just by separating the various parameters for the template tag with ampersands. Now randomize the order, changing the smallest tag to 10 px (because the default 8 is a bit small when you're using pixels rather than points) and the largest to 24 px.

Here's the code in function style:

```php
<?php
    // The arguments
    $args = array(
        'smallest' => 10,
        'largest' => 24,
        'unit' => 'px',
        'orderby' => 'count',
        'order' => RAND
```

```
    );
    // Pass the arguments
    wp_tag_cloud( $args );
?>
```

Simple enough to read and work with, right? Now compare that to the query-string style:

```
<?php
    wp_tag_cloud( 'smallest=10&largest=24unit=px&orderby=count&order=RAND' );
?>
```

This is less than user friendly. The lesson is that there is such a thing as query string, but if you're passing multiple arguments to a parameter, then use the function style. It will make things easier on you. And, as noted previously, this is currently the preferred method.

To recap this code: The order value, RAND, is in capitals. That is intentional; it is just how you pass data to order (the other options are ASC for ascending and DESC for descending). Also, you probably noticed that both smallest and largest were placed before the unit option. It is good form to put the various parameters in the order they are described, as you'll be able to find them more easily whenever you need to edit the code or look something up.

UNDERSTANDING DATA TYPES

There are three types of data you can pass to template tags: strings, integers, and Booleans. Although the template tag's definition (as stated in the WordPress Codex wiki) will tell you exactly how to pass data to that particular template tag, it's important to know what's behind it so that you can select the correct type.

The first data type is *strings,* which are lines of text. The bloginfo('name') example is a string because you tell it that 'name' is the parameter. Strings are found within single or double quotation marks (they do the same thing), although the single version is a lot more common and the one used in the examples in this book.

The second data type is *integers.* Integers are whole numbers, such as 55900 or -3. You can pass them inside quotation marks if you want, but you don't need to. They are commonly used when you need to fetch something that has an ID, which is a lot of things. You'll stumble onto template tags as well as conditional tags that do this later on.

Finally, there are the *Boolean* parameters, which are used when the value can be only true or false. You can pass this information with all capitals (TRUE or FALSE), all lowercase letters (true or false), or using numbers (1 being true and 0 being false).You cannot put Boolean values within quotation marks; they always stand on their own. For example, the get_calendar() template tag takes only one instruction, and that is whether to display the full day or just a one-letter abbreviation. true is the default value and displays the first letter in the name of the day (for example, *M* for "Monday"), so if you want to output Mon instead of M, you need to set get_calendar() to false:

```
<?php get_calendar( FALSE ); ?>
```

Another example of Boolean instructions is the `the_date()` template tag, usually used to output the date of a post. You may, for example, want to use that information in your own PHP script instead and display nothing from the `the_date()` tag. You can change the output format of the date (the first string in the parameter), what goes before the outputted date (the second string), and what comes after it (the third string). The fourth instruction you can pass is a Boolean that tells the system whether to output (`true` by default). Say you want to output a year-month-day date (Y-m-d according to the PHP manual for date functions; WordPress can take them all) within a paragraph. The code would look like this:

```
<?php the_date( 'Y-m-d', '<p>', '</p>' ); ?>
```

However, if you want to use this with PHP outside of the WordPress functions for some reason, outputting nothing, you can set it to `false` with the `echo` option that this template tag has. This goes last and is a Boolean value; hence, you won't put it within quotation marks:

```
<?php the_date( 'Y-m-d', '<p>', '</p>', FALSE ); ?>
```

This would give you the same result, being year-month-day within a <p> tag, but it would output nothing, so if you want to use it with your own PHP code, this is the way to go about it. In other words, this is for assigning `the_date()` to a variable and not for direct output.

Remember that strings are text within quotation marks, integers are whole numbers, and Boolean parameters are true or false without any quotation marks. With this in mind, it'll be a lot easier to understand the template tags you'll use to build really cool WordPress sites later on.

> *Don't hardcode the date format in* `the_date()` *or* `the_time()` *unless you know what you're doing. These are settings that are available in WordPress, so most of the time you don't need to worry about them at all.*

CONDITIONAL TAGS

Conditional tags are very handy. You use them in your theme's template files, and as the name implies, they are for setting various conditions. In other words, you can use them to display different things depending on the situation. A very good example is the conditional tag `is_front_page()`, which checks whether the page you're on is the front page. Use it to output a greeting because that is the polite thing to do:

```
<?php
    if ( is_front_page() ) {
        echo '<p class="welcome">Hey you, welcome to the site. I love new
          visitors!</p>';
    }
?>
```

This would output a paragraph with the class `welcome` and the text within. You have a simple test to determine if the page `is_front_page()` and then an echo with the paragraph if it is in fact the home page. That's very straightforward, so you can go on to try something else.

Suppose you've got a specific category that should have a different sidebar than the rest of the site. You can check for that with the conditional tag `is_category()` and then output another sidebar if appropriate. Whenever it is another page within the site, use the traditional `get_sidebar()` include tag.

The following code will replace the `get_sidebar()` PHP snippet in the theme's template files wherever it matters, which probably means files such as index.php, category.php, and single.php:

```php
<?php
    if (is_category( 'very-special' )) {
       get_sidebar( 'special' );
    } else {
       get_sidebar();
    }
?>
```

Here you're asking if the category is `very-special`, which is the category slug (used in permalinks and such) in this case. You could have asked for the category ID or the category name as well, and although an ID is pretty foolproof, the code is a lot easier to read if you use the slug because it is *nice-named,* meaning that it can't contain nasty special characters and such. If the category is in fact the one with the `very-special` slug, use the include tag `get_sidebar('special')`, where `'special'` is a parameter indicating that you want sidebar-special.php.

Should the category not be the one with the `very-special` slug, the code will move on to the `else` clause and tell WordPress to use the normal `get_sidebar()` include tag, which means that you'll include sidebar.php.

This is all very simple stuff, but it clearly shows how conditional tags can be used to create dynamic pages. You'll do fun stuff with them later.

WHY IS THIS GREAT?

Conditional tags are a great way to get some rudimentary control over your theme. Because you can ask WordPress where the visitor actually is, and under what circumstances, that means you can react to it. Including a different sidebar is a simple example, but you could use conditional tags far beyond that. Features such as loading different template parts depending on where you are on the site means that you can cut down on the necessary amount of template files — or just make your theme a tiny bit more dynamic. Combining conditional tags with a simple `if` clause will get you a long way.

Something often overlooked by beginners is that knowing where the visitors are, and in what situation, also tells you where they are not. If you need to do something for everything that is not a particular circumstance, then you can use the `if not` solution, which means that you'll put an exclamation mark before the conditional tag, like this:

```php
<?php
    if ( ! is_front_page() ) {
        // Do something for every page but the front page
    }
?>
```

This will let you do something whenever `is_front_page()` is false, which would be on every page but the front page.

NEXT UP: THE LOOP

Now that you know that WordPress sites are built on themes, which in turn consist of template files containing different kinds of tags that do funky stuff, it's time to start manipulating the content. This is done with the *loop,* a PHP snippet that is the heart and soul of WordPress. Although you can do a lot with WordPress without knowing about the loop, you certainly have to understand it if you want to truly bend the platform to your will. You can use the loop to make posts show up in a different order and generally display things the way you want.

A lot of the things you'll want to do with WordPress are only possible within the loop. And that in turn means that you sometimes need multiple loops with custom outputs. Or, at the very least, you need to figure out where the loop begins and ends so that you can add the cool template tags and plugin features you no doubt will find or create on your own.

There's no way of getting around it; the loop is important. Better hop to it, then.

CHAPTER

3

THE LOOP

NOW THAT YOU have WordPress installed and the theme concept under control, it's time to look at what really makes the system run. This chapter will teach you about the *loop,* which basically is a PHP query that talks to WordPress and makes it output the content requested. The chapter starts with some basic loop usage and then branches out to multiple loops and some nice little trickery used within to achieve various effects.

You need to understand the loop to create really cool WordPress sites. Although you won't need to be an expert, you should grasp what it does. That way, you can research the many functions and features available when you run into a solution that requires custom content output.

UNDERSTANDING THE WORDPRESS LOOP

The loop is the heart of WordPress, and it resides in your theme's template files. Although you can in fact have a theme without the loop, it would make the fluidness of the content handling, such as displaying the latest posts and browsing backward, quite difficult to pull off. Some template files — for example, 404 error pages — don't have the loop at all, but most do.

Some template tags work only within the loop, so you need to be able to identify it. This is easy, as you will see in the next subsection.

THE BASIC LOOP

If you want to create sites using WordPress, you need to understand the loop. Luckily, the basic one is pretty easy. Here's what you see to begin with:

```php
<?php if ( have_posts() ) : while ( have_posts() ) : the_post(); ?>
```

And at the end:

```php
<?php endwhile; else: ?>
    <p>Some error message or similar.</p>
<?php endif; ?>
```

Actually, you don't need that error message part other than in template files that are used to output errors, but because a lot of themes do have it, it is included here. It can be a "Posts not found" error or a search result message telling the visitor that that particular query didn't return any hits. Technically, the loop starts with `while` and ends with `endwhile`, but it is common for themes to include the `if` statement as well for error messages and such. It is included here for convenience's sake.

What follows is a fully functional loop, with the common template tags for outputting post content. You'll find it, or something pretty similar to it, in either the index.php file or a loop. php file in most themes:

```php
<?php if ( have_posts() ) : while ( have_posts() ) : the_post(); ?>
    <div id="post-<?php the_ID(); ?>" <?php post_class(); ?>>
        <h2><a href="<?php the_permalink(); ?>" title="<?php
          the_title_attribute(); ?>">
            <?php the_title(); ?>
        </a></h2>
        <?php the_content(); ?>
    </div>
<?php endwhile; else: ?>
    <div class="post">
        <h2>Error!</h2>
        <p>Something went wrong! Please try again.</p>
    </div>
<?php endif; ?>
```

Naturally, you'd want a more comprehensive error message than the one in this code, but that's not the point right now.

The basic loop checks whether there are any posts to return, and in turn the loop is controlled by the global blog settings (how many posts to display and such) and your whereabouts on the blog. A single post would return just one post (the one you want, presumably), whereas a category listing would return the number of posts specified in the WordPress settings, but only the ones that belong to that particular category.

If there are posts, a `while` loop is started, and as long as there are posts to return, as controlled by the situation and settings, posts will be returned and displayed. When the `while` loop is done (all posts that should be returned have been output), it ends with `endwhile`, and then the loop ends with `endif`.

Should there be no posts that match the criteria of the particular situation, the `else` clause is called, and that's when the error message (or similar) will be output (or nothing at all, if there is nothing defined). After that, the loop ends.

So the loop actually loops content from the database, based on the WordPress settings and any criteria that the page you're on may bring. Makes sense, doesn't it?

SEPARATING THE LOOP USING THE LOOP.PHP TEMPLATE FILE

There was a time when the loop would always be in the theme's index.php template file, and possibly several other template files as well. These days, not all themes include the loop in index.php. By using the `get_template_part()` include tag (mentioned in Chapter 2, "The WordPress Syntax") along with a separate loop template file, you can separate the loop from your various templates, reusing it when appropriate. In fact, whereas some template files will contain the loop itself and not rely on `get_template_part()` for loop inclusion, others will use loop.php but render the content differently depending on what part of the site is being displayed. A category archive often looks different from a single post, but both of these could be generated by the same loop.php template file (albeit not exactly the same code within said loop.php template) or from completely different files altogether. It is all a matter of where on the site you are and how many template files you've got in your theme.

Recall from Chapter 2 that `get_template_part()` will include the loop.php template file, and that is obviously where you would put the loop.

So the example loop code in the previous subsection wouldn't be found in index.php at all. Instead, you would have this:

```php
<?php get_template_part( 'loop', 'index' ); ?>
```

This will look for loop-index.php first, and failing that, it'll revert to loop.php. You'd put your loop code in either of those files. The purpose of using loop-index.php (in this case) would be to enable you to control the loop on a specific page (index.php in this case), while keeping the general loop (found in loop.php, the one WordPress reverts back to) free of custom stuff for specific pages. So if you want a completely different loop for your category archives, for example, you'd use the following line in category.php, the template file used in the example:

```
<?php get_template_part( 'loop', 'category' ); ?>
```

This looks for loop-category.php first, where you'll put your custom loop, hence making loop. php clean and slim. You'll put this to good use with child themes in Chapter 5, "The Child Theme Concept." For now, you can be content knowing that this is a great way to separate the loop code, which can be quite extensive, from the various template files.

> There's no law that says you need to use loop.php or even that kind of separation of the loop. You could include just about anything with `get_template_part()`, and you might prefer to have the obvious parts of the loop within the actual template file, including specific parts depending on what post format a post can have, for example.

A FEW WORDS ABOUT WP_QUERY

`WP_Query` is the heart of the loop, even though you don't see it spelled out in the most basic code. It is really a class that handles all the loop magic, and you'll find it in wp-includes/query. php if you want to dig deep within the WordPress core files. Refer to the Codex page (http://codex.wordpress.org/Function_Reference/WP_Query) for an explanation of all the properties and methods that go with `WP_Query`.

The basic loop uses `WP_Query`, or rather it uses the default `$wp_query` object. This means that when you use necessities such as `have_posts()` and `the_post()`, you'll in fact use `$wp_query->have_posts()` and `$wp_query->the_post()`. In other words, `have_posts()` and its friends take it for granted that you want to be using `$wp_query`. Whenever you go outside `$wp_query` by creating your own queries, as you'll do in the multiple loops section as well as in examples and adaptations further in the book, you'll have to create an object for it, like this:

```
<?php $brand_new_query = new WP_Query(); ?>
```

Here, you're loading everything into `$brand_new_query` instead of the default `$wp_query`, and that means that you can do stuff outside of the main loop.

Most parts of WordPress connect to the `WP_Query` class, including templates and conditional tags. You can tap into and alter things within the `WP_Query` class, but you should refrain from it if there is an available solution already. As you master WordPress, there may come a time when you want to do things that are truly out of the box, but that's a whole other matter.

USING THE LOOP

Now that you've established where you need the loop (in post listings, no matter if it is one or several) and that you can run several at once, the question becomes how to use the loop most effectively. For one thing, maybe you don't want to display the full post in your category listings — maybe you just want an excerpt? This brings you back to the template tags, and the ones that control the output of the loop.

This section takes a quick look at the most frequently used tags. Chances are, you'll want to display and link the title of the various posts. This little code snippet is present in just about every theme's template files that list several posts, and sometimes in templates that just display one as well:

```
<h2>
    <a href="<?php the_permalink(); ?>" title="<?php
      the_title_attribute( array(
          'before' => 'Permalink to: ',
          'after' => '')
      );
    ?>">
        <?php the_title(); ?>
    </a>
</h2>
```

It's really simple: Using the tags for outputting the post title, you display just that. Around the title is a traditional hyperlink, getting its `href` value from `<?php the_permalink(); ?>`, which of course is the permalink to the post in question. You'll get a proper title for the hyperlink using `the_title_attribute()`, which returns the title of the post. In this case, you have added an array of settings, adding the text `Permalink to:` in front of the title and nothing at all after it. You can use `the_title_attribute()` as is, in which case it will return just an escaped version of the title, as opposed to `the_title()`, which will return the title as is.

To output some content, you use either one of these two template tags:

```
<?php the_content() ;?>
<?php the_excerpt() ;?>
```

The first tag outputs the full post content, unless you're on a page listing several blog posts. In that case, it outputs the content until the point where the `<!--more-->` tag is inserted; if that tag is not used, the full post is displayed (see Figure 3-1). If you're a WordPress user, you know all about that one; it is the More button in the HTML editor, inserting a Read More link.

Incidentally, you can make the Read More link appear in any way you like — for example:

```
<?php the_content( 'Read more here, mate!' ); ?>
```

This would change the default Read More link text to "Read more here, mate!" There are more options for this, and you can even put HTML code in it (or perhaps a graphic instead of text). The important thing is that the template tag `the_content()` outputs the post content, and if it is a blog listing, it breaks it with a Read More link if the `<!--more-->` tag is inserted.

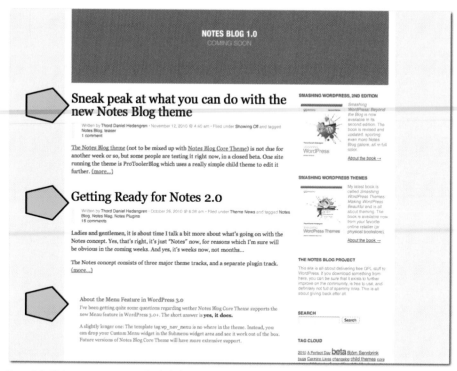

Figure 3-1: All these posts are outputted with the loop.

Naturally, when you're on a single-post page and `the_content()` is used (whether custom Read More text is defined or not), it won't output a Read More link. You'll see the full post.

The second content template tag available is `the_excerpt()`. As its name implies, it outputs only an excerpt of the actual content, by default the first 55 words. All HTML, whether it is images, paragraph breaks, or YouTube videos, is stripped from this excerpt, so it should really be used with caution. Neither are there any parameters, which is a bit weird; you would think that you'd be able to control the length of the actual excerpt, but alas. You can alter the length by adding a filter to the `excerpt_length` hook, though, if you want to alter the number of words used by `the_excerpt()`.

However, `the_excerpt()` does fulfill a purpose. You know that Excerpt box on the Write Post screen in WordPress? (See Figure 3-2; depending on your setup you might have to enable it using the Screen Options settings at the top right, also shown in Figure 3-2.) If you put something there, `the_excerpt()` will output that instead of the first 55 words. So if you put a simple "Hi, this is my post!" message in the excerpt field for a post, the usage of `the_excerpt()` will result in a mere `"Hi, this is my post!"` output, despite it being a lot shorter than 55 words.

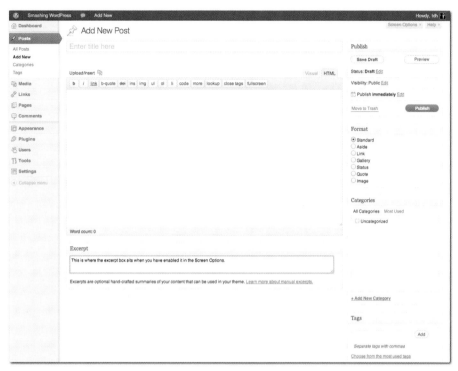

Figure 3-2: The Excerpt box on the Write Post screen in WordPress admin.

What good is `the_excerpt()`, then? It may be useful for lists where you don't want the blog posts to take up so much space, such as in search results or perhaps some kind of archive page. However, the most obvious usage would be as an alternative way of promoting a post. You can have a separate loop that would feature posts with a specific tag and display their titles as usual, but then just output `the_excerpt()` rather than the content. In fact, I'll show you how in the upcoming example.

For clarity's sake, this is the default usage of `the_excerpt()`:

```php
<?php the_excerpt(); ?>
```

Remember not to use `the_excerpt()` on templates displaying just one post, such as single. php. You need `the_content()` to display the full content! And, yes, should you want to, you can use them together.

The following example shows you how to use `the_excerpt()` to create a catchy intro to your posts in the Twenty Ten theme (but just on single posts, of course):

1. Open the Twenty Ten folder (found at wp-content/themes/twentyten/) and find the single.php template file. This is the one used to display single posts, so take a look at it. As you can see, it uses `get_template_part()` to fetch loop-single.php:

```php
<?php
/**
 * The Template for displaying all single posts.
 *
 * @package WordPress
 * @subpackage Twenty_Ten
 * @since Twenty Ten 1.0
 */

get_header(); ?>

		<div id="container">
			<div id="content" role="main">

			<?php
			/* Run the loop to output the post.
			 * If you want to overload this in a child theme then
			 * include a file
			 * called loop-single.php and that will be used instead.
			 */
			get_template_part( 'loop', 'single' );
			?>

			</div><!-- #content -->
		</div><!-- #container -->

<?php get_sidebar(); ?>
<?php get_footer(); ?>
```

2. Now forget about single.php and open loop-single.php instead. Add `the_excerpt()` just above `the_content()` in loop-single.php, around line 33. You'll see that it sits in a `div` with the class `entry-content`:

```php
<div class="entry-content">
    <?php the_content(); ?>
    <?php wp_link_pages( array( 'before' => '<div class="page-link">' . __(
    'Pages:', 'twentyten' ), 'after' => '</div>' ) ); ?>
</div><!-- .entry-content -->
```

3. Add `the_excerpt()` just above, with a `div` of its own around it so that you can style it the way you want:

```php
<div class="entry-content">
    <div class="entry-intro">
        <?php the_excerpt(); ?>
    </div>
    <?php the_content(); ?>
    <?php wp_link_pages( array( 'before' => '<div class="page-link">' . __(
    'Pages:', 'twentyten' ), 'after' => '</div>' ) ); ?>
</div><!-- .entry-content -->
```

4. Save and upload loop-single.php. Now you'll see the default excerpt (the first 55 characters from the post) above the content on single posts. But hang on, there's a weird Continue Reading link there (see Figure 3-3). That won't do!

Figure 3-3: This post shows the excerpt rather than the full post. Note the ellipsis at the end.

That link is due to a function in Twenty Ten that adds the link to the `excerpt_more` filter. (You'll get to hooks and filters in Chapter 6, "Advanced Theme Usage.") You can remove that with two simple lines of code before `the_excerpt()`. You need two lines because there are two conditions where the link shows — if you filled out an excerpt or if it is automatically generated. Add this code to the theme's functions.php, within the `<?php` and `?>` tags, obviously. Figure 3-4 shows the new output:

```
// Remove the excerpt_more filters by Twenty Ten
remove_filter( 'excerpt_more', 'twentyten_auto_excerpt_more' );
remove_filter( 'get_the_excerpt', 'twentyten_custom_excerpt_more' );
```

5. If you fill out a custom excerpt in the appointed box found on the Write Post screen in WordPress admin (see Figure 3-5), the excerpt of your choice will be displayed instead, as shown in Figure 3-6. No more nasty […] stuff!

6. Almost done! Now you need to style it accordingly, so open up style.css and add something like this to it (at the end, or where it makes sense for you). This will make the text in the `div.entry-intro` larger, but you could style it any way you'd like, of course. You can see the result of this particular code in Figure 3-7:

```
div.entry-intro {
        font-size: 130%;
        line-height: 130%;
        font-variant: small-caps;
}
```

Figure 3-4: The link is gone, and there's a default […] treatment instead.

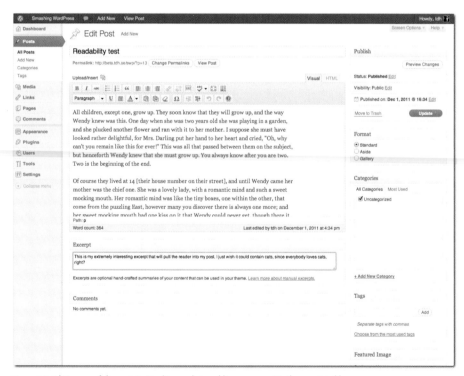

Figure 3-5: Editing one of the posts in WordPress admin, adding an excerpt in the appointed box.

Figure 3-6: The edited post now displays the custom excerpt rather than the automatic one.

Figure 3-7: Uppercase intro text has been added here.

USING STICKY POSTS

WordPress added something called *sticky posts* back in version 2.7. People familiar with online discussion forums will recognize the lingo; it is basically something that sticks to the top of the post listing at all times. No matter how many new posts are added, the sticky post remains the first item at the top of the listing of posts. In the Edit Post screen, you can set a blog post to sticky, hence making it stay on top at all times (see Figure 3-8). If two or more posts are sticky, they will all appear at the top of the list, in chronological order. When you remove the sticky setting from the Edit Post screen, the post will automatically sort itself into place with the others.

Figure 3-8: A sticky post.

There is a `sticky_class()` template tag to output the sticky post class, but with the addition of `post_class()`, it really isn't very useful:

```
<div id="post-<?php the_ID(); ?>" <?php post_class(); ?>>
```

The lovely `post_class()` template tag adds a number of classes to the post, depending on the details of the post. This is very useful for a designer, so this book covers `post_class()` in more depth in Chapter 6.

If the post is marked as sticky, `post_class()` will add a CSS `.sticky` class. That way, you can alter it in any way you want. Maybe you want it to have a light gray background, larger type, or something else? Just add the necessary styles to your style sheet, applying them to the `.sticky` class as in the following example:

```
.sticky {
    padding: 15px;
    background: #eee;
    border: 1px solid #bbb;
    color: #444;
    font-size: 18px; }
```

This CSS code would put the sticky post in a light gray box with a slightly darker frame and 18-pixel-sized default font size. Here it is in action, within a basic loop:

```
<?php if ( have_posts() ) : while ( have_posts() ) : the_post(); ?>
    <div id="post-<?php the_ID(); ?>" <?php post_class(); ?>>
        <h2>
            <a href="<?php the_permalink(); ?>"
              title="<?php the_title_attribute(); ?>">
                <?php the_title(); ?>
            </a>
        </h2>
        <?php the_content(); ?>
    </div>
<?php endwhile; else: ?>
    <p>Some error message or similar.</p>
<?php endif; ?>
```

In plain HTML, you'd get the following containing div. Notice the classes applied by post_ class() in particular:

```
<div id="post-1" class="post-1 post type-post status-publish format-standard
 sticky hentry category-uncategorized">
    <!--POST CONTENT GOES HERE -->
</div>
```

Want to do more with sticky posts? The conditional tag is_sticky() will help you do some funky stuff. Maybe you really want to rub in the importance of this post above all others? Then why not say so:

```
<?php if ( is_sticky() ) echo 'Super important post! Read it! Now!'; ?>
```

A bit over the top, of course, but there may indeed be times when it is a good idea to output or change things if there is a sticky post involved. Say you sell eBooks on your blog; you could use sticky posts to promote your latest one:

```
<?php if (is_sticky()) echo 'The latest e-book release by yours truly'; ?>
```

Not all themes support sticky posts visually, and the functionality is a bit hidden in the admin interface, so keep that in mind when building around the sticky post feature.

WORKING WITH POST FORMATS

Post formats were introduced in WordPress 3.1 and join sticky posts as a separate way to add a bit of control over the content. There are nine different post formats:

- aside: For short updates, usually without a title
- audio: For use with audio files
- chat: Used to publish chat transcripts

- `gallery`: For gallery posts
- `image`: For displaying a single image
- `link`: To link the reader onwards
- `quote`: Used to show quotes
- `status`: For short status updates
- `video`: For displaying a single video

Obviously, you can use these for anything you want, depending on what your theme is doing with them using CSS and conditional tags.

You pick the post format in a box in the right column. Figure 3-9 shows the box for the Twenty Eleven theme, which supports six post formats, not counting the standard (default) one.

Figure 3-9: Pick the post format.

A post published in accordance with the options selected in Figure 3-9 will show up as a titleless post when using Twenty Ten.

So what's the purpose of using post formats? Well, for starters, they add new CSS classes for you to play with. The `aside` post format will add the `format-aside` class, for example (see Figure 3-10), an alternative to using a dedicated asides category. This can be very handy. You'll also get added classes from `body_class()` that should sit in your `body` tag, giving you further control.

The real power comes into play when you use conditional tags within the loop. You can check whether a post is a certain post format or not, and act on it, like so:

```php
<?php
    if ( has_post_format( 'aside' ) ) {
        echo 'This is an aside post so expect it to be short!';
    }
?>
```

Figure 3-10: CSS classes added to the aside post, styled using the `format-aside` class.

To add this functionality to your theme, you'll have to use `add_theme_support()` in your functions.php file, telling WordPress which post formats your theme supports by passing an array. If you want to support the `aside`, `gallery`, and `video` post formats, for example, you would add this to functions.php:

```php
add_action( 'after_setup_theme', 'smashingtheme_setup' );
function smashingtheme_setup() {
    // Add post formats
    add_theme_support( 'post-formats', array(
        'aside',
        'gallery',
        'video'
    ) );
}
```

This would add the `smashingtheme_setup()` function to the `after_setup_theme` hook, which in turn means that it will run the `add_theme_support()` code for the post formats. The ones you want to enable are passed in an array. I'll revisit setting up theme functions properly in the next chapter.

More details on post formats are available in the Codex at http://codex.wordpress.org/Post_Formats.

THE GET_TEMPLATE_PART() AND POST FORMATS

Some theme designers prefer not to put the entire loop in loop.php, but rather use `get_template_part()` for even smaller chunks of code. The Twenty Eleven theme does this pretty well, with the default post output in content.php. What you'll notice should you go digging in Twenty Eleven is that it has additional files for the various kinds of post formats, so you'll find content-aside.php and content-video.php in there. In Twenty Eleven, the start of the loop, the `while` loop covered previously, is a part of the actual template file (index.php, category.php, and so on), but the output for the posts are in content.php. This method can make the template files a bit easier to work with.

When it really shines, however, is when you combine `get_template_part()` with `get_post_format()`. The latter will output the post format of the particular post. In Twenty Eleven, you'll find this bit of code:

```
get_template_part( 'content', get_post_format() );
```

This returns the post format to `get_template_part()` and appends it to `"content"`, much like it did for `"loop"` in your previous look at `get_template_part()` in this chapter. So if the post has the post format `"aside"`, `get_template_part()` will include content-aside.php. This way, you can easily separate different kinds of content and how they are outputted, which is pretty handy.

Naturally, it makes less sense with this setup if you don't use post formats, but it is a handy technique to keep in mind.

PUTTING QUERY_POSTS() TO GOOD USE

Every WordPress loop hacker and ambitious theme designer should know about the nifty `query_posts()` tool. In essence, `query_posts()` represents a way to take the loop WordPress wants to output (most frequently, the latest posts) and do something else with it. Perhaps you want to limit the number of posts, exclude a set number of categories, or change the order of things.

> *A few words of caution: The idea is to apply the `query_posts()` template tag on the main loop, not to use it to build multiple loops. That is possible, but things can get weird if you do, so it's best not to use it that way. See the "Multiple Loops" section later in this chapter to see how to create as many loops as you like.*

To use `query_posts()`, apply it before your main loop, like this:

```
<?php query_posts();
if ( have_posts() ) : while ( have_posts() ) : the_post(); ?>
    <!-- Doing stuff here, styling the posts and so on. -->
<?php endwhile; else: ?>
    <p>Some error message or similar.</p>
<?php endif; ?>
```

You can tighten that code a bit; there is no need for separate PHP tags for `query_posts()` and the `have_posts()` part.

So what does this do to the loop? Nothing really, because you haven't passed any parameters to `query_posts()` yet. There are no default values; this would just return the standard loop according to your WordPress settings. What `query_posts()` does is alert the SQL query from the loop to fit your needs.

Now that you're acquainted with `query_posts()`, you can execute a few examples to get used to it. There are tons of things you can do with this template tag when it comes to controlling the content flow. It really has a lot of settings, and using it with conditional tags is the route to hundreds of possible combinations.

Start by removing all posts from a category from the listings; try that Asides category where you push out your short, nonsensical posts. The first thing you need to do is figure out what ID it has, which is easily done by logging in to the WordPress admin interface and finding your way to the Edit category page. There you'll find the ID hidden at the end of the URL of the Edit page:

```
http://domain.com/wp-admin/categories.php?action=edit&cat_ID=130
```

As you'll probably have gathered, `cat_ID=130` tells you that the ID is 130. Remember, category IDs (or any IDs really) don't relate to the each other in any other way than they are all numerical values. Posts, categories, tags, and everything else are mixed, so you may have one category with ID 3 and the next with ID 749. This is because they are assigned by the database when you create the post or category.

Back to the example: You don't want to display posts from the Asides category, which has the ID 130. The `query_posts()` page in the Codex (http://codex.wordpress.org/Template_Tags/query_posts) says that you can use a number of ways to pass category information to `query_posts()`, but for this example, use the `cat` parameter, which takes IDs:

```
<?php
    // The arguments
    $args = array(
        'cat' => -130
    );
    // Passing the arguments
    query_posts( $args );
?>
```

This, in front of the loop shown previously, will exclude posts belonging to the category with the ID 130. Notice the minus sign in front of the ID: You really need that. If you forget about it, you would get the exact opposite result, which would be to show posts *only* from the category with ID 130.

Next, display posts tagged with `blue`, `green`, or `yellow` by applying this before the loop:

```php
<?php
    // The arguments
    $args = array(
        'tag' => 'blue+green+yellow'
    );
    // Passing the arguments
    query_posts( $args );
?>
```

Here, you obviously use that particular tag parameter. There's a bunch of parameters as well, just as with categories. Other things you can do with `query_posts()` are fetch posts from a specific author, add time-based queries, and order whatever data you choose any way you like. You can even grab the custom fields' data and use it for sorting, for example, which means that posts suddenly can get even more parameters to be sorted with. You'll do a lot of these things later on when you're building cool WordPress-powered sites.

One snag you may run into when working with `query_posts()` is the number of posts being returned. This is still controlled by the main WordPress settings related to how many blog posts to display per page. Luckily, you can control that as well. Say you want your front page to display just five posts, but all other listings should display ten. You can tackle this problem in two ways. You can either create a home.php template and do the `query_post()` magic there or use a conditional tag for your index.php template. Start with the home.php variant because it is the cleanest and easiest one. Using `query_posts()` and the `posts_per_page` parameter, you can control these things:

```php
<?php
    // The arguments
    $args = array(
        'posts_per_page' => 5
    );
    // Passing the arguments
    query_posts( $args );
?>
```

By placing that before the loop on your home.php template, you'll display five posts per page. Simple, huh? Now, put those conditional tags to use and add this functionality to the index.php page instead because you really don't need a separate home.php for this. All you need to do is use the conditional tag `is_home()` in an `if` clause to check if you're on the home page. If not, nothing will happen, but if you are, the `query_posts()` statement will go through. By adding this before the loop in index.php, you achieve the same thing as you did with the home.php template:

```php
<?php
    // Is it home?
    if ( is_home() ) {
        // The arguments
        $args = array(
            'posts_per_page' => 5
        );
        // Passing the arguments
        query_posts( $args );
    }
?>
```

Now, because you can limit the number of posts, naturally you can remove the limit as well. Just set the posts_per_page parameter to -1, and you'll show all posts that fit the loop criteria. Beware of putting that on a blog with thousands of posts, because if you do that on the front page, it will show all your posts, and that's not a fun SQL query to pass to the database at all. That being said, why not show all posts written by the author with the name TDH, published in 2009?

```php
<?php
    // The arguments
    $args = array(
        'author_name' => 'TDH',
        'year' => 2009,
        'posts_per_page' => -1
    );

    // Passing the arguments
    query_posts( $args );
?>
```

As you can see, query_posts() takes its parameters in query string style. This means that you can cram a lot of things into it without it being too complicated.

ALTERNATIVES TO THE LOOP

You may be tempted to create multiple loops or advanced loop queries in your theme's template files when you've figured out how those work. However, whereas that may be the solution to what you want to do in some cases, you should consider alternative methods as well. Doing a lot of funky stuff with the loop, often utilizing query_posts(), is sometimes completely unnecessary. Here's why.

First, ask yourself if it really is another loop you need. Often there are template tags that can do what you need, and that is almost always a better solution. Custom loop magic should be saved for actions that truly deserve and need it. At other times, a conditional tag might be the solution to the problem, which usually is a better approach than another loop.

Second, are there any plugins that can do the work for you? The WordPress community is full of brilliant solutions to common problems, and although it may be a lot cleaner to sort these things from within your own theme, a plugin may enhance the functionality and be easier for you to manage. A lot of the plugins that work with post listings are in fact doing stuff with the loop that you could do yourself, from within your theme. Normally I would recommend the latter solution, but what if you're not the one responsible for maintaining the theme in the long run, as is common when doing theme design work and then leaving it to the clients to nurture? If your clients are reluctant to pay more for customizations, or if the clients think that their in-house HTML skills are enough, then you're probably better off finding a plugin solution than one that will break when they do something with their template files. Granted, plugins come with their own issues, such as suddenly not being developed anymore or relying on WordPress functionality that isn't favored, but still, it is something to consider as an alternative to more loops.

> Chapter 8, "Plugins or functions.php?," dives deeper into the question of when to rely on plugins to replace built-in functionality.

Finally, there is the possible strain on the server and database. Doing loop after loop means a lot of PHP and SQL queries and that will slow down the site. Simple is not always best, but keeping things as simple as possible while managing to get the required result is always a good idea. Both web hosts and WordPress have come a long way since the early days, but that doesn't mean that you should make things more clunky or complicated than they need to be.

My point is this: Always question the need for that extra loop. It may save you some headaches in the future.

MULTIPLE LOOPS

Sometimes you want several loops on a page. Perhaps you have a category for your extremely important posts and want to run those by themselves on the front page, or maybe you just want the latest posts in the sidebar. Either way, whenever you need to fetch posts a second time, you'll want another loop. This is often essential when you want to break from the traditional blog mold, so you may as well master it.

Start with the most basic multiple loop solution, which is to just get another loop on the page. This is done with `rewind_posts()`, which just resets the loop's counter and lets you run it again:

```php
<?php
    rewind_posts();
    while ( have_posts() ) : the_post();
?>
    <!-- And then the basic loop continues... -->
```

Naturally, this would just output the exact same thing as your first loop, which would neither look good nor be particularly useful, so to actually do something with `rewind_posts()`, you need to change something. You could also use `wp_reset_postdata()`, which will restore `$post` to where it was in the original query — something that might be what you're

after should you go off on your own within a loop. You can read more about `wp_reset_`
`postdata()` in the Codex at http://codex.wordpress.org/Function_Reference/
wp_reset_postdata.

Say you want a box at the bottom of the page showing the last five posts from the News
category; this can be achieved by using `WP_Query`, which takes the same arguments as
`query_posts()` (touched upon earlier):

```php
<?php
    // Arguments for WP_Query
    $args = array(
        'category_name' => 'news',
        'showposts' => 5
    );
    // The new loop stored in $new_loop
    $new_loop = new WP_Query( $args );
    while ( $new_loop->have_posts() ) : $new_loop->the_post(); ?>

        <!-- Loop output goes here -->
<?php
    // Loop ends
    endwhile;
    // Reset the query
    wp_reset_postdata();
?>
```

This would then output the five latest posts from the News category, which you would put in
the box mentioned in the previous paragraph.

FEATURED POSTS WITH MULTIPLE LOOPS

Another common usage for multiple loops is to display a featured post at the top of the page.
This allows the WordPress theme to break from the traditional blog layout and has become
quite popular, especially with the so-called magazine themes that mimic their print
counterparts.

To do this, you first need a loop that fetches a single post — the latest one, naturally — from
the Featured category. Then, you need a second loop that does the regular thing, listing the
latest posts from all categories. To pull this off, you need to store the first loop query inside its
own query object. Do that by calling the `WP_Query` object and storing it in a new query.
`WP_Query` is the big huge thing that makes the loop tick. Although you don't see it in the
basic loop, you actually use it with `have_posts()`, for example, which in essence is `$wp_`
`query->have_posts()`; you just don't have to write it all out all the time. `WP_Query` is
huge and somewhat complicated, so messing with it requires some decent coding skills or a
lot of trial and error. As any experienced PHP coder will tell you, a little of both usually does
the trick. Often, however, you'll interact with `WP_Query` by using the various template and
conditional tags.

Recall the `query_posts()` template tag. The usage description says that it is intended to modify the main loop only, so you won't be using that for your new loop. Instead, pass the same variables to `WP_Query`. Here is the code:

```php
<?php
    // Setting a temporary value to avoid errors
    $do_not_duplicate = null;
    // Loop arguments
    $args = array(
        'category_name' => 'featured',
        'showposts' => 1
    );
    // Our featured query and loop
    $featured_query = new WP_Query( $args );
    while ( $featured_query->have_posts() ) : $featured_query->the_post();
    // Save the post ID to $do_not_duplicate
    $do_not_duplicate = $post->ID;
?>
    <!-- Styling for your featured post -->
<?php
    // Featured loop ends
    endwhile;
    // Resetting
    wp_reset_postdata();
?>
    <!-- Put whatever you want between the featured post
       and the normal post listing -->
<?php
    // Loop arguments
    $args = array(
        'showposts' => 9
    );
    // Our second loop
    $second_query = new WP_Query( $args );
    while ( $second_query->have_posts() ) : $second_query->the_post();
    // Let's not output the featured post
    if ( $post->ID == $do_not_duplicate ) continue; update_post_caches( $posts );
?>
    <!-- Your normal loop post styling goes here -->
<?php
    // Second loop ends
    endwhile;
?>
```

Take a closer look at this code. The first thing happening is that `$do_not_duplicate` gets set to null, to avoid any errors should there be no posts in the featured loop. Then there's the arguments that you use in `WP_Query` for controlling what the loop should contain. `WP_Query` is stored in `$featured_query`, which you then use in the actual `while` loop. You've seen this before. Finally, you save the result of the loop to `$do_not_duplicate`, which is the one post ID. Note that although it is easy enough to output two or more featured posts by changing the `showposts` argument for `WP_Query`, you'd have to store these post IDs in an array for `$do_not_duplicate` to work.

The actual output of the loop's content isn't covered in this example. It can be anything, perhaps a featured image, a nice headline, and the post excerpt. Anything you'd normally output within the loop will work. Next, you close the loop with `endwhile` and reset the post data with `wp_reset_postdata()`.

The second loop, which contains the rest of the posts that are meant to go after the featured one, is built in a similar fashion. Do note that `WP_Query` is stored in `$second_query` here. The one thing that truly differs is the check to see whether a post ID is the same as the one used in the earlier featured loop. If it is, the loop will just skip it.

THREE'S A CHARM, BUT FOUR LOOPS ARE WAY COOLER

Using the knowledge you've gained thus far, in this section you'll put the multiple loop concept to the test. In this example, you'll have three featured posts in one loop, and then you'll imagine three columns underneath consisting of the latest posts from one category each. The idea is to mimic the front page of a nonbloggish site. In terms of template files, this would ideally be in the home.php template, which means that it would be loaded only when on the front page. It could also be a Page template belonging to a page set as the front page for the site.

This example will use the same principle as the previous one but with four queries. The top one consists of three featured posts, and below that you have three queries sorted after category. Start with the featured posts:

```php
<div id="featured">

<?php
    // Setting a temporary value to avoid errors
    $do_not_duplicate = null;
    // Loop arguments
    $args = array(
        'category_name' => 'featured',
        'showposts' => 3
    );
    // Our featured query and loop
    $featured_query = new WP_Query( $args );
    while ( $featured_query->have_posts() ) : $featured_query->the_post();
    // Save the post ID to $do_not_duplicate
    $do_not_duplicate[] = $post->ID;
?>
    <div id="post-<?php the_ID(); ?>" <?php post_class(); ?>>
        <h1>
            <a href="<?php the_permalink(); ?>"
              title="<?php the_title_attribute(); ?>">
                <?php the_title(); ?>
```

```
        </a>
      </h1>
      <?php the_excerpt(); ?>
    </div>
<?php
  // Featured loop ends
  endwhile;
  // Resetting
  wp_reset_postdata();
?>
</div>
```

This is very similar to the featured post example from the previous subsection. There are a few things that differ, though. First of all, you display three posts rather than just one, which in turn means that you have to store these three post IDs in an array in $do_not_duplicate[]. You'll ask for them in three subsequent queries.

The rest of the code here is just a simple output of post titles and such. Also, the HTML markup is simple with some IDs and classes so that you can easily target the various parts of the code using style sheets.

Moving on, take a look at the next loop:

```
<div class="column-left">
    <h2>Latest from <span>Apples</span></h2>
    <ul>
    <?php
        // Loop arguments
        $args = array(
            'category_name' => 'apples',
            'showposts' => 10
        );
        // Our query and loop
        $apple_query = new WP_Query( $args );
        while ( $apple_query->have_posts() ) : $apple_query->the_post();
        // Let's not output any featured posts
        if ( in_array( $post->ID, $do_not_duplicate ) ) continue;
          update_post_caches( $posts );
    ?>
        <li>
            <h3>
                <a href="<?php the_permalink(); ?>"
                  title="<?php the_title_attribute(); ?>">
                    <?php the_title(); ?>
                </a>
            </h3>
            <?php the_excerpt(); ?>
        </li>
    <?php
        // Loop ends
```

```
        endwhile;
        // Resetting
        wp_reset_postdata();
    ?>
    </ul>
</div>
```

This is pretty much the same as the first loop, but limited to showing ten posts from the Apples category. You have a similar check for post IDs used in the featured loop as in the previous example, but this time you're checking an array instead. The post output is pretty straightforward, with every post as an item in the list. Resetting the query with `wp_reset_postdata()` is important here; you want a clean slate for your next loop.

There are two more loops, more or less identical to the previous one. The only change is the category and the variable name where you store `WP_Query`. Take a look at the whole thing:

```
<div id="featured">
<?php
    // Setting a temporary value to avoid errors
    $do_not_duplicate = null;
    // Loop arguments
    $args = array(
        'category_name' => 'featured',
        'showposts' => 3
    );
    // Our featured query and loop
    $featured_query = new WP_Query( $args );
    while ( $featured_query->have_posts() ) : $featured_query->the_post();
    // Save the post ID to $do_not_duplicate
    $do_not_duplicate[] = $post->ID;
?>
    <div id="post-<?php the_ID(); ?>" <?php post_class(); ?>>
        <h2>
            <a href="<?php the_permalink(); ?>"
              title="<?php the_title_attribute(); ?>">
                <?php the_title(); ?>
            </a>
        </h2>
        <?php the_excerpt(); ?>
    </div>
<?php
    // Featured loop ends
    endwhile;
    // Resetting
    wp_reset_postdata();
?>
</div>
<div class="column-left">
    <h2>Latest from <span>Apples</span></h2>
    <ul>
        <?php
```

```php
        // Loop arguments
        $args = array(
            'category_name' => 'apples',
            'showposts' => 10
        );
        // Our query and loop
        $apple_query = new WP_Query( $args );
        while ( $apple_query->have_posts() ) : $apple_query->the_post();
        // Let's not output any featured posts
        if ( in_array( $post->ID, $do_not_duplicate ) ) continue;
          update_post_caches( $posts );
    ?>
        <li>
            <h3>
                <a href="<?php the_permalink(); ?>"
                  title="<?php the_title_attribute(); ?>">
                    <?php the_title(); ?>
                </a>
            </h3>
            <?php the_excerpt(); ?>
        </li>
    <?php
        // Loop ends
        endwhile;
        // Resetting
        wp_reset_postdata();
    ?>
    </ul>
</div>
<div class="column-left">
    <h2>Latest from <span>Oranges</span></h2>
    <ul>
    <?php
        // Loop arguments
        $args = array(
            'category_name' => 'oranges',
            'showposts' => 10
        );
        // Our query and loop
        $orange_query = new WP_Query( $args );
        while ( $orange_query->have_posts() ) : $orange_query->the_post();
        // Let's not output any featured posts
        if ( in_array( $post->ID, $do_not_duplicate ) ) continue;
          update_post_caches( $posts );
    ?>
        <li>
            <h3>
                <a href="<?php the_permalink(); ?>"
                  title="<?php the_title_attribute(); ?>">
                    <?php the_title(); ?>
                </a>
```

```
            </h3>
            <?php the_excerpt(); ?>
        </li>
    <?php
        // Loop ends
        endwhile;
        // Resetting
        wp_reset_postdata();
    ?>
    </ul>
</div>
<div class="column-right">
    <h2>Latest from <span>Lemons</span></h2>
    <ul>
    <?php
        // Loop arguments
        $args = array(
            'category_name' => 'lemons',
            'showposts' => 10
        );
        // Our query and loop
        $lemon_query = new WP_Query( $args );
        while ( $lemon_query->have_posts() ) : $lemon_query->the_post();
        // Let's not output any featured posts
        if ( in_array( $post->ID, $do_not_duplicate ) ) continue;
          update_post_caches( $posts );
    ?>
        <li>
            <h3>
                <a href="<?php the_permalink(); ?>"
                  title="<?php the_title_attribute(); ?>">
                    <?php the_title(); ?>
                </a>
            </h3>
            <?php the_excerpt(); ?>
        </li>
    <?php
        // Loop ends
        endwhile;
        // Resetting
        wp_reset_postdata();
    ?>
    </ul>
</div>
```

There you have it: four loops starting with one for featured posts and then three more to display the latest from three different categories. This code can easily be implemented in just about any WordPress theme, but you would need to alter it to fit your category setup to make it work properly.

GETTING MORE COMFORTABLE WITH THE LOOP

The loop can certainly feel tricky to work with at first. The basic loop isn't too hard to identify, and that is really all you need to get started with WordPress. With a little practice, you will find it easier to understand the loop's mechanics, and when you start to build your own themes to power your WordPress site, you'll soon find yourself fiddling with it. The fact that a lot of plugins and template tags that you will want to use have to reside inside the loop makes it important, but the custom stuff, such as using multiple loops or specific content outputs, becomes more important when you begin pushing WordPress.

If you're having a hard time understanding the loop fully after reading this chapter, don't worry. The more examples you read and the more you play with it, the easier it will become to alter the loop to your needs. And that's what you're going to do next: actually start to build stuff. First up are themes, which you'll work with for the next few chapters. This means that you'll see a lot of the loop from now on, but you'll also delve deeper into template tags and other tools supplied by WordPress to control the content.

II

DESIGNING AND DEVELOPING WORDPRESS THEMES

4

WORDPRESS THEME ESSENTIALS

IF YOU WANT to do more advanced stuff with WordPress, you need to understand theme essentials. You could just start hacking the default theme or download any other quality theme listed in Appendix B, "Starter Themes," and go from there, but there are some things that might not be obvious from just using and tinkering with the code if you're new to WordPress. This chapter helps you dive into the WordPress theme concept to get acquainted with themes and how they work. You'll learn how to alter them to fit your needs. After doing that, you'll be able to put your knowledge to good use in the coming chapters.

In this chapter, you'll build a theme from scratch and learn more about the various template files. Those files include the style sheet and the fairly extensive functions.php file, so you can learn how to work with all those elements you encountered in the previous chapters.

THEME BASICS

You may already be somewhat familiar with WordPress themes and the premises under which they operate. In theory, themes are a way to separate the design from the code, but in reality, there is still a lot of coding happening in the more advanced themes out there.

A theme consists of a folder with template files and any other files that may be needed. The only two absolutely necessary template files are style.css and index.php. The former contains the header that identifies your theme (and generally some styling code), and the latter is the basic layout. If you're looking for a challenge, try to create a WordPress theme consisting of just the two necessary files and see what you can do with it. This is an interesting exercise if nothing else.

ELEMENTS OF THE BASIC THEME

Figure 4-1 shows a common blog layout. At the top, spanning the full width, is the blog header, which in fact is the header.php file. Underneath is the actual blog area, with the content to the left (index.php) and the sidebar to the right (sidebar.php). Finally, there is a footer to wrap it up, using the footer.php template file.

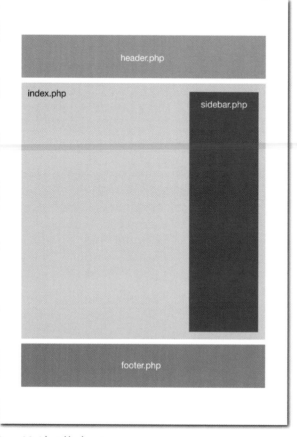

Figure 4-1: A basic blog layout.

This setup is not mandatory; you can change it, exclude parts of it, or expand it further. It is, however, a very common setup, one that the default WordPress themes Twenty Ten and Twenty Eleven both adhere to. You can find a lot of themes using template files in this manner, but it is in no way the only way to do things.

Although you can get by with just style.css and index.php in your theme, it is generally not such a good idea to be so minimalistic. At the very least, you should also have a header.php and a footer.php for your theme. These are called from within index.php, with the template tags `get_header()` and `get_footer()`. You'll also want a comments.php file for commenting functionality, and you call that with `comments_template()`, also from within index.php. The same goes for the sidebar; you should have a template file for that, too, and call it with `get_sidebar()`.

The header.php file consists of the `doctype` heading and everything related. You'll get a closer look at that in a later example section. The header.php file also generally does basic tasks such as getting the right favicon, generating proper title tags, and having the necessary keywords so that search engines can find the pages more easily. However, one thing it must have is a link to the style sheet, and `wp_head()` is also needed to start the whole WordPress shebang.

The footer.php file should include `wp_footer()` to stop WordPress and, of course, all the necessary closing tags. Make sure to close the `body` and `html` tags and anything else you may have opened in header.php.

Finally, comments.php needs the code for outputting comments, as well as the necessary forms so that people can actually post new comments. This is done with simple template tags these days, so comments.php files aren't as messy to work with as they once were. The simplest file of all is sidebar.php, which is just the stuff you want in the sidebar.

As you may have gathered, everything revolves around index.php. However, there are other template files that can replace index.php, depending on the situation. If you're on the front page, for example, home.php takes the top slot, and index.php will be used only if there isn't a home.php file. The same goes for single post view, in which single.php takes precedence over index.php, and for WordPress pages, page.php goes before index.php. Actually, if you use every one of the possible template files, your index.php file will never load. The concept is the same, though, so leave things like that for a little while.

Now that the basics are out of the way, it's time to get your hands dirty!

THIS IS WHAT YOU'RE DOING

How you go about designing your theme is completely up to you. For your needs in this chapter, you'll use the basic blog design shown in Figure 4-2, which actually is a simple plain HTML file. Sometimes this is all you need to get started.

Nothing too fancy, pretty much the same as the blog template dummy shown in Figure 4-1, right? You'll be breaking this simple HTML design into template files and making a WordPress theme based on it.

Figure 4-2: A simple HTML design that will serve as the base for your theme.

If you want to take a closer look at the HTML before moving along, it is available in the download package for this book on the John Wiley & Sons website at www.wiley.com/go/ smashingwordpress3e. Because it takes so much space, I won't reprint it here.

A FEW WORDS ON HTML5

I went with a simple HTML5 markup for this example. This means that the code won't work particularly well in older web browsers, including Internet Explorer prior to version 9. If you want your theme to be backward compatible, as I do to an extent, but still want to use nice semantic HTML5 markup such as `header`, `article`, and `footer`, then you need to do something about that.

Luckily, there are several solutions available. You could just wrap everything in `div` tags and sort out the issues with older web browsers that way, but that will make your code a bit messy, and this sort of misses the point of using the semantic markup in the first place. Another solution is to use JavaScript to make sure that older versions of Internet Explorer understand the code, which is what I've done. Remy Sharp created a bit of JavaScript code that you can either host on your own server or, if you don't mind an additional HTTP request, load from Google, which I've done for convenience's sake:

```
<!--[if lt IE 9]>
<script src="http://html5shim.googlecode.com/svn/trunk/html5.js"></script>
<![endif]-->
```

This is a (non-WordPress) conditional tag checking if the web browser is a version of Internet Explorer prior to version 9. If it is, you'll load the html5.js JavaScript from Google. You can read more about Remy Sharp's solution in his announcement blog post from 2009: http://remysharp.com/2009/01/07/html5-enabling-script. Later in this chapter, you'll enqueue this script properly.

Now, you can break down this HTML file and make a WordPress theme out of it!

CREATING THE TEMPLATE FILES

You'll cut up the HTML file into WordPress templates files, one by one, and by doing so, you'll get your theme. I'll go through them all to give you a complete overview as to how a theme can be constructed, although there are — as you'll see later in this book — various ways to go about these things. Keep it simple for now.

Before you get started, you'll want to create a folder for the theme; in the example, I'm calling it *simple-blog* (more on that when you create the style.css file), and every template file besides style.css will be a PHP file in that folder.

THE THEME DECLARATION IN STYLE.CSS

You need a style.css file for your theme; there's no avoiding it. At the top of this file, you have your theme declaration, and below that, there is just a regular style sheet. You can import other style sheets or keep all your styles in style.css — that's up to you — but you need this file.

I won't reprint the complete style sheet for the HTML design here, but the top of it looks like this when moved into the simple-blog folder:

```
/*
Theme Name: Simple Blog
Theme URI: http://tdh.me/wordpress/simple-blog/
Author: Thord Daniel Hedengren
Author URI: http://tdh.me/
Description: A simple light weight blog theme.
Version: 1.0
License: GNU General Public License
License URI: license.txt
*/
```

After that, there are just regular styles. You'll notice the License and License URI lines; these are basically just the license for the theme and a note telling others that the complete license is available in the theme folder, in a text file called license.txt. It's a good idea to have one of these to avoid confusion.

UP TOP, THE HEADER.PHP FILE

Starting from the top of the HTML file, you obviously have your makings of the header.php file. Figure 4-3 shows what you want to move into that file visually.

Figure 4-3: This is what you want in your header.php file.

Because header.php is loaded as a header for all purposes in this theme (although you can have several headers if you like), you want this file to be general enough to work on all occasions. This is the code I've copied from the HTML file, to a new file called header.php:

```
<!DOCTYPE HTML>
<html>

<head>
    <meta http-equiv="Content-Type" content="text/html; charset=UTF-8" />

    <title>Blog Title</title>

    <link rel="stylesheet" type="text/css" media="all" href="style.css" />

    <!-- Fix for Internet Explorer prior to version 9
        by Remy Sharp http://remysharp.com/2009/01/07/html5-enabling-script/ -->
```

```
    <!--[if lt IE 9]>
    <script src="http://html5shim.googlecode.com/svn/trunk/html5.js"></script>
    <![endif]-->
</head>

<body>

    <div id="outer-wrap">
        <div id="inner-wrap">

            <header id="header-container">
                <hgroup>
                    <h1 id="site-title">Blog Title</h1>
                    <p id="site-description">Description from blog settings</p>
                </hgroup>

                <nav>
                    <div class="menu">
                        <ul>
                            <li><a href="#">Menu item</a></li>
                            <li><a href="#">Another one</a></li>
                            <li><a href="#">Third menu item</a></li>
                        </ul>
                    </div>
                </nav>
            </header> <!-- #header-container ends -->
```

Now, this won't do — you need some WordPress functions in there to make it work as intended. Theoretically, if you just wanted a functional theme, adding `wp_head()` would do, but obviously, you'll want some more stuff than that.

Starting with the head part of this particular code, you want to make sure that WordPress knows the correct character set, that the right title is printed depending on where on the site the visitor is, that you include the style sheet correctly, that there is a pingback URL for blog-to-blog communication, that you load the necessary JavaScript, and that you have `wp_head()` last in the head. So with that in mind, here's the head part of the code, with all these things added:

```
<!DOCTYPE HTML>
<html <?php language_attributes(); ?>>
<head>
    <meta charset="<?php bloginfo( 'charset' ); ?>" />
    <title>
    <?php
        // The title
        wp_title( '|', true, 'right' );
        // Add the blog name.
        bloginfo( 'name' );
    ?>
    </title>
```

```
<link rel="profile" href="http://gmpg.org/xfn/11" />
<link rel="stylesheet" type="text/css" media="all" href="<?php
  bloginfo( 'stylesheet_url' ); ?>" />
<link rel="pingback" href="<?php bloginfo( 'pingback_url' ); ?>" />
<!-- Fix for Internet Explorer prior to version 9
     by Remy Sharp http://remysharp.com/2009/01/07/html5-enabling-script/ -->
<!--[if lt IE 9]>
<script src="http://html5shim.googlecode.com/svn/trunk/html5.js"></script>
<![endif]-->
<?php
    // Always have wp_head() before closing of head
    wp_head();
?>
</head>
```

You'll notice that the contents of the `title` tag are built using an `if` clause. Because you don't know where the user will be on the site, this is necessary if you want the `title` tag to be remotely true. You're using conditional tags to check whether the user is on an archive, a single post, or a page and to act accordingly after that. Also worth noting is that I've chosen to keep the Internet Explorer HTML5 fix separate within HTML conditional, rather than load said JavaScript with `wp_enqueue_script()`, which normally would be the right thing to do. I'm keeping it separate to make sure that the HTML browser check works as intended and because I really don't want any browser besides Internet Explorer versions prior to 9 to load this JavaScript. Finally, there's the queuing of the JavaScript for comment replies, loaded only on single posts and pages as that's the only way it can be used — and last but not least, the ever-important `wp_head()`. You always want `wp_head()` just above your closing `head` tag, as this is where a lot of plugins and theme-enabled features will insert code that is supposed to be run in `head`, and you want to do that after you've gotten everything else out of the way.

Moving on, you need to take care of the rest of header.php. Here you want to make sure that the `body` tag gets the proper classes (good for styling with CSS, obviously), make sure that the correct site title and site description is outputted, and make sure that the menu doesn't have to be hardcoded but can be used using WordPress's menu feature:

```
<body <?php body_class(); ?>>

    <div id="outer-wrap">
        <div id="inner-wrap">
            <header id="header-container">
                <hgroup>
                <?php if (is_home() || is_front_page()) { ?>
                    <h1 id="site-title">
                        <a href="<?php echo home_url(); ?>" title="<?php
                          bloginfo( 'name' ); ?>">
                            <?php bloginfo( 'name' ); ?>
                        </a>
                    </h1>
                    <h2 id="site-description">
                        <?php bloginfo( 'description' ); ?>
```

```
            </h2>
        <?php } else { ?>
            <div id="site-title">
                <a href="<?php echo home_url(); ?>" title="<?php
                  bloginfo( 'name' ); ?>">
                    <?php bloginfo( 'name' ); ?>
                </a>
            </div>
            <div id="site-description">
                <?php bloginfo( 'description' ); ?>
            </div>
        <?php } ?>
        </hgroup>
        <nav>
        <?php
            // Top navigation menu
            wp_nav_menu( array(
                'theme_location' => 'top-navigation'
            )
        ); ?>
        </nav>
    </header> <!-- #header-container ends -->
```

This is pretty straightforward stuff. When you get to the actual content, you'll see that just as you have a `body_class()` supplying style sheet classes for the `body` tag, you'll have one for your posts as well. The idea is to give more control over the design and make it possible for you to style specific parts of the site. Maybe you want the background for pages belonging to a specific category to be yellow; well, this is the way you do that — just add the appropriate style to your style sheet, and you'll be good to go.

The site title is outputted with `bloginfo()`, nothing fancy there. However, I believe that the site title shouldn't be wrapped within h1 tags on single pages but only on the front page as that is the only place the site title is the most important item. This is why I've put another conditional check here, wrapping the site title in h1 or `div` tags, depending. The same obviously goes for the site description, which is within this check as well.

Finally, there's the menu. This code replaces `div.menu` and `ul` list with `wp_nav_menu()`. This is the tag to output menus, but to make it work, you'll have to add support for it in functions.php. You'll get to this later; for now, just leave it there. Should you want to test your theme before fiddling with functions.php, just comment this part out to avoid confusion.

And that's it — header.php is done! Now that wasn't so hard, was it?

THE FOOTER, WITH FOOTER.PHP

The footer is really simple to get right in this theme, so you might as well just get it out of the way. Skipping everything in between, such as the content and right column, you'll move along to the bottom part. Just like the header.php file, this is something that needs to be global, although you can have several footers if you like. Figure 4-4 shows what you'll be working with here.

Figure 4-4: This is what will go in footer.php.

Returning to the HTML file, you'll see that the following is the code copied to a file named footer.php:

```
<footer id="footer-container">
    <nav>
        <div class="menu">
            <ul>
                <li><a href="#">Menu item</a></li>
                <li><a href="#">Another one</a></li>
                <li><a href="#">Third menu item</a></li>
            </ul>
        </div>
    </nav>

    <p>Copyright &copy; 2012, and similar information</p>
</footer> <!-- #footer-container ends -->

</div> <!-- #inner-wrap ends -->
```

```
        </div> <!-- #outer-wrap ends -->

</body>

</html>
```

There's not much to do here. You've got another menu that you want to make user-editable with `wp_nav_menu()`, just like in header.php, and there's the copyright text to take into account. Finally, you want to wrap up everything with `wp_footer()` just before the closing `body` tag, just as you did with `wp_head()` before the closing `head` tag.

The following is the code with these things added, along with a simple echo of the year using regular ol' PHP for the copyright text:

```php
        <footer id="footer-container">
            <nav>
            <?php
                // Bottom navigation menu
                wp_nav_menu( array(
                    'theme_location' => 'bottom-navigation' )
                );
            ?>
            </nav>
            <p>
                Copyright &copy; <?php echo date( 'Y' ); ?>
                <a href="<?php echo home_url(); ?>" title="<?php
                  bloginfo( 'name' ); ?>">
                    <?php bloginfo( 'name' ); ?>
                </a>
            </p>
        </footer> <!-- #footer-container ends -->
        </div> <!-- #inner-wrap ends -->
    </div> <!-- #outer-wrap ends -->
<?php
    // Wrapping up WordPress just before the closing body tag
    wp_footer();
?>
</body>
</html>
```

The menu feature needs to be taken care of in functions.php, so you'll just let that one slide for now. There really is just one thing I want to talk about briefly here, before you move on to more interesting things, and that is the whole copyright thing. I put it there just to show how it could work, but if you release a theme, do keep in mind that not all people will want that. In fact, they might want to offer their content free for anyone to use or license it using any of the Creative Commons (http://creativecommons.org) licenses. The best solution is a theme setting for this, something you'll get to later in this book. Just something to keep in mind for now.

THE RIGHT COLUMN: SIDEBAR.PHP

Before you get to the actual content, take a look at the right column, more commonly known as the *sidebar* in blog speak. Figure 4-5 shows the area in question.

Figure 4-5: The right column.

Now, you could load a bunch of different right columns depending on where on the site the user is, but for your needs here, you'll stick with just one. The following HTML code is what I've copied and pasted into a file called *sidebar.php*:

```
<aside id="sidebar-container">
    <ul id="sidebar">
        <li class="widget-container">
            <h3 class="widget-title">Widget title</h2>
            <p>Donec eu libero sit amet quam egestas semper. Aenean ultricies mi
              vitae est. Mauris placerat eleifend leo.</p>
        </li>
```

```
<li class="widget-container">
    <h3 class="widget-title">Another widget title</h2>
    <p>Donec eu libero sit amet quam egestas semper. Aenean ultricies mi
      vitae est. Mauris placerat eleifend leo.</p>
</li>
    </ul>
</aside> <!-- #sidebar-container ends -->
```

Obviously, you don't want the sidebar littered with dummy content, so that has got to go. The actual content will be dynamic, an area where the site owner can drop widgets, also known as *a widget area.* Most themes have one or several widget areas that let the site owner add whatever functionality he or she wants, either from the available widgets in WordPress by default or widgets added by plugins. The right column in this theme is a widget area, which means that you need to make some changes:

```
<aside id="sidebar-container">
    <ul id="sidebar">
    <?php
        // If the sidebar is empty, output the static content
        if ( !dynamic_sidebar( 'right-column' ) ) : ?>
        <li>Please add some widgets to the <em>Right column</em> widget area!</li>
    <?php endif; ?>
    </ul>
</aside> <!-- #sidebar-container ends -->
```

The dummy content has been replaced by a PHP check that looks for a sidebar called *Right column,* but should it be empty, an `li` with some instructive text is outputted.

For sidebars to work, you need to declare them in functions.php. You'll do that in a bit; for now this is all you need with sidebar.php.

THE CONTENT FLOW, USING INDEX.PHP

It's time to get the actual content under control. Figure 4-6 shows the content flow from the HTML design, which in this case is just two posts but should be able to be a bunch of posts, obviously.

All your previous template files have been parts of the site, and so is index.php as well. However, it is a bit different from all other templates because index.php is the fallback template if there is no dedicated template for the particular page. You'll look more closely at that later on, but it is good to know that index.php needs to be there to save you should you forget to add a template or if new features come along.

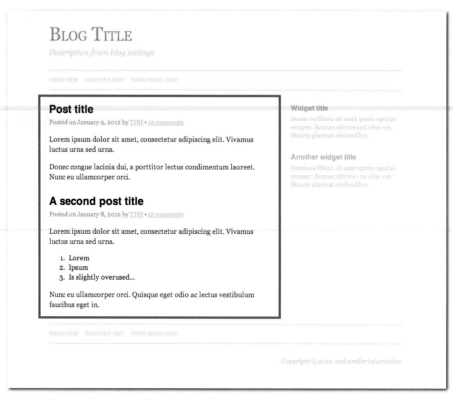

Figure 4-6: The content flow is destined for index.php, and more!

Now, this is the HTML code I've copied and pasted into index.php. You'll notice the right column part, which you recently moved to sidebar.php. That's okay; you'll fix that in a little bit.

```
<div id="main-container">
    <section id="content-container">
        <article class="post">
            <header>
                <h2 class="entry-title">Post title</h2>
                <p class="entry-meta">Posted on <time datetime="2012-01-09">January 9,
                    2012</time> by <a href="#">TDH</a> &bull; <a href="#comments">12
                    comments</a></p>
            </header>
            <p>Lorem ipsum dolor sit amet, consectetur adipiscing elit. Vivamus
                luctus urna sed urna.</p>
            <p>Donec congue lacinia dui, a porttitor lectus condimentum laoreet.
                Nunc eu ullamcorper orci.</p>
        </article>
```

```
        <article class="post">
            <header>
                <h2 class="entry-title">A second post title</h2>
                <p class="entry-meta">Posted on <time datetime="2012-01-08">January 8,
                    2012</time> by <a href="#">TDH</a> &bull; <a href="#comments">12
                    comments</a></p>
            </header>
            <p>Lorem ipsum dolor sit amet, consectetur adipiscing elit. Vivamus
                luctus urna sed urna.</p>
            <ol>
                <li>Lorem</li>
                <li>Ipsum</li>
                <li>Is slightly overused...</li>
            </ol>
            <p>Nunc eu ullamcorper orci. Quisque eget odio ac lectus vestibulum
                faucibus eget in.</p>
        </article>
    </section> <!-- #main-container ends -->

    <aside id="sidebar-container">
        <ul id="sidebar">
            <li class="widget-container">
                <h2 class="widget-title">Widget title</h2>
                <p>Donec eu libero sit amet quam egestas semper. Aenean ultricies mi
                    vitae est. Mauris placerat eleifend leo.</p>
            </li>
            <li class="widget-container">
                <h2 class="widget-title">Another widget title</h2>
                <p>Donec eu libero sit amet quam egestas semper. Aenean ultricies mi
                    vitae est. Mauris placerat eleifend leo.</p>
            </li>
        </ul>
    </aside> <!-- #sidebar-container ends -->
</div>
```

First things first: You need to get the references for header.php, footer.php, and sidebar.php in there. You'll use `get_header()`, `get_footer()`, and `get_sidebar()` to achieve this, and all you need to do is add the first one to the top and the second one to the bottom and then replace the code for the right column with the last one — like this:

```
<?php get_header(); ?>

<div id="main-container">
    <section id="content-container">
        <article class="post">
            <header>
                <h2 class="entry-title">Post title</h2>
                <p class="entry-meta">Posted on <time datetime="2012-01-09">January 9,
```

```
            2012</time> by <a href="#">TDH</a> &bull; <a href="#comments">12
            comments</a></p>
        </header>
        <p>Lorem ipsum dolor sit amet, consectetur adipiscing elit. Vivamus
            luctus urna sed urna.</p>
        <p>Donec congue lacinia dui, a porttitor lectus condimentum laoreet.
            Nunc eu ullamcorper orci.</p>
    </article>

    <article class="post">
        <header>
            <h2 class="entry-title">A second post title</h2>
            <p class="entry-meta">Posted on <time datetime="2012-01-08">January 8,
                2012</time> by <a href="#">TDH</a> &bull; <a href="#comments">12
                comments</a></p>
        </header>
        <p>Lorem ipsum dolor sit amet, consectetur adipiscing elit. Vivamus
            luctus urna sed urna.</p>
        <ol>
            <li>Lorem</li>
            <li>Ipsum</li>
            <li>Is slightly overused...</li>
        </ol>
        <p>Nunc eu ullamcorper orci. Quisque eget odio ac lectus vestibulum
            faucibus eget in.</p>
    </article>
  </section> <!-- #main-container ends -->

<?php get_sidebar(); ?>

</div>

<?php get_footer(); ?>
```

You'll remember that these three tags will include the contents from header.php, footer.php, and sidebar.php.

Next up is getting index.php ready for actually displaying content. To do that, you need the loop, covered in the previous chapter, "The Loop." You'll use the dummy content as a basis for how the actual output should look. Add the loop, clean out the dummy content, and see how it looks:

```
<?php get_header(); ?>

<div id="main-container">
    <section id="content-container">

    <?php
```

```php
        // Start the loop
        if ( have_posts() ) : while ( have_posts() ) : the_post();
    ?>

        <!-- LOOPED CONTENT GOES HERE -->

    <?php
        // Loop ends
        endwhile;
        // Nothing in the loop?
        else :
    ?>

        <article id="post-0" class="post no-results not-found">
            <header>
                <h2 class="entry-title">Nothing Found</h2>
            </header>
            <p>We're sorry, but we couldn't find anything for your. Please try and
                search for whatever it was you were looking for.</p>
            <?php get_search_form(); ?>
        </article>

    <?php
        // And we're done
        endif;
    ?>

    </section> <!-- #main-container ends -->

<?php get_sidebar(); ?>

</div>

<?php get_footer(); ?>
```

Because you learned all about the loop in the previous chapter, I'm pretty sure you'll recognize the `if ( have_posts() ) : while ( have_posts() ) : the_post();` part. After that, you'll find a commented placeholder for where the actual output will be, and then you've got an `else` clause for those occasions when there are no posts available to loop out. Then you need a different message obviously, so that's what you get. Nothing particularly weird here; if you need to refresh your memory, just revisit the previous chapter.

Moving on, you'll get the actual output in there as well, replacing the comment. Looking at the dummy content, you need to replace it all with template tags that output the actual content, such as the title, correct date and time, and author:

```
<article id="post-<?php the_ID(); ?>" <?php post_class(); ?>>
    <header>
        <h2 class="entry-title">
            <a href="<?php the_permalink(); ?>" title="<?php the_title_attribute();
              ?>" rel="bookmark">
                <?php the_title(); ?>
            </a>
        </h2>
        <p class="entry-meta">
            Posted on <time datetime="<?php echo get_the_date(); ?>"><?php
              the_time(); ?></time>
            by <?php the_author_link(); ?>
        <?php
            // Are the comments open?
            if ( comments_open() ) : ?>
            &bull; <?php comments_popup_link( 'No comments', '1 comment', '%
              comments' ); ?>
        <?php endif; ?>
        </p>
    </header>
    <?php
        // The content
        the_content();
    ?>
</article>
```

There's not much to talk about here, really. There are some checks to see whether the comments are open, and if they are, they are outputted; otherwise they are not. The latter comment check is meant for fallbacks mostly because it will be true only on single posts and pages (that's what the conditional tag is_singular() checks for), but it could come in handy should the theme lack a single.php template for some reason.

Putting it all together, you've got this index.php file:

```
<?php get_header(); ?>
<div id="main-container">
    <section id="content-container">
    <?php
        // Start the loop
        if ( have_posts() ) : while ( have_posts() ) : the_post();
        // Show the date once per page
        the_date( '', '<h3 class="the_date">', '</h3>' );
    ?>
    <article id="post-<?php the_ID(); ?>" <?php post_class(); ?>>
        <header>
            <h2 class="entry-title">
                <a href="<?php the_permalink(); ?>" title="<?php
                  the_title_attribute(); ?>" rel="bookmark">
                    <?php the_title(); ?>
                </a>
```

```
        </h2>
        <p class="entry-meta">
            Posted on <time datetime="<?php echo get_the_date(); ?>"><?php
                the_time(); ?></time>
            by <?php the_author_link(); ?>
        <?php
            // Are the comments open?
            if ( comments_open() ) : ?>
            &bull; <?php comments_popup_link( 'No comments', '1 comment', '%
                comments' );
            endif;
        ?>
        </p>
    </header>
    <?php
        // The content
        the_content();
    ?>
</article>
<?php
    // Load comments if singular
    if ( is_singular() ) {
        comments_template( '', true );
    }
    // Loop ends
    endwhile;
    // Nothing in the loop?
    else :
?>
    <article id="post-0" class="post no-results not-found">
        <header>
            <h2 class="entry-title">Nothing Found</h2>
        </header>
        <p>We're sorry, but we couldn't find anything for your. Please try and
            search for whatever it was you were looking for.</p>
        <?php get_search_form(); ?>
    </article>
</section> <!-- #main-container ends -->
<?php get_sidebar(); ?>
</div>
<?php get_footer(); ?>
```

There are two minor additions to this code, not mentioned previously. First, there's the the_date() heading, which will only output the day's date once per instance, so if you have two posts on the same date, you will see it only once. This line is found directly after the loop:

```
// Show the date once per page
the_date( '', '<h3 class="the_date">', '</h3>' );
```

Then there's the conditional tag that checks whether this is a singular page or post and outputs `comments_template()` if it is, like this:

```
// Load comments if singular
if ( is_singular() ) {
    comments_template( '', true );
}
```

At this stage, you actually have an almost-working theme. There are some elements that need to be declared in functions.php, which you'll do in a bit, but before you wrap this up, you should do this right and add some more template files.

BREAKING OUT THE LOOP

Although it isn't mandatory, I find it useful to break out the loop from the template files. Either that or the output of the loop, depending on if you want the whole thing in a separate file or just the content part. In this case, just break out the content part. Look at the preceding code block; what you want to do is to move the `article` block to a file of its own. Because this is the default post look and feel, you'll just call it content.php. With the `article` block in content.php, you'll replace it in index.php with this:

```
get_template_part( 'content', get_post_format() );
```

This looks for content-X.php to include, where X is the post format, fetched with `get_post_format()`. If the post in question is a regular post, it'll just default to content.php, but if it is in the Gallery post format, the code will look for content-gallery.php first — and should that not exist, it'll default to content.php. The purpose of this is obviously to be able to reuse content.php files for various post formats wherever you want.

The following is the complete new index.php file:

```
<?php get_header(); ?>
<div id="main-container">
    <section id="content-container">
    <?php
        // Start the loop
        if ( have_posts() ) : while ( have_posts() ) : the_post();
        // Get the correct content type
        get_template_part( 'content', get_post_format() );

        // Load comments if singular
        if ( is_singular() ) {
            comments_template( '', true );
        }
        // Loop ends
        endwhile;

        // Nothing in the loop?
        else :
```

```
        ?>
            <article id="post-0" class="post no-results not-found">
                <header>
                    <h2 class="entry-title">Nothing Found</h2>
                </header>
                <p>We're sorry, but we couldn't find anything for your. Please try and
                    search for whatever it was you were looking for.</p>
                <?php get_search_form(); ?>
            </article>
        </section> <!-- #main-container ends -->
<?php get_sidebar(); ?>
</div>
<?php get_footer(); ?>
```

For the record, here are the contents of the content.php file as well:

```
<article id="post-<?php the_ID(); ?>" <?php post_class(); ?>>
    <header>
        <h2 class="entry-title">
            <a href="<?php the_permalink(); ?>" title="<?php the_title_attribute();
                ?>" rel="bookmark">
                <?php the_title(); ?>
            </a>
        </h2>
        <p class="entry-meta">
            Posted on <time datetime="<?php echo get_the_date(); ?>"><?php
                the_time(); ?></time>
            by <?php the_author_link(); ?>
        <?php
            // Are the comments open?
            if ( comments_open() ) : ?>
            &bull; <?php comments_popup_link( 'No comments', '1 comment', '%
                comments' ); ?>
        <?php endif; ?>
        </p>
    </header>
    <?php
        // The content
        the_content();
    ?>
</article>
```

With that established, it's time to create some more template files!

SINGLE POSTS AND PAGES

Most themes sport both single.php and page.php templates. The former is for single posts, and the latter is for pages. A simple theme such as the one you're building now really doesn't need these; a few conditional tags could do everything without complicating the index.php file. But forget about that and create a single.php and page.php template.

Start with single.php, which really doesn't differ too much from index.php. In fact, it is basically a simplified index.php, without the fallback stuff and with `get_template_part ( 'content', 'single' )` instead of one for a specific post type because a single post should look the same no matter what, in this case at least.

Here's the complete single.php:

```php
<?php get_header(); ?>

<div id="main-container">
    <section id="content-container">

    <?php
        // Start the loop
        while ( have_posts() ) : the_post();

        // Get the correct content type
        get_template_part( 'content', 'single' );

        // Comments
        comments_template( '', true );

        // Loop ends
        endwhile;
    ?>

    </section> <!-- #main-container ends -->

<?php get_sidebar(); ?>

</div>

<?php get_footer(); ?>
```

Thanks to `get_template_part()`, single.php will try to load content-single.php first, and failing that, it'll load content.php. Create a content-single.php file as well, based on the original content.php but without a linked title, using `h1` instead of `h2` and no check whether it is a single post or page either (because you already know that). Here it is:

```php
<article id="post-<?php the_ID(); ?>" <?php post_class(); ?>>
    <header>
        <h1 class="entry-title">
            <?php the_title(); ?>
        </h1>
        <p class="entry-meta">
            Posted on <time datetime="<?php echo get_the_date(); ?> <?php
                the_time(); ?>"><?php the_date(); ?> <?php the_time(); ?></time>
            by <?php the_author_link(); ?>
        <?php
            // Are the comments open?
```

```
            if ( comments_open() ) : ?>
                &bull; <?php comments_popup_link( 'No comments', '1 comment', '%
                    comments' ); ?>
            <?php endif; ?>
            </p>
        </header>
</article>
```

Actually, besides the preceding changes, which I'm sure you'll have no trouble finding if you compare this to content.php, I did add an additional post `meta` line that lists the category separated by commas. If there are any tags for the post, those are also added after the category. Having this in listings is sometimes preferred, but here it serves as an example of when a separate single.php template file is warranted.

Moving on to page.php, you will see that it is very similar. In fact, you could just copy the contents from single.php, paste it into page.php, and be done with it. Well almost, because pages.php doesn't have categories of tags. Fix that in content-single.php because that is now used on page.php. If you wanted a different look and feel for your pages, you would probably create a content-page.php file and use `get_template_part( 'content', 'page' )` instead, but that's not the case here. In content-single.php, you'll wrap the post `meta` part in a conditional tag, `is_single()`, that returns `true` only if you're viewing any sort of single post of a post type. This includes attachments but not pages.

Here's the updated content-single.php:

```
<article id="post-<?php the_ID(); ?>" <?php post_class(); ?>>
    <header>
        <h1 class="entry-title">
            <?php the_title(); ?>
        </h1>
    <?php if ( is_single() ) : ?>
        <p class="entry-meta">
            Posted on <time datetime="<?php echo get_the_date(); ?> <?php
                the_time(); ?>"><?php the_date(); ?> <?php the_time(); ?></time>
            by <?php the_author_link(); ?>
        <?php
            // Are the comments open?
            if ( comments_open() ) : ?>
            &bull; <?php comments_popup_link( 'No comments', '1 comment', '%
                comments' ); ?>
        <?php endif;
            // Show categories and tags on single posts
            if ( is_singular( 'post' ) ) :
        ?>
            <br />Filed in <?php the_category( ', ' ); ?>
            <?php the_tags( ' and tagged with ', ', ', '' ); ?>
        </p>
    <?php
        endif;
    endif; ?>
```

```
    </header>
    <?php
        // The content
        the_content();
    ?>
</article>
```

So what about the comments, then? Well, you need to use comments.php, which is the template file used to style your comments. The following is an altered version of the comments.php file that ships with Twenty Eleven, ready for styling:

```
<div id="comments">
<?php
    // Is the post password protected?
    if ( post_password_required() ) : ?>
    <p class="nopassword">
        This post is password protected. Please enter your password.
    </p>
</div>
<?php
        // Go back
        return;
    endif;

    // Looking for comments
    if ( have_comments() ) : ?>
    <h2 id="comments-title">
        There are <?php comments_number( 'no comments', 'one comment', '%
            comments' ); ?>
    </h2>

    <?php
        // Comment navigation
        if ( get_comment_pages_count() > 1 && get_option( 'page_comments' ) ) : ?>
        <nav id="comment-nav-above">
            <div class="nav-previous">
                <?php previous_comments_link( '&larr; Older comments' ); ?>
            </div>
            <div class="nav-next">
                <?php next_comments_link( 'Newer comments &rarr;' ); ?>
            </div>
        </nav>
    <?php endif; ?>

    <ol class="commentlist">
    <?php
        // Listing the comments
        wp_list_comments();
    ?>
    </ol>
```

```php
<?php
    // Comment navigation
    if ( get_comment_pages_count() > 1 && get_option( 'page_comments' ) ) : ?>
    <nav id="comment-nav-above">
        <div class="nav-previous">
            <?php previous_comments_link( '&larr; Older comments' ); ?>
        </div>
        <div class="nav-next">
            <?php next_comments_link( 'Newer comments &rarr;' ); ?>
        </div>
    </nav>
    <?php endif;

// And we're done
endif; ?>

<?php
    // Leave a comment form
    comment_form();
?>

</div>
```

The comments within the code should help you along. What's important here is that `wp_list_comments()` is what's outputting the actual comments. This template tag takes a few parameters, and you can even tune the output of it using the callback parameter to point to a function in functions.php should you want to. For your needs here, you'll just use the default output, which is a simple list to work with. If you want to know what you can do with `wp_list_comments()`, read up on it in the Codex at http://codex.wordpress.org/Function_Reference/wp_list_comments.

ARCHIVE TEMPLATES

There are several possible archive templates you can use in a theme. The index.php template, when used for listing posts, is basically an archive. What kind of archive templates you want and need in your theme depends on your type of content. The archive.php template is a general fallback template in most themes, and you could stick with that. For categories, you've got category.php, and for tags, you've got tag.php. There is also date.php for date archives and so on. All available templates are listed later in this chapter in the section "Understanding Template Files"; they all work more or less the same.

For the Simple Blog theme, you'll settle for an archive.php template, which will be used for all archives (rather than just have them revert to index.php), and you'll use conditional tags to output the correct heading for the various types of archives:

```php
<?php get_header(); ?>

<div id="main-container">
    <section id="content-container">
```

```
            <header class="page-header">
                <h1 class="page-title">
                    <?php if ( is_day() ) : ?>
                        Daily archives for <span><?php echo get_the_date(); ?></span>
                    <?php elseif ( is_month() ) : ?>
                        Monthly archives for <span><?php echo get_the_date( 'F Y' ); ?>
                            </span>
                    <?php elseif ( is_year() ) : ?>
                        Yearly archives for <span><?php echo get_the_date( 'Y' ); ?>
                            </span>
                    <?php elseif ( is_category() ) : ?>
                        <?php single_cat_title('Currently browsing '); ?>
                    <?php elseif ( is_tag() ) : ?>
                        <?php single_tag_title('Currently browsing '); ?>
                    <?php else : ?>
                        Archives
                    <?php endif; ?>
                </h1>
            </header>

    <?php
        // Start the loop
        while ( have_posts() ) : the_post();

        // Get the correct content type
        get_template_part( 'content', get_post_format() );

        // Loop ends
        endwhile;
    ?>

    </section> <!-- #main-container ends -->

<?php get_sidebar(); ?>

</div>

<?php get_footer(); ?>
```

Basically, this is the index.php template without the fallback stuff, but with a conditional `if else` statement at the top outputting various headings for the different situations. This handles day, month, year, category, and tag archives, along with a general fallback just in case. You should be pretty comfortable with these template files by now, right?

404, SEARCH, AND SCREENSHOTS

There are additional templates a theme should have. Two very prominent ones are a 404 template, for those cases when a user reaches a URL on your domain that doesn't exist, and a search template for displaying search results. Called *404.php* and *search.php*, these two are pretty straightforward. The following is a simple 404.php file, which really should contain more help for the user, but you'll get to that later in the book.

```php
<?php get_header(); ?>

<div id="main-container">
    <section id="content-container">

        <article id="post-0" class="post no-results not-found">
            <header>
                <h1 class="entry-title">404 Page Not Found</h2>
            </header>
            <p>Oops, this page doesn't seem to exist. Maybe the link pointing here
              was faulty?</p>
            <p>Would you like to search for whatever you were looking for?</p>
            <?php get_search_form(); ?>
        </article>

    </section> <!-- #main-container ends -->

<?php get_sidebar(); ?>

</div>

<?php get_footer(); ?>
```

Basically, it's a simple template file with the error message in itself. This will be shown when a nonexistent page is accessed.

The search.php template is closely related to index.php. In fact, if you don't have a search template, index.php will be used. You can either copy index.php and edit it accordingly or just add some tags for when search results are displayed. For this theme, you'll go with the latter, adding this to index.php, just after the `section#content-container`:

```php
<?php
    // If it is a search result
    if ( is_search() ) :
?>
    <header class="page-header">
        <h1 class="page-title">
            You searched for<br />
            <span><?php the_search_query(); ?></span>
        </h1>
    </header>
<?php endif; ?>
```

This has a simple conditional check to find out if the page in question is a search result, and if it is, the search query is outputted in an `h1` tag. Sometimes you don't need more than that.

Oh, and don't forget to put a screenshot.png file depicting your theme in the theme folder. The file should be 300 x 225 pixels and will be used in the Themes section of the WordPress admin interface. Make it look nice, but more importantly, make it look like the theme — otherwise, you'll confuse your users, and you won't get to use your theme in the WordPress.org themes directory should you want to.

FEATURES WITH FUNCTIONS.PHP

The primary toolbox of theme designers is called *functions.php.* This file is loaded with the theme and lets you do cool stuff, almost plugin-like. This is where you activate features such as custom backgrounds and headers, featured images, menus, and a lot more. You'll revisit functions.php later in this chapter for a more in-depth look, and you'll revisit it again several times in this book. But first, take a look at the really short and simple functions.php used in your Simple Blog theme:

```php
<?php
// Set content width for the theme
if ( ! isset( $content_width ) )
    $content_width = 500;
// Theme setup
add_action( 'after_setup_theme', 'simpleblog_themesetup' );
function simpleblog_themesetup() {
    // Automatic feed links
    add_theme_support( 'automatic-feed-links' );
    // Add nav menus function to "init" hook
    add_action( 'init', 'simpleblog_register_menus' );
    // Add sidebars function to "widgets_init" hook
    add_action( 'widgets_init', 'simpleblog_register_sidebars' );
    // Queue JavaScript files on "wp_enqueue_scripts" hook
    add_action( 'wp_enqueue_scripts', 'simpleblog_load_scripts' );
}
// Register menus
function simpleblog_register_menus() {
    register_nav_menus(
        array(
            'top-navigation' => 'Top navigation',
            'bottom-navigation' => 'Bottom navigation'
        )
    );
}
// Register widget areas
function simpleblog_register_sidebars() {
    // Right column widget area
    register_sidebar( array(
        'name' => 'Right column',
        'id' => 'right-column',
        'before_widget' => '<li id="%1$s" class="widget-container %2$s">',
        'after_widget' => '</li>',
        'before_title' => '<h3 class="widget-title">',
        'after_title' => '</h3>',
    ) );
```

```
}
// Queue JavaScripts
function simpleblog_load_scripts() {
    // Queue JavaScript for threaded comments if enabled
    if ( is_singular() && get_option( 'thread_comments' ) && comments_open() )
        wp_enqueue_script( 'comment-reply' );
}
?>
```

First of all, `$content_width` tells WordPress what the basic width for the content is in pixels, which is 500 pixels in this case. Next, you have the theme setup function. This hooks on to the `after_setup_theme` hook, which means that all the functions you're including in `simpleblog_themesetup()` will be used then. These functions are further down, with `simpleblog_register_menus()` for creating two menus using `register_nav_menus()`, `simpleblog_register_sidebars()` for creating the right column widget area, and finally, `simpleblog_load_scripts()` to load whatever JavaScript is needed. All these functions are referenced in the `simpleblog_theme_setup()` function, which is hooked on to `after_setup_theme`.

Not too confusing, right? It can be, though, when you add theme options and a ton of other features. You'll take a closer look at that in Chapter 6, "Advanced Theme Usage," and onward; for now, this is all you need to do.

And you know what — that's it for the basic theme. The only thing left is to style it appropriately because without any styling in style.css, it just won't look any good, as Figure 4-7 so clearly shows.

Figure 4-7: Believe it or not, this theme only needs some CSS love to look good.

UNDERSTANDING TEMPLATE FILES

A theme consists of template files, at least one style sheet, and possibly additional files such as functions.php. There is some confusion about this at times because people refer to the theme as a *template*. That's wrong; a theme is a theme, which in effect is a folder (that needs to be situated in the wp-content/themes/ directory to be used) containing several files, some of which are template files.

Template files can be used in a wide variety of ways. Their exact use depends on what you put in them, of course. You can make them behave in almost any way you want by changing the loop or leaving it out altogether, and you can use template tags to generate a specific behavior. Likewise, you can make pages a lot more dynamic by using conditional tags, and if you really want to shake things up, you can always use plugins to extend WordPress beyond any of the built-in functionality.

There are a few things you need to know upfront about template files. First, you need to know which ones are necessary for the basic functionality. Second, you have to work out which template file is used when. Third, you should figure out which template files are necessary for what you want to achieve.

Suppose you want the home page to be the same as the index.php pages, except with an added image or welcome text. Should you use a home.php template in addition to index.php? It would be a lot more convenient to add an `is_home()` conditional tag in index.php to output the additions on the front page only. The same goes for single posts: If there is not much difference between single post view and the front page, you can use `is_single()` to alter the parts that need to be different (not linking the post title, for example).

WHICH TEMPLATE FILE IS USED WHEN?

The following are the various template files and the uses of each:

- Home and front page: front-page.php takes precedence. If a static Page is set as the front page, it will be used, then home.php, and finally index.php.
- Single posts: single-X.php where X is the post type (for example, single-book.php if the post type is "book"), then single.php, and finally index.php.
- Pages: The selected Page template comes first, then page-X.php where X is the Page slug, then page-Y.php where Y is the Page ID, then regular page.php, and finally index.php.
- Category archives: category-X.php where X is the category slug, then category-Y.php where Y is the category ID, then category.php, archive.php, and finally index.php.
- Tag archives: tag-X.php where X is the tag slug, then tag-Y.php where Y is the tag ID, then tag.php, archive.php, and finally index.php.
- Custom taxonomy archives: taxonomy-X-Y.php where X is the taxonomy slug and Y is the term slug (for example, taxonomy-person-waldo.php would be the term "waldo" in "person"), then taxonomy-X-php where X is the taxonomy slug, then taxonomy.php, then archive.php, and finally index.php.

- Custom post type archives: archive-*X*.php where *X* is the slug for the custom post type, then archive.php, and finally index.php.
- Author archives: author-*X*.php where *X* is the slug, then author-*Y*.php where *Y* is the ID, then author.php, archive.php, and finally index.php.
- Date archives: date.php, then archive.php, and finally index.php.
- Search results: search.php and then index.php.
- 404 (Not Found): 404.php and then index.php.
- Attachments: Per MIME type, such as image.php for images, video.php for videos, text. php, and so on; then attachment.php; single-attachment.php; single.php; and finally index.php.

Remember, a theme doesn't need to include all the possible template files. In fact, you shouldn't use more of these than you really need to because that only means that you'll have more files to maintain should WordPress change or if you want to alter something in your design.

Some of these templates may be confusing. Take a look at the category.php template, for example. By default, this template displays the post listing from any given category. However, should there be a category-*X*.php template, where *X* is the ID of the category in question, that template file will be used rather than the category.php template. The same goes for tags: tag-*X*. php is displayed before tag.php. The same goes for category and tag slugs, so the category Monkeys with the slug `monkeys` and an ID of 42 can be reached at category-monkeys.php as well as category-42.php.

In short, WordPress will look for a specific template file, and if that one isn't present, it will fall back to the next best template file, and lacking that, fall back again, and so on.

Keep in mind that page.php and Page templates are actually two different things. You may have noticed that you can set a template when creating WordPress Pages. These are Page templates, not controlled by page.php but rather sporting their own header information much like style.css. They can be very useful, so you'll play with them in a little while.

THE TEMPLATE HIERARCHY

Now that you know what the template files are, you need to know which one is loaded when and what happens if there is no template at all. As you know, index.php is the fallback template for everything, and you can settle for using only that. Figure 4-8 illustrates the hierarchy of the template files. For a more comprehensive version, along with conditional tags, see the WordPress Codex at http://codex.wordpress.org/Template_Hierarchy.

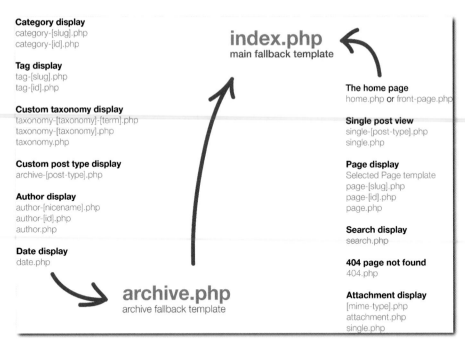

Category display
category-[slug].php
category-[id].php

Tag display
tag-[slug].php
tag-[id].php

Custom taxonomy display
taxonomy-[taxonomy]-[term].php
taxonomy-[taxonomy].php
taxonomy.php

Custom post type display
archive-[post-type].php

Author display
author-[nicename].php
author-[id].php
author.php

Date display
date.php

index.php
main fallback template

The home page
home.php or front-page.php

Single post view
single-[post-type].php
single.php

Page display
Selected Page template
page-[slug].php
page-[id].php
page.php

Search display
search.php

404 page not found
404.php

Attachment display
[mime-type].php
attachment.php
single.php

archive.php
archive fallback template

Figure 4-8: The hierarchy of template files.

PAGE TEMPLATES

WordPress Pages are meant for static content that is less time-dependent than your average blog post (which probably is static, after all). Pages can have subpages, which are typically used for information about the site, contact forms, and so on. However, you can take it way beyond that if you want to. First, you can give the page.php template a nice styling that fits the kind of content you want to display on your Pages (rather than just have them mimic your blog posts). Second, you can create Page templates that you can apply to individual Pages from the Write page section in WordPress admin.

These Page templates are basically normal template files, except that they need a little code snippet at the top of the file before the actual code begins so that WordPress can find them (much like your theme's style.css, in other words).

Just put the following lines on top of the Page template file, which you can name whatever you like as long as it is suffixed with .php:

```php
<?php
/*
Template Name: My Page Template
*/
?>
```

The preceding one, for example, could be named mypagetemplate.php. It may be a good idea to name Page templates pagetemplate-[something].php for semantic reasons, but that's entirely up to you. Just keep in mind that you shouldn't name them page-[something].php because page-[slug].php is a template file that WordPress might look for, and you could get a clash there.

With that code snippet on top and then any kind of template file content you like, the Page template will show up in the Page template box in the Write page section in WordPress admin. Just pick it, save, and there you go.

A common usage for Page templates is an archive page. Maybe you want to have a link to your archives that displays all authors, categories, tags, and the 50 latest posts using template tags. This just won't work with a normal Page because you can't put template tags within the post itself through WordPress admin (at least not without using plugins that open up the editor), so you need a Page template. Add a simple Page template to your new theme, designed for use with simple blog archives:

```php
<?php
/*
Template Name: Archives
*/

get_header(); ?>

<div id="main-container">
    <section id="content-container">

    <?php
        // Start the loop
        while ( have_posts() ) : the_post();
    ?>

        <article id="post-<?php the_ID(); ?>" <?php post_class(); ?>>
            <header>
                <h1 class="entry-title">
                    <?php the_title(); ?>
                </h1>
            </header>
            <?php
                // The content
                the_content();
            ?>
            <h2>Browse by month</h2>
            <ul>
            <?php
                // Arguments
                $args = array(
                    'type' => 'monthly'
```

```php
        );

        // The archives
        wp_get_archives( $args );
    ?>
    </ul>
    <h2>Browse by category</h2>
    <ul>
    <?php
        // Arguments
        $args = array(
            'title_li' => ''
        );

        // The categories
        wp_list_categories( $args ); ?>
    </ul>
    <h2>Browse by tag</h2>
    <?php
        // Arguments
        $args = array(
            'smallest' => 8,
            'largest' => 28,
            'number' => 0,
            'orderby' => 'name',
            'order' => 'ASC'
        );

        // The tag cloud
        wp_tag_cloud( $args ); ?>
    </article>

<?php
    // Loop ends
    endwhile;
?>

</section> <!-- #main-container ends -->

<?php get_sidebar(); ?>

</div>

<?php get_footer(); ?>
```

Other common uses are Pages created just to display a specific loop. You can just take your index.php template file, for example, make a Page template out of it (put the code snippet on top), and then change the loop to output whatever you want using `query_posts()`. You can also have a Page containing multiple loops or perhaps PHP code that isn't related to WordPress at all.

Putting Page templates to good use is a huge step toward creating the site you want using WordPress.

USING FUNCTIONS.PHP

One theme file you haven't touched very much yet is functions.php. It is a bit mysterious, and most people take a brief look at it and then shy away. Not all themes have functions.php files, but the ones that do usually support widgets and may even have their own options page inside WordPress admin. This is possible thanks to the functions.php file.

What, then, does functions.php do? Basically, it does whatever you want it to because it more or less acts like a plugin that is called within the WordPress initialization, both when viewing the public site and when loading the admin interface. Because of that, you can add admin functionality to functions.php.

You'll look at widgets and how to set up widget areas later, but first, add a simple function to functions.php:

```php
<?php
    function hellomate() {
        echo 'Hello mate, how are you doing?';
    }
?>
```

If you put that simple little code snippet in functions.php and then call the function somewhere within your theme, it will output the "Hello mate, how are you doing?" text. You call the function as you would call any PHP function:

```php
<?php hellomate(); ?>
```

So that would echo the text. Not very useful, perhaps, but it does show you something that functions.php can do. If you have code snippets you use all the time and want them easily accessible, this is your solution.

Many themes use admin options pages to let the user set his or her own color schemes or font styles, or perhaps change the header. This is all managed with functions.php. You'll dive further into functions.php in Chapter 6 and onward.

SETTING THE DEFAULT WIDTH

A commonly forgotten feature is the content width setting. Content width, which is a simple little snippet added to functions.php, tells WordPress the maximum width that the theme can manage, which in turns means that the theme will resize images accordingly. Sure, you have Media Settings in the WordPress admin interface, where you can control the size of images (see Figure 4-9), but the user may forget to change these things when changing themes.

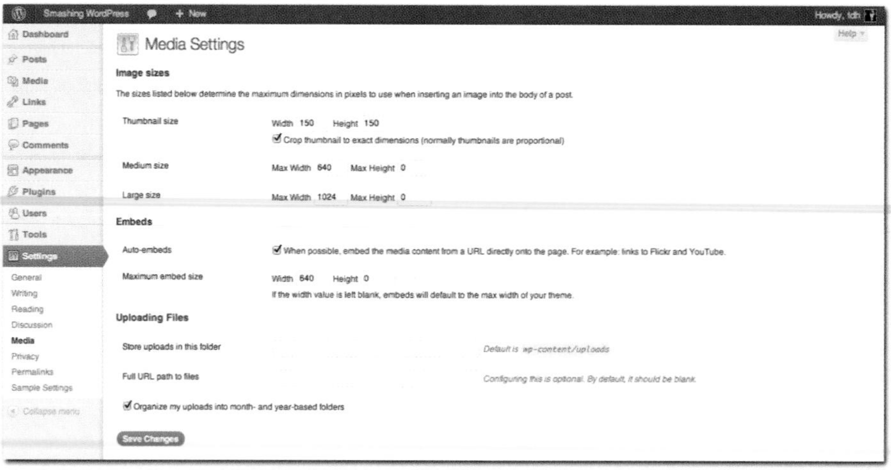

Figure 4-9: The Media Settings in WordPress admin isn't the only way to control image width.

This is where `$content_width` comes in. It sets the width for large-sized images. Remember, when uploading an image to WordPress you get a total of four images: the ones listed on the admin page and the original one. And with `$content_width`, the large image will fit perfectly with your theme.

It is easy to add. Just put this snippet in functions.php (within the PHP tags of course):

```
$content_width = 580;
```

`580` is the width in pixels, so you need to change that to whatever is the maximum width for content in your theme.

INSERTING PROMOTIONS WITH FUNCTIONS.PHP

A lot of blogs and sites show promotional elements after the post, usually to get people to subscribe to the RSS feed. This is easily done in the theme's template files, but it can also be handled by your functions.php file and some action hookery.

Say you want to encourage your readers to subscribe to your RSS feed. You want to output a `div` with the class `promotion`, and within it an h4 header and a line of text. Thanks to the magic of CSS, you can style it graphically any way you want just by applying styles to the `div` — maybe something like this:

```
div.promotion {
    background: #eee;
    border: 1px solid #bbb;
    padding: 10px; }

div.promotion h4 {
    color: #f00;
```

```
    font-size: 14px;
    margin: 0 0 5px 0;
    padding: 0; }

div.promotion p {
    font-size: 12px;
    color: #444;
    margin-bottom: 0; }
```

That would probably look decent. To really bling it up, you should add a background image featuring a nice RSS graphic or something to the `div`, but forget about that for now. This is the full HTML you want to output after your marvelous posts:

```
<div class="promotion">
    <h4>Never miss a beat!</h4>
    <p>
        The smashing <a href="http://tdh.me/feed/">RSS feed</a> keeps
        you up-to-date!
    </p>
</div>
```

How, then, do you get this thing to output itself without hacking the template files? Easily enough: You can use functions.php and attach it to the `the_content` filter hook. (You know, the one that outputs the actual content, after which you want to add it.) Here's the functions.php code:

```
function Promotion($content) {
        if( !is_feed() && !is_home() ) {
            $content.= '<div class="promotion">';
            $content.= '<h4>Never miss a beat!</h4>';
            $content.= '<p>The smashing <a href=/"http://tdh.me/feed/">
              RSS feed</a> keeps you up-to-date!</p>';
            $content.= '</div>';
        }
        return $content;
}
add_filter ( 'the_content', 'Promotion' );
```

The function creates a variable called `Promotion`, which you're storing with the HTML code. Naturally, you can just as easily write the whole HTML in one long string, rather than have four lines of `$content`, but this way makes it a bit simpler to write. Then you return `$content`, which means that `Promotion` is now stored with the HTML you want to output. Finally, you use `add_filter` to add it after `the_content`.

And there you have it; whenever it is not a home page or a feed listing (see the `if` clause — you may want to add more conditions there, by the way), you'll output the promotional box that asks the reader to subscribe to the RSS feed.

Why would you do this rather than just hack the template files? The only real reason is that this method is pretty theme-independent, so you can just copy and paste it between your themes and add the necessary CSS to the style sheet. Having a set of functions for the most common content you want to output, and even hooking them onto template tags when possible, is a way to streamline your WordPress themes even more.

As you can see, functions.php can be very handy, and it is certainly a lot more than just the widget declarations that just about every theme has these days. That said, the widgets are the most commonly used feature originating from functions.php, so you'll look at those next.

UNDERSTANDING WIDGETS AND WHEN TO USE THEM

Widgets add drag-and-drop functionality, which allows the administrator to add features to a WordPress site from within the admin interface. This can be anything from a simple text block in the sidebar to category listings, recent comments, or the latest updates from RSS feeds. That is just core widget functionality built in to WordPress; add widget-ready plugins, and you get a lot more.

When used correctly, widgets can be a great asset for a site administrator because the hands-on way you use and alter them makes them really easy to work with. In the coming chapters, you'll see how you can use widget areas for tasks other than just displaying a lot of clutter in the sidebar of typical blog 1A.

DECLARING WIDGET AREAS

It is easy to make your theme widget-ready. Do so using functions.php within your theme, where you declare the widget areas, and then add the necessary code in your various theme files (usually sidebar.php) where you want the widget area to show up.

The simplest way of doing it is just creating the default sidebar in functions.php:

```
register_sidebar();
```

Although this will work, the proper way to register a sidebar is by hooking on to `widgets_init`, which means that you need to write a function for `register_sidebar()` and then pass that to the hook, like so:

```
add_action( 'widgets_init', 'smashing_register_sidebars' );
function smashing_register_sidebars() {
    // Register sidebars
    register_sidebar()
}
```

This will hook `smashing_register_sidebars()` to `widgets_init`, which in turn means that `register_sidebars()` will be run.

Then add this to the part of sidebar.php where you want the widgets to show up. It should go within the `ul` tags:

```
<ul id="sidebar">
<?php dynamic_sidebar(); ?>
</ul>
```

For a more detailed example of how sidebar.php can look with default content in it, see the "The Right Column: sidebar.php" subsection of "Creating the Template Files" earlier in this chapter.

USING MULTIPLE WIDGET AREAS

Some themes have more than one widget area. You can accomplish this by declaring the widget areas in functions.php a little differently. If you want two sidebar areas, a header area, and a footer area that are widget-ready, just add the following code to functions.php:

```
add_action( 'widgets_init', 'smashing_register_sidebars' );

function smashing_register_sidebars() {
    // The first sidebar
    register_sidebar( array(
        'name' => 'First sidebar',
        'id' => 'first-sidebar',
        'before_widget' => '<li id="%1$s" class="widget-container %2$s">',
        'after_widget' => '</li>',
        'before_title' => '<h3 class="widget-title">',
        'after_title' => '</h3>'
    ) );
    // The second sidebar
    register_sidebar( array(
        'name' => 'Second sidebar',
        'id' => 'second-sidebar',
        'before_widget' => '<li id="%1$s" class="widget-container %2$s">',
        'after_widget' => '</li>',
        'before_title' => '<h3 class="widget-title">',
        'after_title' => '</h3>'
    ) );
    // Sidebar in the header
    register_sidebar( array(
        'name' => 'Header widget area',
        'id' => 'header-sidebar',
        'before_widget' => '<li id="%1$s" class="widget-container %2$s">',
        'after_widget' => '</li>',
        'before_title' => '<h3 class="widget-title">',
        'after_title' => '</h3>'
    ) );
    // Sidebar in the footer
    register_sidebar( array(
```

```
            'name' => 'Footer widget area',
            'id' => 'footer-sidebar',
            'before_widget' => '<li id="%1$s" class="widget-container %2$s">',
            'after_widget' => '</li>',
            'before_title' => '<h3 class="widget-title">',
            'after_title' => '</h3>'
    ) );
}
```

Speaks for itself, right? This is basically the same declaration as for one (default) widget area but with the names of every area defined. This will have to carry on to the code that defines the actual areas in the template files. That doesn't require any fancy footwork; just add the widget area ID (preferably) to the first PHP tag for defining an area, like this:

```
<?php dynamic_sidebar( 'the-widget-area-ID' ); ?>
```

So the footer area would look like this:

```
<?php dynamic_sidebar( 'footer-sidebar' ); ?>
```

Simple and straightforward. Naturally, anything that goes for single widget areas can be used when you have multiple widget areas, so if you need them to behave differently, by all means go for it.

CUSTOMIZING WIDGETS

Sometimes you may not want the widgets to output the way they do by default. Maybe you want to enclose them in div tags, for example. To do so, register them in functions.php using an array:

```
<?php
    register_sidebar( array(
        'before_widget' => '',
        'after_widget' => '',
        'before_title' => '',
        'after_title' => '',
    ) );
?>
```

The wrapping code goes inside the single quotation marks at the end of each line.

Now, wrap the widget in a div with the class customwidget and enclose the title in a div with the class customtitle:

```
<?php
    register_sidebar( array(
        'before_widget' => '<div class="customwidget">',
        'after_widget' => '</div>',
```

```
        'before_title' => '<div class="customtitle"',
        'after_title' => '</div>',
    ) );
?>
```

You should use this custom stuff with caution. After all, most themes and widgetized plugins are created with the unordered list in mind.

Now that you've gotten deep into the theme's template files and have looked into how to widgetize areas, you can do something about those comments. Yes, you did indeed look at the comments.php template file earlier in this chapter, but there is more to comments than just getting the functionality working. They need to look good.

MAKING COMMENTS LOOK GOOD

Not all sites need comment functionality, but chances are that a lot of the sites you'll be building with WordPress will. Most blogs allow readers to comment on the posts, and the same goes for the vast majority of editorial sites out there, from newspapers to magazines. This is just a good way to connect with the readership, and although the sites in question may have different motives for doing this and may have different comment policies, the basic functionality remains the same.

From a WordPress theme designer's point of view, comments can be a bore, mostly because making them look good can be a problem. The actual code isn't all that hard, though, and if you like the default comment view, you won't even have to create the comments.php template file if you don't want to.

The following list notes the most important considerations for designing the comments section of a site:

- Clearly delineate the comments section from other content. You don't want the readers to mix up comments with the editorial content.
- The comments need to be easy to read, just like the rest of the site.
- Proper spacing between comments, along with alternating colors or dividing lines, helps provide visual separation. Any method that accomplishes this separation is fine.
- The comment author must be evident.
- The Post Comment form should be obvious to use, be properly tabbed, and use a readable font in a decent size. Think about it: If you want the readers to write long and insightful comments, you should make it as easy on them as possible to do so.

A few less essential points come to mind as well:

- What's the comment policy? Link to it or put it in small print along with the Post Comment button.
- Do you allow HTML code? If so, which tags are acceptable?

- Do the comments go into moderation before publication? If they do, you should let the readers know or at least output a big note when a posted comment goes into moderation.
- Do you require sign-up and/or login to comment? Then make that process as simple and obvious as possible.

Think the comment functionality through, and you'll be fine. You'll also have a much easier time designing it, and possibly altering the functionality when required as well.

THREADED COMMENTS

Threaded comments were introduced as early as WordPress 2.7 and require activation from within the WordPress admin interface, under Settings → Discussion. Any theme that uses the proper template tag for listing the comments, which is `wp_list_comments()`, supports threaded comments should you want them.

If you activate threaded comments, you'll get a Reply link at the end of each comment. Clicking it will alter the Post Comment section somewhat and add a Cancel Reply link as well. This is all built-in stuff, so you needn't worry about it.

What you do need to consider, however, is the following:

- How deep will the threaded comments go? This is an admin setting, and you need to make sure that you support it within your design.
- You need to ensure that the Reply link is properly styled.
- You need to ensure that the Cancel Reply link is properly styled as well.

Replies to comments end up within that particular comment's `li`, inside a `ul` with the class `children`. The comment hierarchy is basically like this (with some code cut out to illustrate the point):

```
<li>
    [The top level comment content]
    <ul class="children">
        <li>
            [First level reply]
            <ul class="children">
                <li>
                    [Second level reply]
                </li>
            </ul>
        </li>
    </ul>
</li>
<li>
    [Next comment on the top level]
</li>
```

How many `uls` with the `children` class are allowed is determined by the threaded comment depth setting in admin. Five is the default, so your themes should support that many at least. The whole concept of threaded comments is built on hierarchy, so you should probably set the margin or padding for the `children` class to 10 pixels or so. It all depends on your theme, but you should make every reply indent a bit.

Styling the Reply link is easier. The link resides in an `a` with the class `comment-reply-link`, so just style that any way you want. You can make it float to the right and in a font size of 12 pixels easily enough by adding this to the style sheet:

```
a.comment-reply-link {
    float:right;
    font-size: 12px; }
```

The same applies to the Cancel Reply link that is outputted just below the Post a Comment header in the Respond section of the comment area. Again, this all depends on how your comments.php template looks, of course, but usually you'll find it here. It is in an `a` with the `cancel-comment-reply` ID by default. You can make that bold just as easily as you managed the Reply link:

```
a#cancel-comment-reply { font-weight: bold; }
```

Threaded comments are a great way to make longer conversations more manageable, so do consider using them if the topics on the site in question spark debates.

AUTHOR HIGHLIGHTING

Highlighting the post author's comments is a good idea, especially if the site is of the teaching kind. Say, for instance, you're doing tutorials. The readers may have questions, in which case it is a good idea to be very clear about which comments are the author's.

Comments are listed in a list (`ol`), with every comment being a list item (`li`). This is where you can make a difference because `wp_list_comments()` applies some CSS classes to each `li`. Among those classes are `bypostauthor`, if it is in fact the post author who wrote a comment. That means that the post author needs to be logged in when commenting; otherwise, WordPress won't recognize him or her.

You can give the post author comments a yellow background by adding this to style.css:

```
li.bypostauthor { background: yellow; }
```

You may want do something fancier as well, but changing the background of the comment is a good idea, as is upping the font size and/or color a bit. And if you want to, you can take it really far because everything related to the particular comment is found within the `li.bypostauthor` tag. This means that you can change the way the avatar is displayed (`img.avatar` is the CSS class you're looking for) or alter the comment metadata (`div.comment-author` and `div.comment-meta`) as well as the actual comment text. Set the comment text font size to 18 pixels, just for the fun of it, and keep the comment background yellow:

```
li.bypostauthor { background: yellow; }

li.bypostauthor div.comment-body p { font-size: 18px; }
```

Use post author highlighting with caution. After all, it is not always all that important that the post author's comments are highlighted this way. A smaller note, however, will never hurt.

ADDING CUSTOM FIELDS

Custom fields open up even more advanced options to the theme and plugin designer. They provide a way to store custom data in the database, and that in turn means that they can open up new functionality. See the "Using Custom Fields" section in Chapter 6 for hands-on examples on how custom fields work; in this section, I explain what you can do with them as a designer.

COMMON USAGE

Custom fields were initially thought of as a way to store metadata for a post, and that's still the way they are presented in the Codex, as well as how the default output (which you'll get to) behaves. However, that is not the most common usage for custom fields these days. Most often, custom fields are used to attach a reference of an image to a post and use it in listings or to achieve what is often referred to as *magazine-style headlines*. However, custom fields needn't be limited to managing magazine-style headlines or showing off alternative post thumbnails in listings. You can use custom fields for a number of things, such as applying custom CSS styles depending on the post as a way to add further unique styling to posts. Or you can use custom fields to create and identify a series of posts (the key would be `Series`, and the value would be the various series' names) and then create a Page template with a custom loop that limits the output to posts with a specific Series value.

Another image-based custom field implementation would be to not only apply headline and listing images for the post, but also alter the complete body background!

Custom fields can be taken pretty far, so whenever you need to step outside the boundaries of traditional WordPress template tags and functions, custom fields are definitely worth a look.

THE USABILITY FACTOR

My main gripe with custom fields is that they look so messy. Just look at that Custom Fields box in WordPress admin; it isn't at all as user-friendly as the rest of the interface. Just the *key* and *value* nomenclature, and then the whole design of the box . . . No, it just isn't something I'd trust a client with.

This is the most serious issue with custom fields, in my view. After all, when you've used them once, it is easy enough to pick the key you need and copy and paste the image you want in the value field, for example. But although that may not seem daunting to you, a client may feel different.

This is something you need to keep in mind when doing work for clients. Is it feasible to assume that the person(s) updating the site can handle custom fields? The most common usage of custom fields is, after all, headline images and things such as that, and they almost always involve finding a URL to the image and copying and pasting it to the value field of the appropriate key. Can the client handle that?

Custom fields are great, but until they are presented in a more user-friendly way, they are limited to the more web-savvy crowd, which isn't afraid to do some manual inputting. You probably fall into that category, but whether your clients (or partners, collaborators, or whoever) do is up to you to decide. If not, you are probably better off finding another solution. Luckily, there are a few plugins that solve this (which you'll get to later in the book), or you can create more stylized meta boxes yourself.

DEVELOPING A STARTER THEME

If you're a theme designer, or just an aspiring one, and you want to develop WordPress-based sites, you really need a basic starter theme. Here's why:

- It is a timesaver. Every time you need to start a new WordPress project, you have a basic and easy-to-edit/alter/break theme to begin with.
- It is familiar. When you've spent hours and hours hacking a theme, possibly for several different projects, you'll feel right at home when going at it again and again.
- It is easy to keep up to date. If you keep your starter theme up to date, you won't have to struggle with new functionality all the time: Just update once, and there you have it.
- It may make client updates easier. Assuming that you're building your sites as child themes standing on your starter theme's shoulders, updating client sites with new functionality shouldn't be a problem.

As you will discover in Chapter 5, "The Child Theme Concept," child themes are your friends. If you set up a solid starter theme that you build your WordPress sites on, you'll make everything easier on yourself.

You can use any theme as your own basic starter theme to build upon, whether you do this by hacking the theme directly to fit your needs or by applying the child theme concept to it. There are lots of free themes to use in just about any way you like, for personal sites or as a basis for commercial projects. You'll find some in Appendix B, if you haven't found a favorite yet. It is important to pay attention to the license for any theme you choose because you want to be able to use your basic starter theme any way you like without paying for every setup. If your starter theme of choice is a commercial theme, there is most likely a developer's license that gives you these rights, but if you're reading this book, chances are you're better off spending some time creating your very own starter theme.

Should you not want to use an existing theme, you can create your own basic starter theme from scratch (or copy and paste your way, with sensibility of course). This means that you'll get everything the way you want it, but it does take some extra time because you'll be doing all the work. Chances are you're interested in that sort of thing, though, because you're reading this book!

So what should your starter theme do? Well, everything you think you need on a regular basis, and absolutely nothing more. The last thing you want is a bloated starter theme that may look good in itself, or perhaps suit one kind of WordPress site, but be entirely overkill for others. It is a better idea to keep an extras library with stuff you won't need all the time, from custom code to small code snippets and template files, and deploy these things only when needed. After all, you want the final theme to be as tight as possible, without being hard to maintain.

To sum up:

- Analyze your needs and set up a basic starter WordPress theme based on those needs.
- Use an existing theme framework, if possible, to save time.
- Pay attention to theme licenses!

Say you're the generous kind and want to share your brilliant starter theme, or a variant of it at least, with the general public. Good for you; that's very much in line with the open source spirit. But if you're gonna do it, then make sure that you do it right!

RELEASING A THEME

The WordPress community always appreciates the release of a new theme. The official theme directory offers theme installation from within the WordPress admin interface, which makes it all the more interesting to host your theme there. That way, the WordPress site will also make sure that sites use the latest version of the theme or offer users the option to upgrade automatically through the admin interface. That is assuming you keep your theme up to date in the directory, of course.

When you release a theme, it should, of course, be fully functional, preferably validated, and not a complete copy of someone else's work. See the following theme checklists for more details on what you should consider before releasing your theme.

It may be tempting to sell your theme. Commercial (or *premium,* as they are sometimes called) themes are a reality, and there are licenses for sale with support programs, as well as other solutions that work around the GPL license that WordPress carries. Why should that matter to you and the theme you want to sell? Well, because WordPress is licensed under GPL, that means everything relying on WordPress is also covered. This is rocky ground to say the least, and you should carefully consider how you license your theme. It may also be good to know that the directory on WordPress.org accepts only themes compatible with the GPL license, which has (happily) sparked a mass conversion of premium themes to GPL.

THEME CHECKLISTS

When releasing a WordPress theme, and to some extent also when delivering one to a client or rolling out one of your own projects on a theme, there are some mandatory elements. Naturally, the theme needs to work — that's the first thing — and that means you need at the very least the style.css file with the theme information at the top, as well as the index.php file and whatever other template files you may want to use.

But that's not all. Before releasing your theme, you should ensure that it meets all the standards in the following checklists. These checklists can help you avoid the mistake of releasing a theme and then having to patch it right away.

Development issues

- Is the theme validated?
- Is there a proper `doctype` in the header?
- Do you call `wp_head()` and `wp_footer()`? (Because you really should!)
- Is there an RSS feed link in the header declaration? Web browsers need that to see the feed and add that pretty little icon to the right of the URL.
- Have you gotten rid of everything from your local development environment? This can be anything from local image references to code relating to your svn.
- Are you using JavaScript properly? Remember, a lot of themes are shipped with WordPress, and there is even a `wp_enqueue_script()` function for this purpose; see Chapter 11, "Design Trickery," for more information.
- Are the widget areas working as they should, and do they display default content? If they are, make sure that the content is relevant and appropriate; otherwise, they shouldn't output anything at all.
- What about menu areas? Are there any, and how are you handling them? The menu feature in WordPress helps end users a lot, so you should use it if you can!
- Have you added Edit links to posts, Pages, and possibly even comments that are displayed only when administrators are logged in? This is very handy.
- Do the Gravatars work properly?
- Did you remember to add CSS for threaded comments, even if you don't think you'll use it? It should support all the settings users can select in the admin interface.
- Is your theme ready for localization? Should it be?
- Are all the dates and times displaying properly? Try not to code this into the template files by passing parameters to `the_date()` and `the_time()`: It is a lot better to have the user control these elements in the WordPress admin settings.
- Have you set the content width variable in functions.php?
- Are you supporting custom backgrounds and custom headers? Should you?
- Have you enabled support for the post format? Do you need it?
- What about all the other nice things you can add support for: feeds and a custom style sheet for the visual editor in WordPress admin?

- If you have built-in support for plugins, have you made sure that the theme works even when the plugins aren't installed?
- Are your readme.txt and theme information in style.css up to date? Do you fulfill whatever demands your license of choice puts on the theme?
- Have you done the basic tests to make sure that the correct posts are displayed in listings, posting comments works, and things like that? Don't forget the most basic stuff: You can break a lot of WordPress functionality with your theme, so test it from the ground up!

Things the user will notice

- Is there proper 404 error handling?
- Is there a search form, and is the search results page actually usable?
- Are all the archive templates in your theme, or have you considered them in any other way? Make sure that archives for categories, tags, author, dates, and so on work in the way you want them to.
- Do nested categories and Pages display correctly when used? If there are widget areas where they should not be used at all, have you made sure that the user is aware of this?
- Have you styled the single post view properly?
- Have you styled the Page view properly?
- Did you make sure that you're not using `the_excerpt()` anywhere you should be using `the_content()`?
- Is pagination working: previous/later posts on post listing pages, and possibly previous/next post links on single posts?
- Does the author name display the way you want?
- Have you checked that all attachments (images, videos, and so on) are displayed properly? You may need to make a template file for this if your design is limited in any way.
- Do image galleries look good?
- Have you enabled featured images?
- When comments are turned off, what happens? Make sure that the response looks good and displays a message the way you'd like it to.

Formatting

- Have you styled every element from the visual editor in WordPress admin to be displayed properly? This includes block quotes, tables, and both ordered and unordered lists.
- Do block quotes, lists, and so on work within the comments?
- Are you styling comments and trackbacks differently? And do you highlight author comments?
- Have you put in special styling for sticky posts? Is special styling needed?
- Have you checked that headings 1 to 6 look good (even if you don't expect to use them all)?
- Do images inserted from within WordPress display properly? This includes images floating to the left and right as well as centered images.

- Do image captions work?
- What happens if an image that is too wide gets published? Does it break the design?

Naturally, there are tons of things that are directly related to your theme that you need to test out as well. You need to check whether menu links work and that all text is readable. The preceding checklists will help you avoid common WordPress-related mistakes with your theme. You should add anything that is related to your design and code to those checklists for even more assurance that your sites will look good and work as expected.

COMMERCIAL THEMES AND THE GPL LICENSE

Commercial (or premium) GPL themes cannot be submitted to WordPress.org at this time. However, if you're a theme reseller, you can get featured on the commercial themes page, which currently is just a links page containing screenshots of some popular themes, but no hosting. In other words, this means that the commercial GPL theme you're selling won't work with automatic updates from within the WordPress admin interface because WordPress.org won't let you host it there unless you make it free for all to download. Naturally, if you do that, hosting may be approved, and you can make money on providing support or customizations to the design, or whatever your theme business is all about.

The commercial themes page is a fairly new addition to WordPress.org, and the debate on how commercial GPL themes should be managed continues. If you intend to profit from commercial GPL themes in any way, you should keep up to date on developments in this area. You can read more at http://wordpress.org/extend/themes/commercial.

SUBMITTING TO WORDPRESS.ORG

If the theme checklists didn't raise any obstacles and your theme is licensed under a GPL-compatible license, you can submit it to the WordPress.org theme directory. Hosting your theme there is good for several reasons, the most prominent being the ability to reach WordPress users through the official channel, which incidentally now also resides within the admin interface. It also lets you update to new versions and hosting and provides nice linkage with the WordPress.org support forums.

Before you start thinking of submitting your theme, you should install and run the excellent Theme Check plugin (http://wordpress.org/extend/plugins/theme-check), which is based on the tests that the theme review team runs on your theme. This plugin will let you know what problems there are and also recommend fixes, so it is a great help and also a timesaver for the review team. If you're comfortable with messing with wp-config.php, you should also enable WP_DEBUG, which means that you'll set it to `true`:

```
define( 'WP_DEBUG', true );
```

When done, just change this to `false` again. This will give you more information about any errors you might have, especially the ones that WordPress might've suppressed because they're not crucial for the site and/or platform to function. If you just want to debug the WordPress JavaScript, then use this:

```
define( 'SCRIPT_DEBUG', true );
```

As with `WP_DEBUG`, just set this to `false` when done.

Your theme needs to be complete and saved in a single zip file. This should contain all the theme's template files, where style.css is extremely important. This is where the version is listed, along with the tags that are used to sort your theme. You also need to include a screenshot.png file, which has to be a screenshot of your theme in action, not a logo or something similar. Other rules include avatar support (usually done with Gravatar [http:// gravatar.com]), widget support, exposed RSS feeds, showing the blog title and tagline, and listing both categories and tags by default.

Remember the Tags label at the top of style.css? That's where you define how your theme will be sorted on WordPress.org, should it be approved. Tags are separated by commas, like this:

```
Tags: light, two-columns, right-sidebar, fixed-width, custom-menus
```

That would go at the top of the style.css file, along with the other things that define the theme.

The following are the tags currently used for sorting your theme on WordPress.org (a definitely up-to-date version is available at http://wordpress.org/extend/themes/about).

Colors
- black
- blue
- brown
- green
- orange
- pink
- purple
- red
- silver
- tan
- white
- yellow
- dark
- light

Columns
- one-column
- two-columns

- `three-columns`
- `four-columns`
- `left-sidebar`
- `right-sidebar`

Width

- `fixed-width`
- `flexible-width`

Features

- `blavatar`
- `buddypress`
- `custom-colors`
- `custom-header`
- `custom-background`
- `custom-menu`
- `editor-style`
- `featured-image-header`
- `featured-images`
- `front-page-post-form`
- `full-width-template`
- `microformats`
- `post-formats`
- `rtl-language-support`
- `sticky-post`
- `theme-options`
- `threaded-comments`
- `translation-ready`

Subject

- `holiday`
- `photoblogging`
- `seasonal`

Take good care to make the tags as accurate as possible because it is via these tags that people will find your theme in the WordPress.org theme directory, whether they're browsing it from the WordPress.org website or from within their WordPress install (under Appearance and then Add New Themes).

You can submit your theme at http://wordpress.org/extend/themes/upload.

MOVING ONWARD WITH THEMES

Now you know how the WordPress syntax is constructed (refer to Chapter 2, "The WordPress Syntax"), how the loop works (as shown in Chapter 3, "The Loop"), and also how a theme is built from the ground up.

At this point, you may have started to consider creating your own starter theme, tuned to your needs. By all means go for it, and be sure to pick the best from the themes you like as well as altering the code to fit your needs. There is no reason for you not to start fiddling with themes now, although the following two chapters may open up some more doors for you.

Next up are child themes, a way for you to build on a theme without actually altering it. Think about that and the possibilities for a while, or just turn the page and get on with it.

5

THE CHILD THEME CONCEPT

AS A WORDPRESS designer, one of the things you need to keep in mind is the addition of new features with new versions of WordPress, and in turn the deprecation of old ones. A theme created a few years ago will probably still work, but it will definitely be lacking some of the functionality of more modern themes. And the question is, will it still work in another few years? The backward compatibility in WordPress is pretty extensive, but there is a limit.

Compatibility is one of the many reasons why you create core themes to build on and why using child themes to extend them is such a great idea.

In a way, the child theme concept is all about moving the individual styling for the sites you create another step from the code because the child theme will consist mostly of visual enhancements and changes to the parent theme. This means that the user can update the core theme without breaking anything.

This chapter is dedicated to the brilliance of child themes and how you can use them effectively for your own projects.

THE BRILLIANCE OF CHILD THEMES

Child themes let you create themes that rely on other themes, called *parent themes,* as templates, by changing parts of the parent theme to suit your own needs. For example, say you love a particular theme but dislike the fonts and colors. You may also think that it needs a few Page templates to meet your needs. There are two ways to tackle this problem. The most obvious method is the direct route: Just open the theme's files and edit them to your heart's content. In this case, that would mean making some changes in style.css (for the fonts and colors) and adding a couple of Page templates. No big deal, right?

Wrong. What happens when the theme author updates the theme with brand-new functionality, and you, giddy with joy, upload the new version and see all your edits go away? Obviously, your edits, with the colors you changed and your Page templates, aren't included in the original author's theme, so now you'll have to re-create all your adaptations so that the theme fits your needs again. You can of course keep notes of what you change and back up your altered files, but the new version of the theme may have several changes and (re)applying your edits will be at best a nuisance — at worst, tricky and time-consuming.

Editing a theme may be a simple solution, but if you want to be able to upgrade it with new versions with your edits intact, there is a better way. You can create a child theme, using the original theme as the parent theme (or *template,* as it is called when defining it). The child theme sits in its own folder, and so do all its associated files, so when you upload the new version of the original theme that you've built your site on, you'll overwrite only that theme's files, and not your child theme, which contains all your changes. In other words, none of your edits will go away when updating the main theme. The whole idea is to separate the main theme functionality, code, and content from your own edits and adaptations. And because those will reside in your child theme's area, they are safe from the parent theme's updates. Figure 5-1 illustrates the child theme concept.

HOW CHILD THEMES WORK

Any theme can be the parent of a child theme. The parent theme must be located in your wp-content/themes/ folder (because otherwise you can't use its files) and the child theme in its own folder, just like a regular theme. For example, to use the Notes Blog theme as a parent theme, make sure that it is in the wp-content/themes/ folder and then add your very own Small Notes child theme (or whatever you want to call it) in its own folder, also within wp-content/themes/.

After that, you need a style.css file to tell WordPress that it is a theme, and in fact a child theme, and point to the parent theme. Whenever a template file is called for, WordPress will look for it within the child theme, and if it isn't there, it'll load up the one in the original parent theme.

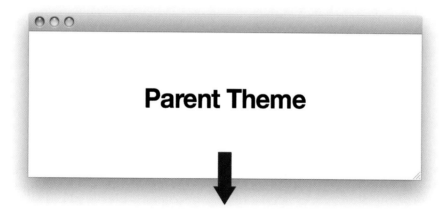

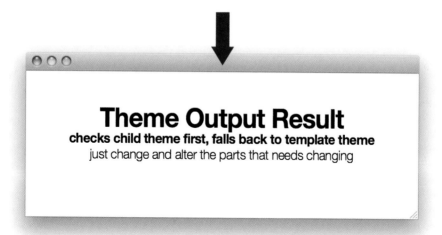

Figure 5-1: The child theme concept.

Here's the basic style.css for a theme, omitting some of the tags necessary only for WordPress. org submission:

```
/*
Theme Name: Your Theme Name
Theme URI: http://your-theme-homepage.com
Description: Oh what a lovely description of your theme you'll put here!
Author: Your Name
Author URI: http://your-website.com
Version: A version number
*/
```

You need to add a `Template` line if you want the style sheet to declare that it is a child theme, like this. The template line contains the word *Template:* and the name of the folder in which the parent theme resides:

```
Template: The name of the parent theme's folder goes here (child themes only)
```

Here's the style.css file again, filled out with dummy content to fit the hypothetical Small Notes child theme for Notes Blog:

```
/*
Theme Name: Small Notes
Theme URI: http://notesblog.com/blog/small-notes/
Description: This is Small Notes, a child theme for Notes Blog.
Author: Thord Daniel Hedengren
Author URI: http://tdh.me
Template: notes-blog
Version: 1.0
.
You need to have both Small Notes and Notes Blog in your wp-content/themes/ folder
  for this theme to work.
.
*/
```

Remember, this is the child theme's style.css file. You can activate it just like a normal theme from the Appearance page in WordPress admin.

Now that you have your style sheet for the Small Notes child theme, you can change those fonts and colors. First, you must decide whether to completely replace the parent theme's style.css file (Notes Blog in this case) or build on it. For this example, you will build on the Notes Blog style.css, so you need to import the style sheet from Notes Blog. You do that with the `@import` tag:

```
@import url("../notes-blog/style.css");
```

Add that line below the style.css theme header information and add anything you want to alter below it. Change some colors and some fonts, just for fun:

```
@import url("../notes-blog/style.css");

div#content { font-family: Georgia, Times New Roman, serif; }

ul.sidebar { color: #444; }
```

Nothing fancy there, but you will have the font family starting with Georgia on everything in the `div` with `id="content"`, and the color of type in the `ul.sidebar` tag will be dark gray. This will be read *after* everything in the style sheet from Notes Blog is read; `@import` is declared and read first.

So the full style.css file for the Small Notes child theme, with the changes mentioned so far, would look like this:

```
/*
Theme Name: Small Notes
Theme URI: http://notesblog.com/blog/small-notes/
Description: This is Small Notes, a child theme for Notes Blog.
Author: Thord Daniel Hedengren
Author URI: http://tdh.me
Template: notes-blog
Version: 1.0
.
You need to have both Small Notes and Notes Blog in your wp-content/themes/ folder
  for this theme to work.
.
*/


@import url("../notes-blog/style.css");

div#content { font-family: Georgia, Times New Roman, serif; }

ul.sidebar ( color: #333; }
```

Remember the Page templates you wanted? Creating them is easy. Just create them like you would if you hacked the Notes Blog theme and put them in the Small Notes child theme folder. Now they are available for use whenever the Small Notes child theme is activated, just like with a regular theme.

Every template in the child theme is ranked higher than its equivalent in the parent theme. That means that even though there is a sidebar.php in the Notes Blog parent theme, your sidebar.php from Small Notes will be loaded instead. If you don't want to make any changes to the sidebar.php file from the parent theme, just don't add that file to the child theme.

There is one exception to this rule, and that is functions.php. The parent theme's functions. php file will be loaded even if there is a functions.php in the child theme folder, but the child theme's functions.php is loaded first. This is a good thing because it means that you can use the child theme's functions.php to alter whatever features and functions you'd like from the parent theme. In other words, if you want to do something slightly different in your child theme, you can override parts of the parent theme's functions.php by just altering the particular code that's bothering you in your child theme's functions.php, leaving the rest of the parent theme's functions.php fully functional. The great advantage to this process is that only changes go in your child theme, so whenever the original parent theme is updated, you can update your parent theme too, knowing that your changes are intact in the child theme. Better yet, your child theme will reap the benefits of the parent theme update, while otherwise remaining untouched.

THE BEAUTY OF TEMPLATE FILE OVERRIDING

The fact that most template files in a child theme will override the parent theme's equivalent means that you can target specific parts of the parent theme and alter just that. This usually means that you'll add new template files to your child theme that take precedence over the parent theme. For example, say that you want another look and feel for your category archives; you'll just create the category.php template file in your child theme, and it will be used instead of the parent theme's category.php. Chances are you need to add some CSS as well, but all you need to do is add the necessary style to your child theme's style sheet.

It is not just regular template file overriding that makes child themes so great. Say that you actually just want a specific category to look and feel different. By adding category-awesome.php to your child theme, you can target that particular category, with the slug "awesome" in this case, without changing anything else. You could add category-awesome.php to your parent theme as well, but that might be a problem when updating the theme, and chances are you don't want it to be a global thing.

THE WONDERFUL LOOP.PHP TEMPLATE

Child themes and using additional template files containing the loop are a great mix. A lot of themes are putting the complete loop in the loop.php template file, further separating the heavy code from the basic markup and design. This really helps when it comes to child themes because it lets you pinpoint a specific loop in your child themes, instead of overwriting a complete template file.

Suppose you want to alter the loop on category archives. Your parent theme of choice has a fully functional category.php file, which in turn includes a loop template called loop-category.php, with this now familiar code snippet:

```php
<?php get_template_part( 'loop', 'category' ); ?>
```

As you know, this will first look for loop-category.php, and failing that, loop.php.

Previously, you would have had to create a brand-new category.php template file to get to the loop used there, but no more. If you want to alter the actual loop in your child theme, just put a loop-category.php template file in there. Because the child theme's file will take precedence, the loop-category.php file that your parent theme's category.php wants to include will be pulled from your child theme instead (assuming you've put it there, of course). In other words, you can get to the loop included in the parent theme's category.php without having to put a complete category.php template in your child theme — just the loop. Sweet, huh?

The same technique obviously works just as well for other template files that are included this way. Say that you've got a menu that differs around the site. You're including it with `get_template_part()`, looking for nav-X.php and defaulting back to nav.php. The following code would look for nav-archives.php and, failing that, settle for nav.php:

```php
<?php get_template_part( 'nav', 'archives' ); ?>
```

In your child theme, you could easily target nav-archives.php if you wanted to, just like you can target specific loops. This way, you can change parts of the site that aren't just the loop as well, using child themes, which will save time and effort when maintaining the theme.

EVENT CHILD THEMES

One of the cooler, albeit not as groundbreaking, usages of child themes is the possibility of short-term event themes. Think about it: If you have a theme that you're happy with but suddenly want full of snow and reindeer and such to celebrate that cold time of the year, then why not just create a child theme that swaps out the colors, background images, and even the graphics?

Or, to be blunt, say you want to make money by selling parts of your design to a company for promotion. Background images, slightly altered header files, and the like are all a breeze using child themes. Sitewide ads and roadblock-like functionality are easily implemented in this way.

Using child themes for minor events, promotions, and other custom hacks is a great way to keep the main theme clean. Any good theme designer will consider this option.

A Few Words on Theme Semantics

Child themes can certainly spin things around. Say that you love a particular theme, and it has a class called `column-right`, which is used to place the ever-present sidebar to the right side of the main content, in a suitable column. Fair enough. Problem is, you want it on the left side, which you can easily fix by just applying `float: left` in the style.css file of your child theme. It works, but it is ugly to have an element named `column-right` positioned to the left.

This may seem a bit nerdy, even trivial, but writing code that makes sense is important when several people are collaborating on a project, and also good form in general. The whole point of naming elements in design after what they actually are supposed to be is that you, and the people you work with, will have an easier time finding your bearings in the design.

So `column-right` should really be on the right side. That's where you'll look for it, thanks to the name.

Another popular example of this is the sidebar. A lot of people think that the sidebar.php template, or at least the actual term *sidebar*, should be retired. It is something of a relic from the past, from the time when WordPress was about blogging only. Today WordPress is a CMS, and you use it for a lot more than just publishing blog posts. Why call it *sidebar*; why not *sidecolumn*? You can take the reasoning another step; what says that it will be on the side of things at all? Single-column designs often position the sidebar.php content at full width below the main content, above the footer. There's nothing wrong with that, other than that the sidebar obviously isn't to the side.

Now, perhaps that's taking it a bit too far. WordPress and its community will most likely keep using the *sidebar* lingo for quite some time, but that doesn't mean that you need to name things `column-right`. It is something to think about when designing themes because although a certain name may make a lot of sense in the present context, there's nothing to say that you won't be moving that `column-right` to the left side. And if someone were to use your theme as a parent template theme for a child theme, that is even more likely to happen.

So think about the semantics. It'll make things easier on everyone.

THE FLIP SIDE OF INHERITANCE

You already know that most template files in a child theme take precedence over the parent theme's counterpart. A child theme's style.css trumps the style.css of the parent theme, and so does the child theme's index.php compared to the parent theme's index.php, and so on.

The child theme inherits the contents of the parent theme, but only if it needs it.

This brings up some issues, the most obvious probably being "what if they don't match, designwise?" Well, the whole idea with child themes is to make customizations to themes you like. In other words, if you create a child theme based on a parent theme that you end up changing altogether, with new template files for just about everything, you may have defeated the purpose. After all, that is just like taking the original theme and making a new version of it, which means that you're missing out on the smooth upgrading perks that child themes can claim.

A child theme is most warranted when most of your changes go in style.css, at most a few template files, and possibly some changes using functions.php. The former can alter the look and feel of the theme, whereas the latter two can change the necessary functionality.

So what's the verdict: Are child themes a good idea? In most cases, yes. If you discover you're creating a brand-new theme rather than making standalone changes to an existing one, you're better off creating what you need from scratch, or rather, from that core theme you may have ended up creating by now.

COMMON ISSUES TO KEEP IN MIND

There really are just two things with child themes that can cause confusion. The first is purely user-based, and that is the fact that the child theme just won't work unless the parent theme is in the wp-content/themes/ folder. This is pretty obvious when you think about it, but most users are used to just uploading a theme and then activating it, and that won't work with a child theme unless the parent theme is there. Or, rather, it may work, but it will definitely look awful and behave badly, too.

The second issue with child themes is technical, and it involves the template path. Most of the time when you want to point to the theme directory, for example to display an image, you'll use `get_template_directory_uri()` and echo it for use. That won't work in a child theme, as the template directory is in fact the parent theme's directory! Hence this code, to display an image, would point to the parent theme's theme folder rather than the child theme's folder:

```
<img src="<?php echo get_template_directory_uri(); ?>/images/the-image.gif" alt=
"My image" />
```

Luckily, there is a solution to this. If you use `get_stylesheet_directory_uri()` rather than `get_template_directory_uri` in your child theme, WordPress will look in the folder with the theme's style sheet instead. And guess what, that's your child theme! So the preceding code would have to be altered to this to work in a child theme:

```
<img src="<?php echo get_template_directory_uri(); ?>/images/the-image.gif"
alt="My image" />
```

This is a common issue, with images suddenly not working or perhaps the wrong one being displayed because of it existing in the parent theme as well.

When you are working with child themes, it is important to remember that functions pointing to a template actually refer to the parent theme, not the child theme. The preceding example illustrates this. It makes a lot of sense, actually, because the child theme uses the parent theme as a template, whereas a parent theme (or rather, a nonchild theme) is its own template, so to speak.

MANAGING SEVERAL SITES USING CHILD THEMES

If you're one of those people running your own blog network or just a number of sites built on the same basic design, then child themes are just right for you. Think about it: You can put more resources into creating features and deploying new functionality in the parent theme and store all the custom stuff for the various sites in child themes. That way, you'll speed up development and make upgrades easier.

If your users have access to several themes and pick whichever they like to use, remember to not make the parent theme available to them in Network Admin (see Figure 5-2). By just enabling the child themes, you give your users the features of your parent theme, but they can choose only from the child themes you have enabled. This way, you can make sure that they aren't using a theme that might not be meant for public usage.

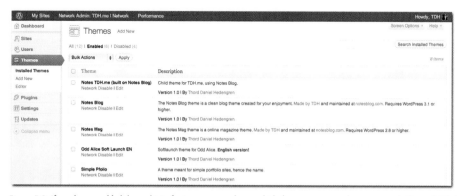

Figure 5-2: If you have enabled the multisite feature, you can choose which themes your users have access to in Network Admin.

MANAGING DESIGN FOR MULTIPLE SITES

First, find the common elements in your design. Granted, because most people don't launch a series of sites built on the same basic look but rather pilfer themes and designs left and right, it may even be a better idea to start from scratch and create a basic design to build on and customize. There are several big-name blog networks that employ this method today, so look around.

Second, after finding all the common elements your sites will need, you should wireframe the main parent theme design. Make room for everything, think about what may go where, and plan ahead.

Third, create the parent theme. This should be as simple and stripped down as possible, containing only the things that *all* your sites will use. If an element isn't common to all your sites, ignore it and define it in the child themes instead. A common mistake is to overstyle the parent theme because it just looks bland and boring otherwise. Don't do that; you'll just end up overriding your own code in the child theme's template files, and that is code that has already been read once. Why make your themes slower to load, after all?

After these three steps, things get a bit more fluid. Start creating child themes that fit the various sites in your network and roll them out. When your network is built completely on child themes, and you want to add a common feature, you only have to do that in the main parent theme. Upgrade it across the network, and suddenly all the sites will have this new feature. Compare that to having to actually implement it in every theme, which is at best a tedious copy-and-paste exercise, and you'll understand that there is time and potentially money to be saved by using child themes.

DON'T FORGET ABOUT FUNCTIONS.PHP

It is not just on the design front where you can benefit from using one main parent theme and any number of child themes across your network: Pure functionality can gain from this, too. Remember, you can have your very own functions.php file for every theme, both the main one and the child themes, which means that if you're PHP-savvy, you can create plugin-like functionality on the theme side of things.

Another of the things people running multiple sites need to tackle is the maintenance of plugins. Granted, this is a lot easier these days, with upgrade functionality from within the WordPress admin interface, but some of the tasks you use plugins for can in fact be done just as well from within your themes. Although you can have those cool things in your theme's template files, whether it is a parent or child theme, it just isn't all that convenient. Besides, the whole idea with themes in the first place is to separate design from code, so filling the template files with more PHP snippets than usual kind of works against that purpose.

This is where functions.php may be an acceptable middle ground. After all, it is a template file outside of the design part of the theme, existing purely to add extra functionality through PHP coding. So it may be a better idea to write general functions in the functions.php file of the main parent theme rather than maintaining plugins that do the same thing across all sites. This strategy can also help reduce the maintenance burden for a network with several sites. Just don't forget about data portability; after all, you want your site to work as intended even when you swap themes, right?

THERE IS SUCH A THING AS TOO MUCH

Child themes are great and something you should consider using; that much should be clear by now. However, there is such a thing as too much, as well, just like for regular themes. For example, although the functions.php file in your child theme can be useful, you should probably consider creating a brand-new theme if it gets too advanced. The same goes if you end up overwriting a lot of template files in the parent theme: Perhaps it is a better idea just to fork the theme and create a new one instead.

There's also the issue of updating the child theme. If you end up with a child theme with a ton of new functionality that needs to be maintained, you might have missed the point of using child themes in the first place. In a perfect world, everything you need to maintain is in the parent theme, and minor changes and additions are in the child theme. Don't forget about that; if things get complicated and just keep growing, you should consider creating a new parent theme instead.

WHAT ABOUT THEME FRAMEWORKS?

There's a lot of talk about theme frameworks within the WordPress community. You may wonder how child themes fit with that notion, and the answer is, of course, that they fit perfectly well. Most so-called theme frameworks are semiblank themes that are designed for you to modify, using either child themes or similar concepts. Some want you to put custom code in folders within the theme, for example, so it pretty much depends on how the theme designer envisions the usage of the creation.

However, this doesn't mean that you're limited to doing only what the designer intended. Any theme is really a possible theme framework in this sense, and any theme can be used as the parent theme for a child theme. You can always just use the theme as the parent theme and then create your own child theme.

Some of the functionality in these themes designed to be used as frameworks for your own creations rely on *action hooks.* This is basically a way for the theme to pass implementation and data to the theme using functions.php. Then, your child theme (or pseudo-functions file within the theme framework if that's the solution of choice) can do things with these action hooks, including removing them should they not be wanted. You'll get to action hooks in the next chapter, "Advanced Theme Usage."

So any theme (that isn't a child theme) is a possible parent theme, and the themes that try to pass themselves off as theme frameworks are basically just creations more suited for being used as the basis for new designs. That is worth keeping in mind, I think.

LET'S TALK ABOUT PARENT THEMES INSTEAD

This is all very confusing, especially because the term *framework* is used so loosely within the WordPress community, and hence here as well. Theme designers often call their themes *frameworks,* which obviously is in their right. However, I'd like to argue that most frameworks are just themes that are more suited for building new themes upon. These new themes could possibly be child themes; that would depend on what you want to achieve. Add to that the use of terms such as *starter themes,* and things get a bit muddy.

The thing to take away from this is to not think too much about what the theme designer calls a theme. Any theme that will work standalone is a possible parent theme, and when it comes to child themes, that's the only important thing.

TAKING THEMES TO THE NEXT LEVEL

Understanding child themes is the first step in taking WordPress theme development to the next level, or at least expanding it to a wider scale. You can put all your core functionality in one theme, everything you usually put into themes anyway, and then lean on that one theme by using a child theme that builds on it.

I'm a firm believer in saving time and making updating easier, so I think child themes are a great idea in most cases, although there are exceptions. For example, with a very traffic-heavy blog, you would want to cut down on anything that adds bandwidth, and in such a case, you should consider as tight a theme as possible.

6

ADVANCED THEME USAGE

TO MOVE BEYOND traditional WordPress sites, which build on the platform's blog basics, you need to be aware of some of the more advanced features that are available to the theme developer. Most of these features build on the template tags and conditional tags that you have been using thus far, but the usage may differ. Some techniques, however, will change or add to the functionality of WordPress from within your theme, which may not be such a good idea if you're looking to release it for general use but may be a good fit for the project you're working on right now.

That's what it all boils down to, really: taking WordPress and putting it to good use for the task at hand. Building a WordPress theme and

releasing or even selling it is one thing, but building a fully fledged WordPress-powered site is something completely different. This chapter is all about taking that extra step and putting WordPress to good use. This includes having a sound theme concept, styling the content the way you want, adding custom features such as custom headers and backgrounds, and working with custom taxonomies when the default categories and tags won't cut it. This chapter also covers adding even more hooks to your theme for easy inclusion of more features. Yes, there really is a lot you can do with your WordPress theme, so why not get to it?

OUTLINING THE THEME

The first thing you should do when you're starting a new WordPress project is consider what functionality you need from the theme. Simple blog designs usually aren't very complicated — you just start from the top and go from there — but if you want to build a newspaper-like site using WordPress, you will have to consider other factors. One of the most obvious concerns is how to make the site look customized because although we all love WordPress, one of the reasons for developing your own themes is to make your site look the way you want, rather than just rely on the default theme.

Before starting to design and code a site, you need to figure out a few basics, outlined in the following list:

- The main website layout: What sections, pages, and major elements do you need to make room for, and how will you populate these with content from WordPress? This usually involves planning multiple loops and determining what template files are needed where.
- Sorting the content: This is usually all about what categories to choose and which parts of the site are static enough to be Pages. Also, will there be a need for public tagging? If not, you can use tagging for customizing post designs and similar tasks without having to think of public tag archives.
- The small stuff: Will you need dynamic elements in this site, where you can drop poll widgets and special promotions? These areas should probably be widgetized.
- Commenting: Most, but not all, modern websites with editorial content have commenting functionality, so you need to decide whether to incorporate this into your project.
- Special functionality: Is there anything you need that WordPress can't do out of the box? If so, you need to figure out if there is a plugin that can help (or develop your own) or perhaps even find an external service to integrate into the site.

Knowing what you want to pull off is essential to outlining the perfect theme for a more advanced project. When you have worked through these items, you can start mocking up, doing paper sketches, playing around with code snippets, and whatever else is in your workflow when creating fabulous websites.

I've been developing WordPress sites on a professional basis since version 1.5, and I've been a user since before that. My sites range from simple blogs to magazines to entirely different functions. Later in this book, you'll learn how to create completely different things using WordPress, showing that it can be a framework as well as a CMS, but for now, all you need to know is that I'm constantly trying to push it to do new things.

When I start up a new project, I always consider what it needs to do and how I can meet those needs: What types of content will be presented, and how will it be displayed to give the user the best possible experience? The following three subsections outline my top three tips for doing this. This approach likely won't fit everyone or every project, but it will help you think through your own approach.

RULE #1: STYLE BY CATEGORY, SORT BY TAG, AND TUNE WITH POST FORMATS

Categories are great for rough sorting, such as a category for Music and another for Books, but they should never be too niche. Tags, on the other hand, can be as precise as needed, which means that a book review may belong to the category Books and have tags that identify the book's author, genre, title, publishing house, and so on. The purpose of this isn't just nomenclature; there are technical reasons behind the decision. First, it's easy to create custom looks for category listings using the category.php and even category-*X*.php (*X* is the ID) template files. These can let you list one kind of content in one way and a second kind in another.

Tags, on the other hand, are niched in themselves and should be viewed partly as search keywords that get grouped together and partly as descriptions of the content. They can be useful as both, especially when you want to collect all those J. K. Rowling book reviews without having to force a traditional (and not so exact) search. By carefully considering how you set up categories and tags and how they relate to each other, you can achieve a great deal.

Need more control? Sometimes the default category and tag taxonomies won't cut it. That's when you create your own taxonomies to provide even more specificity. Custom taxonomies are great because although you can use them for additional organization, much like tags and categories, you can also keep them completely hidden from the visitor. Using a custom taxonomy to add more control over post styling is great, for example.

Need even more? Post formats give you additional control over posts and how they can be styled and managed. In typical blog fashion, this is often a more suitable solution than using categories for styling, so weigh these against each other.

RULE #2: CAREFULLY CONSIDER CUSTOM FIELDS

Custom fields are very useful. They can store data as well as images, and they can fill in the blanks when you need more than just a title, a slug, the content, and an excerpt, or when you want to sidestep the categories and tags. That's great. They are not, however, very user-friendly, as I've already argued, and that means you need to be wary. A lot of funky WordPress-powered sites need to rely heavily on custom fields, but in such cases, you need to educate the people running them. A plugin, which can do the same thing but just not show it, may be a better idea.

> *Keep in mind that using custom fields to do simple stuff like asides is completely unnecessary, thanks to post formats. Use custom fields primarily for data.*

RULE #3: BUILD WITH PAGES AND EXTEND WITH CUSTOM POST TYPES

Pages have a great strength in that you can have just about as many as you want, and each one can have its own Page template if you like. This means that anything you can do with

WordPress can be accessible at the address of your choosing. Hence, most of my Page templates don't include the actual Page's content or the traditional WordPress loop at all. Rather, they do other things, and although they may be a bit rough to manage by themselves — you have to hack the template file because there's nothing more than a title and a slug in WordPress admin — they can step outside the box.

Think about it. Say you need to show off your work stored at another service. You can include it by using the service's own JavaScript widget code, and you can even have it exist in itself that way; all functionality is included. Unfortunately, WordPress wouldn't let that code through. The solution is to just create a Page template and put the code there. The same goes for Google Custom Search Engine result listings, for showing off RSS feed content, or your lifestream.

The Page template is a powerful tool. Use it wisely.

Need even more control here? You can always add custom post types tailored to your needs. Want a completely separate hierarchy of Pages like, er, pages? No problem; just create your own custom post type mimicking Pages. Custom post types are an excellent solution when you need more control over your content and how it is organized in the install as well as on the site.

IS THAT ALL?

Of course, the preceding three rules don't cover everything, but they are the main points I tackle when I start to build a site using WordPress. Other things to consider include whether the user should be able to subscribe to RSS feeds, what screen resolutions you should design for, and if you need additional support for mobile devices. There's more as well, depending on the site you're building, such as the search needs of the user and not to mention how heavy the site can be — not everyone has a broadband connection. Keep an open mind and try to look at the site from your target audience's point of view.

INDIVIDUAL STYLING TECHNIQUES

Adding some individual styling can make both posts and Pages more interesting. At first glance, this may seem hard to accomplish, especially when it comes to posts because they are all governed by one single template file: single.php. Luckily, there are great methods to add a little extra flair to the posts, thanks to the excellent addition of the `post_class()` template tag and some nifty little CSS.

But first, you need to understand the more obvious individual styling technique. I'm talking about Pages, which can be easily styled to act in any way you like because all you really need to do is create a Page template that behaves in the way you want. You can take this even further than is possible with blog posts by loading different sidebars, headers, footers, or whatever you want, really. The strength of the Page template is that it can be set up any way you want, and all you need to do is create it and choose it for your Page.

The same applies to category and tag listings. If you want to add a header graphic to a specific category, for example, all you need to do is alter that particular category's template file. You may remember that category-X.php takes precedence over category.php (which in turn beats first archive.php and then index.php) and that X is the category ID or category slug. So category-37.php would be the template file whenever a listing of posts in the category with ID 37 is called for, just as category-cows.php is the template file of choice when viewing the Cows category. Hence, you can just edit the category-37.php (or category-cows.php) template file to reflect how you want that listing to look.

In short, it is easy enough to add a little extra styling to the parts of your site where there are template files to control that style. Consult Chapter 4, "WordPress Theme Essentials," for more information on which template file is loaded when, and take that information into account when shaping up your site.

STYLING THE POSTS

Styling the individual posts may be a bit trickier. They are all governed by single.php, which means that you need other means of making them stand out when needed.

Enter the `the_ID` and `post_class()` template tags, which go in your `div.post` container, like this:

```
<div id="post-<?php the_ID(); ?>" <?php post_class(); ?>>
    <!-- The post output stuff goes here -->
</div>
```

You'll find this (or something similar, at least) in most WordPress themes. The `the_ID()` template tag returns the post ID, giving the `div` container the ID of `post-X`, where X is the returned ID. That means that this is a way to catch a specific post and make it behave the way you want. ID 674 would hence give you a `div` with `id="post-674"` to play with. Style it any way you like.

Most of the time, however, you don't want to style individual posts per se, but rather posts belonging to a certain category. You can check for this using a conditional tag and a short PHP snippet, of course, but `post_class()` already has you covered. This template tag returns a line of classes for you to style any way you want, depending on where the post belongs and so on.

First, you'll get the post ID as a class as well, so your post with `id="post-674"` will also have the class `post-674`. You'll also get every category that the post belongs to, with `category-` in front of the category slug. So a category called *Website News*, which usually gets the slug `website-news`, would return the class `category-website-news` from `post_class()`. The same goes for tags; if you tag something with `funny`, you'll get that returned as the class `tag-funny`.

You'll also get the classes `post` and `hentry`, the former making sure that `post_class()` is compatible with older WordPress themes, which usually describe the `div` containers for posts with the post class, and the latter telling us the `div` belongs to an entry. In fact, that usage is still there, too.

So what good does this do? First, you can change the category styling, which is probably the most common usage for these classes. Say you've got a news category called *News,* with the slug `news`; hence, you'd get `class="category-news"` from `post_class()` whenever it was used. And say you want the links in this category to be green, and why not put a green border line to the left side as well, to really make it obvious? This can be easily achieved:

```
div.category-news {
    padding-left: 20px;
    border: 5px solid green;
    border-width: 0 0 0 5px; }

div.category-news a { color: green; }
```

Now every post belonging to the News category would get green links and a green border line to the left. This is great because categories can be used to control design elements, and tags in turn should be used to further sort the posts. For example, I might have a tag for My Fave, a feature I'm running. Every post that is one of my faves will get a My Fave graphic in the top right — not clickable or anything, just a marker so that people know it is one of my favorites:

```
div.tag-my-fave { background: url(myfave.gif) top right no-repeat; }
```

This would output a background image, myfave.gif, in the top-right corner (and not repeat it) every time `post_class()` returns the tag with the slug `my-fave`. Naturally, it is no lucky coincidence that that is the actual slug for my My Fave tag, now is it?

Finally, you can pass a specific class to `post_class()`, which may be useful at times. Maybe you want to add the class `stars` to single posts? If so, just edit your `post_class()` code in the single.php template to this:

```
<div id="post-<?php the_ID(); ?>" <?php post_class( 'stars' ); ?>>
```

As you can see, adding a class to `post_class()` is as easy as adding a parameter. A similar solution is used when you need to retain post-specific styling through `post_class()`, but it acts outside the loop. Then, you need to tell `post_class()` to return the ID, which is done by altering the code to this:

```
<?php post_class( '', $post_id ); ?>
```

As you can see, `post_ID()` can let you add pinpointed style to one particular post, but `post_class()` is more useful because it lets you style sets of posts, and also that one post should you need to. In fact, you can question if the `post_ID()` part is still needed, but as long as it is in the default theme, it obviously is, and it may be useful in the future.

BODY CLASS STYLING

Another way to apply some styling to various parts of a WordPress site is the `body_class()` template tag, introduced in version 2.8. Basically, it is for the `body` tag what `post_class()` is for the blog post `div` container. This is how you use it:

```
<body <?php body_class(); ?>>
```

Depending on where you are on the site, the `body` tag will get different classes. Say you're reading a post with the ID 245 and you're logged in. That would return this `body` tag:

```
<body class="class="single single-post postid-245 single-format-standard
  logged-in">
```

A category listing would return other classes, and a tag listing another set again. Pages, the front page, search — every imaginable part of your site will return more or less different classes for your `body` tag.

Why is this good for you? Say you want a different size for your h2 headings, depending on whether they are loaded in a listing or in a single post. You can define this by adding classes to the various template files, or you can do it in CSS with the classes outputted by `body_class()`.

First, you need to find out what classes are returned and when. See the class listing later in this section to get a bearing of what you have to play with, but for now, it is enough to know that the class `single` is passed to the `body` tag when viewing a single post and `archive` is passed for most listings pages (much like the template tag archive.php, which is called for both category and tag listings should category.php and tag.php not be present in the theme). That means you'll work with these classes. Here is the code you may want to put in your style sheet:

```
body.single h2 { font-size: 48px; }

body.archive h2 { font-size: 36px; }
```

This indicates that whenever `body_class()` returns the `single` class, which is in single post view, you get 48-pixel h2 headings, whereas whenever `body_class()` returns `class="archive"`, you get 36-pixel h2 headings.

Body class styling can be taken a long way because the addition of `body` classes depending on whereabouts on a site you are is placed so high up in the hierarchy. Most themes designed prior to the addition of the `body_class()` template tag won't be able to truly put this to good use, but if you reconsider your CSS code, you'll see that you can control more of your design from the classes passed to `body` rather than by adding classes to every element in the template files.

The following classes are available (and are listed in order of importance), depending on where you are on the site. Most likely, you don't have to style them all:

- `rtl`
- `home`
- `blog`
- `archive`
- `date`
- `search`
- `paged`
- `attachment`
- `error404`
- `single-postid-X` (where X is the post ID)
- `page-id-X` (where X is the Page ID)
- `attachmentid-X` (where X is the attachment ID)
- `attachment-MIME` (where MIME is the MIME type)
- `author`
- `author-USER` (where USER is the author's nice name)
- `category`
- `category-X` (where X is the category slug)
- `tag`
- `tag-X` (where X is the tag slug)
- `page-parent`
- `page-child parent-pageid-X` (where X is the Page ID)
- `page-template page-template-FILE` (where FILE is the template filename)
- `search-results`
- `search-no-results`
- `logged-in`
- `paged-X` (where X is the page number, referring to listings)
- `single-paged-X` (where X is the page number, referring to listings)
- `page-paged-X` (where X is the page number, referring to listings)
- `category-paged-X` (where X is the page number, referring to listings)
- `tag-paged-X` (where X is the page number, referring to listings)
- `date-paged-X` (where X is the page number, referring to listings)
- `author-paged-X` (where X is the page number, referring to listings)
- `search-paged-X` (where X is the page number, referring to listings)
- `tax-X` (where X is the taxonomy name)
- `term-X` (where X is the term name)

- `admin-bar`
- `custom-background`

Using the classes outputted by `body_class()` is a great way to add more precise visual control to the various sections of a site. A lot of template files in older themes have become redundant because of minor visual tuning now being easily managed by the classes outputted by `body_class()`. That's a lot better than resorting to template file–specific classes.

STICKY POSTS

When sticky post functionality was introduced way back in WordPress 2.7, you needed to add the `sticky_class()` template tag to your post `div` containers. That added the class `'sticky'`, which could then be styled accordingly. You don't need that anymore, thanks to `post_class()`. In addition to the various tasks already mentioned, `post_class()` also applies the `'sticky'` class to posts that are marked as *sticky* from within WordPress admin.

the sticky posts stand out a bit is easy enough; just add something to `div.sticky` yle sheet:

```
20px 20px 8px 20px;
: #f8f8f8; )
```

ancy there, as you can see (see Chapter 3, "The Loop," for more on sticky posts). The thing to keep in mind when it comes to sticky posts is that you don't know how many of them will be used. If there are two sticky posts, the most recent one will end up on top, and then the next newest one below. This means that several sticky posts need to look good when placed together.

What are sticky posts good for? The most obvious use would be in a traditional bloggish site, nailing the larger, important posts at the top using the sticky feature and unstickying them whenever there's something new to lift to the top. Something of a limited headline area, so to speak.

Another obvious usage is for announcements. If you're selling eBooks, for example, you can stick the "Hey you! You should buy my spanking new book; I have pay the rent after all!" post up on top, as shown in Figure 6-1. More traditional announcements such as new site launches or a call to action for an important cause would also work well.

Finally, you can go a step further by using the `is_sticky()` conditional tag. You can query WordPress (using a loop and `query_posts()` to get the desired effect) for your sticky posts and manage them separately. One idea is to have a headline area outside the normal loop and just include a set number of sticky posts in it, excluding everything else. In fact, you can use sticky posts to manage a full headline, but the same effect can be achieved with either custom fields or a specific tag, for example, and because the sticky post check box is more or less hidden away, the former may be a better call.

Figure 6-1: When this book comes out, you may see this on http://notesblog.com.

USING CUSTOM FIELDS

Custom fields are database fields with content defined entirely by the user and are always used within the loop. You'll find the Custom Fields box on the Add New Post screen within the WordPress admin; however, you might have to enable it using the Screen Options feature in the top right and then checking the box for Custom Fields. The Custom Fields box lets you add one or several custom fields and a value for each (see Figure 6-2).

Custom fields are actually metadata, but they are called *custom fields* within the WordPress admin interface. Most of the time, metadata belongs to posts and consists of two things: a key and a value. You can add new keys whenever you want, and after you've used them once, they show up in a drop-down box, which is nice because you may misspell or forget about them otherwise. Metadata can also belong to comments and users.

CUSTOM FIELD BASICS

Getting started with custom fields is easy; just write a post and add something in the key field and then something in the value field, and click the Add Custom Field button to save. You've now stored your custom field data, although it won't show up anywhere unless you call it within the loop. The idea is to reuse the key across posts, in a way like a categorization of the kind of data you're storing, and just alter the value.

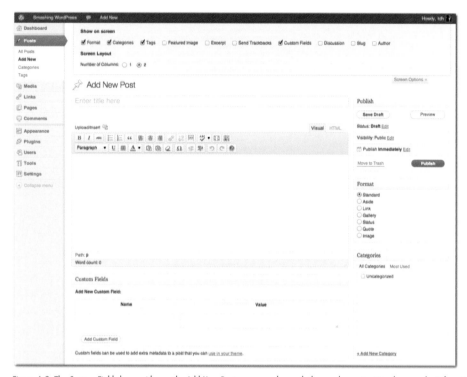

Figure 6-2: The Custom Fields box resides on the Add New Post screen, underneath the regular post-writing box — don't forget to enable it if needed!

The template tag you use to make things happen with custom fields is the_meta(). By default, it outputs an unordered list (or a ul tag with list items, lis, in HTML speak) displaying the post's custom fields. That works great if you just store things such as how happy you are and what you're reading right now, or perhaps a grade for a review or something. The ul will have the class post-meta, and then there's an li for each custom field; within this li there is a span with the class="post-meta-key" that wraps around the key for that particular custom field. After that is the value in plain text.

Suppose you have a custom field with a key called Actor with the value Harrison Ford. Then you have another custom field called Director with the value Steven Spielberg. Finally, you have a custom field called Movie Title with the value Indiana Jones and the Raiders of the Lost Ark. All these custom fields and their values belong to a specific post, and if you put the template tag the_meta() somewhere within the loop, and this post shows, it will output this code:

```
<ul class='post-meta'>
    <li>
        <span class='post-meta-key'>Actor</span> Harrison Ford
    </li>
    <li>
        <span class='post-meta-key'>Director</span> Steven Spielberg
```

```
    </li>
    <li>
        <span class='post-meta-key'>Movie</span> Indiana Jones and the Raiders of
            the Lost Ark
    </li>
</ul>
```

CREATING META BOXES

One way to make it a bit easier to work with metadata is to bypass the custom field's interface altogether and create your own meta boxes. This is done with add_meta_box(). Go ahead and create a meta box for your theme, featuring a simple input field and some explanatory text.

You'll create the meta box in a function, smashing_add_meta_boxes(), which in turn will be hooked to load-post.php and load-post-new.php:

```
// Hook on to load-post.php and load-post-new.php
add_action( 'load-post.php', 'smashing_add_meta_boxes' );
add_action( 'load-post-new.php', 'smashing_add_meta_boxes' );
```

Next, you need to create the smashing_add_meta_boxes() function as well:

```
// Create meta boxes
function smashing_add_meta_boxes() {
    // Creating our demo box
    add_meta_box(
        'smashing-post-demo',
        'Example Box',
        'smashing_post_demo_meta_box',
        'post',
        'side',
        'default'
    );
}
```

You can create several meta boxes within this function, but for this example, just create one. The meta box you're creating has the ID smashing-post-demo, the title Example Box, and the callback function (I'll get to that in a little bit) smashing_post_demo_meta_box, and it should appear only on posts in admin thanks to post and show up on the right side, with the default priority. You can read up more on what arguments you can pass to add_meta_box() in the Codex at http://codex.wordpress.org/Function_Reference/add_meta_box.

You need to create another function called smashing_post_demo_meta_box(), used with the callback in add_meta_box(), to actually create the box:

```
// Display the demo meta box
function smashing_post_demo_meta_box( $object, $box ) { ?>
    <?php wp_nonce_field( basename( __FILE__ ), 'smashing_post_demo_nonce' ); ?>
    <p>
```

```
        <label for="smashing-post-class">
            This is a demo box where you really can't do anything just yet.
        </label>
    </p>
    <p>
        <input class="widefat" type="text" name="smashing-post-demo"
            id="smashing-post-demo" value="<?php echo esc_attr( get_post_meta(
 $object->ID,
            'smashing_post_demo', true ) ); ?>" size="30" />
    </p>
<?php
// Function ends, back to business
}
```

The function includes a nonce field to make sure that any forms within are verified by WordPress. If you are unfamiliar with nonces, you should read up on them at http://codex. wordpress.org/Function_Reference/wp_nonce_field.

The rest is simple HTML, which is easier to manage outside of PHP, so that's why I'm leaving that for a bit. The input field fetches the value with `get_post_meta()` and the ID using `$object-_>ID`. It is sanitized with `esc_attr()`.

Now you have a meta box on your Add New Post and Edit Post screens! Figure 6-3 shows it in action.

Figure 6-3: Look at that meta box.

This meta box won't do anything, though; it won't save data or anything. It is just there. You will have to use `add_post_meta()`, `update_post_meta()`, or `delete_post_meta()` to actually save something from this box, or something completely different depending on what you might want to achieve. You can read up on these functions in the Codex, where there are many examples as well:

- `add_post_meta()`: http://codex.wordpress.org/Function_Reference/add_post_meta
- `update_post_meta()`: http://codex.wordpress.org/Function_Reference/ update_post_meta
- `delete_post_meta()`: http://codex.wordpress.org/Function_Reference/ delete_post_meta

FANCY CUSTOM FEATURES

It may be misleading to call these "custom" features because support for custom menus, custom headers, and custom backgrounds is built in to WordPress, albeit not in every theme. It's easy to add support for these elements in your theme, and having them can be very useful for the user. The following subsections take a look at these pieces.

PROPERLY ADDING FUNCTIONS IN FUNCTIONS.PHP

Before I get into these functions, I'll revisit how to properly add them to your theme's functions.php file. You might remember the `after_setup_theme` hook from the Simple Blog functions.php file in Chapter 4. The idea is to add all your theme features to this hook by keeping them in a function, which you'll then add to the hook — like this, in functions.php:

```
// Theme setup
add_action( 'after_setup_theme', 'smashing_theme_setup' );
function smashing_theme_setup() {
    // Add your functions here
}
```

So if you want to add support for post thumbnails (see the following subsection), you would add it like this:

```
// Theme setup
add_action( 'after_setup_theme', 'smashing_theme_setup' );
function smashing_theme_setup() {
    // Add support for post thumbnails
    add_theme_support( 'post-thumbnails' );
}
```

Naturally, this function could contain more than just one feature like this. Again, if you need to, revisit Chapter 4 and the functions.php file from Simple Blog.

It is preferred to use functions and hooks like this in functions.php rather than just drop the code there. You could, but it is better to know for sure when the code will initiate using hooks.

The following subsections will omit the hook and function to save space. Just add the features to the preceding function, and you'll be fine.

FEATURED IMAGES

Featured images, of *post thumbnails*, if you will, are a theme feature that lets the user select an image representing the post using a simple dialog box on the Edit Post page in the admin interface (see Figure 6-4). Enabling it is easy enough, just use `add_theme_support()` and pass the parameter `post-thumbnails` to it, in functions.php:

```
add_theme_support( 'post-thumbnails' );
```

This will enable the Featured Image box for posts in the admin interface. It is possible to add support for post thumbnails on custom post types as well, for example. Figure 6-4 shows the Featured Image box, which lets the user pick an image as a featured image for a post.

Figure 6-4: The Featured Image box in the bottom right.

You might want to add an additional image size for your featured images. With `add_image_size()`, you can register new image sizes, which will be created with every upload much like the thumbnail and medium image sizes, for example. The following code, which should be used with the `after_setup_theme` hook, will add an image size called `top-feature`, scaled to 500 x 225 pixels. If you want it to just scale by width and not height, change `225` to `9999` instead.

```
add_image_size( 'top-feature', 500, 225 );
```

Just enabling the post thumbnail feature won't make the featured images show up in your theme, however. Using `the_post_thumbnail()` within the loop, you can output the image. If you need additional control, you can combine it with the conditional tag `has_post_thumbnail()`.

```
<?php the_post_thumbnail(); ?>
```

Used like this, `the_post_thumbnail()` will output the thumbnail version of the image. By passing any of the parameters `thumbnail`, `medium`, or `large`, you'll get those versions instead. If you added an image size, such as the previous `top-feature` one, you can pass that as well. You can also pass an array with a custom resolution, like so:

```
the_post_thumbnail( array( 320, 130) );
```

Featured images are often used on the top of posts or in headlines to make the post more appealing. For some additional control, you can pass a CSS class to the featured image to get some more styling options:

```
the_post_thumbnail( 'medium', array( 'class'  => 'headline' ) );
```

This will add the class `headline` to the img tag outputted by `the_post_thumbnail()`. By default, you'll get the `wp-post-image` class, as well as the class `attachment-X`, where `X` is the chosen version of the image (for example, `attachment-large`).

CUSTOM MENUS

You might recognize custom menus from the example in Chapter 4, but for clarity's sake, I'll revisit them quickly. Adding support for menus is really simple. Start by adding a menu area for your theme, called *Smashing Menu* in this example. Do this in functions.php:

```
register_nav_menus( array(
    'smashing-menu' => 'Smashing Menu',
) );
```

That's all there is to it. Now the user can add a menu to the Smashing Menu area in the theme as well, using the `wp_nav_menu()` template tag, like so:

```
<?php wp_nav_menu( array( 'theme_location' => 'smashing-menu' ) ); ?>
```

This will let you populate this particular menu from the menu interface found under Appearance → Menu in the admin interface. That's it. Simple, huh?

CUSTOM HEADERS

Adding support for a custom header isn't particularly complicated, but it does require a few lines of code in functions.php. First, you declare the header's text color as well as the default header image, and then you tell WordPress the width and height of the images, like so (using the `after_setup_theme` hook):

```
define( 'HEADER_TEXTCOLOR', 'ffffff' );
define( 'HEADER_IMAGE', get_template_directory_uri() . '/img/header-
  default.jpg' );
define( 'HEADER_IMAGE_WIDTH', 940 );
define( 'HEADER_IMAGE_HEIGHT', 130 );
```

You also need to define how the header should be outputted:

```
// The site header function
function site_header_style() { ?>
    <style type="text/css">
        div#header {
            background: url(<?php header_image(); ?>);
        }
    </style>
<?php }
```

This is simple CSS, using `header_image()` as the background. That's a template tag that does only one thing: outputs the URL to the header image. You could put the tag to other use as well, such as putting `header_image()` in your theme. The preceding code would apply the chosen custom header image as the background for `div#header`. You can change that to whatever suits your theme.

Because the headers are managed in the admin interface, you need to make it look decent there:

```
// The admin header function
function admin_header_style() { ?>
    <style type="text/css">
        #headimg {
            width: <?php echo HEADER_IMAGE_WIDTH; ?>px;
            height: <?php echo HEADER_IMAGE_HEIGHT; ?>px;
        }
    </style><?php
}
```

The #headimg ID is used in the admin interface, but it needs the proper width and height, hence the added styles.

Finally, you enable the whole thing. Without that, you have no custom header functionality, so don't forget this little bit of code:

```
// Enable custom header image
add_custom_image_header( 'site_header_style', 'admin_header_style' );
```

CUSTOM BACKGROUND IMAGES

So what about the custom background image? It's simple: The following code in functions.php is all you need, preferably used with the after_setup_theme hook as usual:

```
// Activate the admin panels
add_custom_background();
```

That's it. Any settings, be it a background image or just a background color, will be added to wp_head() in a style sheet. Enabling custom backgrounds must be the easiest thing so far, right?

MASTERING ACTION HOOKS

Action hooks are all the rage these days, just like theme frameworks. Actually, they are probably so hot *because* of the theme frameworks, because the frameworks are littered with these babies. But I'm getting ahead of myself. First you need to understand what an action hook is.

Your theme is most definitely already using action hooks. The familiar wp_head and wp_footer calls in the header.php and footer.php template files are action hooks. They are there so that developers can hook in and add stuff to the beginning of WordPress or after it has finished loading. Plugin developers use these all the time, and I imagine that any of the web statistics plugins utilizing Google Analytics, Woopra, or whatever hook on to either the wp_head or wp_footer action hook and add their tracking code. But that's not all: A lot of hooks actually happen when standard template tags are used, such as `the_content()`, for example. Chances are you can hook on to most of the template tags in your theme already.

You can add your own hooks as well. This is the primary way theme framework designers use hooks — basically adding a number of hooks to various parts of the theme and then letting the user or child theme developer alter the look and add features by hooking on to them. Hooks can be used for a multitude of tasks, from populating a menu or advertisement spot with proper coding to actually removing elements from the design. In a sense, using hooks is a good way to make a very complete design and then let the users decide which parts of it should be used. Add an admin options page that does this for you, and you don't have to worry about hacking functions.php as a user, as naturally that's where all the action is.

I tend to lean the other way, though. Although it may be tempting to just add everything imaginable and then have the users check or uncheck boxes to decide what should be displayed, this practice can quickly bloat the theme. In my opinion, a good framework is something to build on, not to cut away from.

Either way, with action hooks, you can add functionality, either by adding your own (you'll get to that in a little bit) or by freeloading the hooks from WordPress. There are a lot of piggyback possibilities within WordPress, with helpful hooks such as `wp_head` (which you'll find referenced in most themes' header.php file) and `wp_footer`. There are way too many to list here, so I'll just point you to the (hopefully up-to-date) Action Reference page in the WordPress Codex: http://codex.wordpress.org/Plugin_API/Action_Reference.

HOOKING ON

If you want to hook on to one of WordPress's action hooks, say by adding some web statistics code to the `wp_footer` hook, you do it in functions.php. You write a PHP function containing the stuff you want to add, and then you add it to the hook.

Start with the function. The actual analytics script code is just nonsense, so if you want to use this particular hook you should, of course, swap the code for your own:

```
<?php function my_webstats() { ?>
    <script for your web statistics tracker />
<?php } ?>
```

This gives you the `my_webstats()` function to use, loaded with the (obviously faulty) `script` tag. This is what you want to hook on to `wp_footer`. Notice how I cut the PHP tag to make it easier to manage the HTML. You do that by using the `add_action` function and placing it before the actual function:

```
add_action( 'wp_footer', 'my_webstats' );
```

You're telling `add_action` that you want to add to `wp_footer` (the first parameter), and then you tell it to add the function `my_webstats`, which you define below. The full code would look like this, in your functions.php file:

```
<?php
    add_action( 'wp_footer', 'my_webstats' );
    function my_webstats() {
?>
    <script code for your web statistics tracker />
<?php } ?>
```

This would add the script at the end of your theme when loaded. Some excellent WordPress hookery right there.

CREATING YOUR OWN ACTION HOOKS

Creating your own action hooks is easy. First, you create your PHP function as you did before. It can be anything, really: a simple echo or something way more advanced. The only difference between creating and using your own action hooks, compared to the built-in ones, is that you need to add them to your theme. Remember, wp_head and wp_footer already sit there, so there's no need to add them, but your brand-new action hook won't be so lucky.

The code for adding action hooks is simple:

```
<?php do_action( 'the-name-of-the-hook' ); ?>
```

Just put in your intended hook name and put the code wherever you want it in your theme. If you have a hook named 'welcome_front', that means you'll put the following wherever you want to be able to hook on to the welcome_front() hook:

```
<?php do_action( 'welcome_front' ); ?>
```

To hook on to your custom hook, just use the add_action() function as you did previously. In fact, wp_head() and wp_footer() are really just wrappers for do_action('wp_head') and do_action('wp_footer'), so it is really the same.

To recap: add_action() is used to add actions to hooks, most likely in functions.php, whereas do_action() creates your own hooks and resides in your theme files.

REMOVING ACTIONS FROM HOOKS

If you're working with a child theme that uses a parent theme with a lot of hooks, you might want to remove functionality. There are several alternatives here, depending on the situation, but they all work more or less the same. Say that you want to remove an action attached to the_content() with add_action(); you would use remove_action(). For example, say the parent theme has the following code snippet, which adds the function superfunction to the_content():

```
add_action( 'the_content', 'superfunction' );
```

Now you don't want that, so you'll use `remove_action()` to remove it:

```
remove_action( 'the_content', 'superfunction' );
```

That's it! What's important to remember is that you need to be specific about what you want to remove, and if you have passed additional information in `add_action()` when adding the action, you need to pass it to `remove_action()` as well.

The `remove_filter()` tag works the same, but for filters.

USING TAXONOMIES

Taxonomies are both cool and useful. Basically, they enable you to create your very own versions of categories or tags. This means that you can have several different sets of tags, for example. Just to get the lingo straight right away: A taxonomy has *terms* associated with it. The tags in the standard Tags taxonomy are in fact terms, as are the categories in the default Categories taxonomy.

By adding taxonomies, you add more ways to categorize and tag your posts. You could say that the default categories and tags are both taxonomies that are there by default, so you have one taxonomy called *Categories* and one called *Post Tags* to start with. Suppose you want more, say a separate way of tagging posts, called *Topics*; you can add that, which gives you two tagging taxonomies that can each take their own set of tags, separate from each other. And finally, you may want a third one called *Frequently Asked Questions*, which would leave you with three tagging boxes: the default one and the two new ones (see Figure 6-5).

Figure 6-5: Multiple tag taxonomies.

Naturally, there is a template file for taxonomies, called *taxonomy.php*. Create it and treat it like any other archive, which means that it needs the loop, of course, and it will be used for post listings generated by a click on a taxonomy link. As you might expect, you can create a taxonomy-*X*.php template file for a specific type of taxonomy, and you can even target a specific taxonomy term by creating taxonomy-*X*-*Y*.php (where *Y* is the specific taxonomy value) as you can with tag.php or categories.php.

PURPOSES FOR CUSTOM TAXONOMIES

There are tons of things you could use custom taxonomies for. The strength of them, whether you use them for hierarchical (such as Categories) or nonhierarchical (such as Tags), is that they add yet another layer to your content organization. Here are some ideas:

- Collect series of posts with a nonhierarchical taxonomy, and style the archives for this taxonomy differently to make it more link-friendly.

- Add another navigational layer with a custom taxonomy. Say you run a video game site and want to mark your posts with the video game platforms such as Xbox 360, iOS, and Wii, but not mix this with the regular categories or tags. With a custom taxonomy called *Platform* (or something else), you can.

- Separate various kinds of terms. With a specific taxonomy for person, companies, and brands, you can create term clouds consisting of just persons, for example, and style each kind of archive differently.

- Create your own post formats. The post format feature really is a custom taxonomy given some special love within the core. There is nothing that stops you from forgetting about the post formats and just creating your own taxonomy with the same purpose, but tailored for your needs.

The possibilities might not be endless, but there surely are a lot of options in terms of organizing and connecting the content thanks to custom taxonomies.

GET YOUR MIND WORKING

It goes without saying that being able to add new taxonomies, essentially new separate sets of tags, can come in handy. Sites looking to work with data in almost database-style can definitely put it to good use, as shown with previous suggestions, but it can also be a different way to tackle the sorting of content. In particular, the addition of more taxonomies can make it possible to further push the categories to a design-driven feature within a site. After all, tagging offers so much more focused control where it matters, and you get that when you add your own taxonomies as well. You can have a taxonomy for design tagging only, for example. The tags in this taxonomy would be used only by the theme, by adding classes to the post `div` or perhaps the `body` tag. There's no default support for this, but it can be used nonetheless by adding it to the theme using a few snippets of code.

You can also imagine some taxonomies overlapping with custom fields because some usage of this feature is all about sorting posts. Taxonomies are better suited for this by nature. Taxonomies reach their full potential, however, when larger amounts of content need to be controlled. Taxonomies are, after all, a sorting feature, and that means they work best when there is actually something to sort.

At first, it can be a bit daunting to wrap your mind around the possibilities that custom taxonomies offer. This feature can be put to good use; no doubt several WordPress-powered sites are already putting taxonomies to useful work. You, as an end user, may not see it, but the developer may not have to write a bunch of plugins or strain the not-so-user-friendly custom fields to achieve the content sorting and presentation needed. So don't forget about taxonomies; they might be your best bet for your project.

TAXONOMIES AND PORTABILITY

Custom taxonomies are great, and I'm sure that you already have a ton of ideas for how you can use them. However, you need to remember that although you can create them from your theme's functions.php file, that part actually belongs in a plugin most of the time. The reason for this is that you want to keep your custom taxonomies around when you switch themes, so make sure that the taxonomy creation belongs in a plugin whenever possible, and let your theme worry about the output in terms of template files.

You can read more about data portability in Chapter 8, "Plugins or functions.php?."

THE POWER OF CUSTOM POST TYPES

Custom post types are an extremely powerful tool. Thanks to this feature, you are no longer restricted to just posts and pages; you can create your own post types tailored to your needs. If you want a post type that is almost identical to WordPress standard pages (which is a post type in itself) but with tags, then you can create a post type that does just that.

Being able to create and name post types that work alongside posts and pages has another benefit as well: They are very user friendly. The user will instantly know what to do because the custom post type resides in the left menu in the admin, much like posts and pages, and working with it works in the same way.

USING CUSTOM POST TYPES

Custom post types come in handy in a lot of cases, but the more you need to divide the content, the more useful they get. In a lot of ways, custom post types are what really made WordPress a great CMS option for larger traditional sites. Although everything could be solved previously with posts and pages and some clever thinking, custom post types make it so much easier to build sites with lots of different types of content.

Custom post types are not just for that; plugins use them to store data. From feedback plugins that looks like e-mail forms to forum software, custom post types have a lot of uses. Thanks to the WordPress template system, it is really easy to create interesting content and features in themes because it is just like working with any other part of a site. One thing worth remembering, however, is that content from custom post types won't show up in your theme's front page loop, in search results, or the like unless you alter the loop.

You'll do some fun stuff with custom post types in Chapter 14, "Uncommon WordPress Usage." Before that, you'll look at how you work with custom post types in themes in the following subsection, and the next chapter, "The Anatomy of a WordPress Plugin," will help you create your first custom post type.

THEMING CUSTOM POST TYPES

Custom post types work much like any other post type when it comes to making them look and feel the way you want. You use archive-*X*.php, where *X* is the slug for the custom post type (for example, if you have a post type with the slug `product`, archive-product.php would be the template file to use), to control the custom post type's archive, much as you would use category.php or tag.php to work with category or tag archives. Single custom post type posts use single-*X*.php, where *X* is the slug. Refer to Chapter 4 for a list of which template files are used under what circumstances.

For more hands-on examples on how custom post types can be put to good use, refer to Chapter 14. In the next chapter, you'll create some custom post types.

There are also plugins that will create custom post types, such as the bbPress (http://bbpress. org) forum plugin. Because these plugins are using custom post types, you can easily work with their output by using the appropriate template files with your theme. Very handy.

THEME OPTION PAGES

Sometimes, you just need one place to provide the necessary data to make the site behave like you want it to. This data can obviously be coded into the theme's template files, but a popular alternative to having to hack the templates is to have an options page.

A *theme option page* is a page in the WordPress admin interface containing information or options for your theme. You create it by adding code to your theme's functions.php file and actually building the whole thing from there. Theme option pages have been around for quite some time, and the default WordPress theme uses the technique to offer color customizations to the rounded header, among other things.

The specific options that will be available in your theme options page depend on the kind of theme you've built. Some themes let the user alter the design by changing default font sizes and similar elements, whereas others let you save custom code that will be outputted some-where in the theme through action hooks. Either way, you should make sure that you know why you may want an options page and what you need it to do. This means that you have to sit down and figure out what option settings make sense for your theme and build the option page from that. This will of course vary a lot from theme to theme. Some themes might benefit from font options, whereas others might need a feature to show or hide the sidebar via a setting on the option page.

Theme option pages are created using the Settings API (http://codex.wordpress.org/Settings_ API), which is covered in the next chapter.

ISSUES WITH THEME OPTIONS

Besides the obvious issues faulty code can cause, there are really just two big considerations when it comes to theme option pages and using functions.php this way: usability and speed.

Consider usability. There are themes with tons and tons of theme options, which might sound like a good idea at first glance. After all, with all those options, you should be able to do whatever you like, right? Although that might be true, chances are that the theme code itself has gotten a bit bloated, but just as important, the end user might have a hard time getting a grasp of the options. If there are too many items to choose from and if some combinations just work out poorly (which is often the case with font and color settings, for example), then what's the benefit of having all those theme options? Keep the theme options to a minimum is my advice — your end users will thank you.

That being said, using functions.php is great for small options settings. More advanced things should be handled outside, by calling other files or in a plugin. It is all a matter of what you want to do, so the only really good advice here would be that you have to consider if you're executing your actions the right way, and if you can, move the code (or at least parts of it) somewhere else if your functions.php is growing too much.

One thing you shouldn't cut down on, though, is localization, at least not if you plan on releasing your theme. I'll tackle that next.

MULTIPLE LANGUAGE SUPPORT

Just as you can get WordPress in your language of choice thanks to language files, you can do the same for your theme, and plugins as well for that matter. Just as with WordPress, you need to provide an .mo file that is tailored to your theme, which in turn is created from a POT (portable object template) file via the .po file. It is all a pretty messy business because a lot of the tools used to generate these files are pretty clunky to use, but using the software is worth it.

First you need to understand why a certain language file gets loaded if it is available to WordPress. There is (usually) no menu setting for what language you want a specific theme or plugin to be in; rather, WordPress looks for the setting defined in the installation, which is to say the one you added to WPLANG in wp-config.php (see Chapter 1, "The Anatomy of a WordPress Install," for more detail). This means that if your WordPress install is in German, a translated theme containing German language files will use those if possible.

The translation process consists of three steps. First you need to create a POT file. The software of your choice (see the following "Working with Language Files" subsection for related links) will parse your theme and build a POT file containing all the words and phrases you have marked for translation.

Step two is to create a .po (portable object) file from your POT file. This process saves the original language (usually English) and the translated language in one file. This is where the translation actually occurs, the actual localization.

The third step in the translation process is to create the .mo (machine object) file, using appropriate software. This file is created from the .po file so that it becomes machine-readable, and that makes the translation a lot faster to read and thus output. The .mo file is the file used by WordPress and your theme.

But how does the software that generates the POT file know what should be made available for translation? This is where you come in, as the theme (or plugin) author. You have to mark the parts of your theme that should be up for translation by wrapping the word or phrase in a PHP snippet and then applying it to a domain. The domain is really just a translation set, and that in turn will be defined in functions.php.

Say you want to make the text "Hello you!" available for translation. That would look like this:

```php
<?php _e( 'Hello you!', 'mydomain' ); ?>
```

That would output "Hello you!" as if written in plain text, but if there is a translation available and `mydomain` is defined in functions.php, you'll get that instead. If not, you'll just get "Hello you!" in plain old English.

You can also write it like this, using two underscores before the opening parenthesis rather than one and the e:

```php
<?php __( 'Hello you!', 'mydomain' ); ?>
```

Call up the trusty Twenty Eleven theme for an example. In the index.php file, you'll find the following result outputted whenever a page isn't found:

```php
<h1 class="entry-title"><?php _e( 'Nothing Found', 'twentyeleven' ); ?></h1>
```

That would output "Your search result:" if there was a defined domain called `twentyeleven`.

Sometimes you want these translations within tags. This is how you've done it with the `the_content()` template tag, to make the Read More link outputted by the `<!-more->` code snippet in posts available for translation:

```php
<?php the_content( __( 'Read more', 'twentyeleven' ) ); ?>
```

A double underscore and then the translation. So why the double underscore method? Well, the `_e()` is an `echo` statement, and the double underscore, or `__()`, is a `return` statement. Doing `echo` within PHP functions can create some weird results because it prints out the content, whereas `return` saves it for future use.

So how, then, do you tell the theme to use the translation file in the first place? Just dropping the translation file in the theme won't do it; you need to declare that a specific text domain should be used (`"twentyeleven"` in the earlier examples). Just add this line in the functions.php file (within the PHP tags, of course, just like almost everything else in the functions.php file):

```
load_theme_textdomain( 'twentyeleven' );
```

This tells you

- That the theme is internationalized; otherwise, there's not much point in using the `load_theme_textdomain` functionality.
- That every translation string with the domain `'twentyeleven'` is considered.
- That you still need a translation.

The actual translation should be in an .mo file, and that in turn comes from a .po file, which you created from a POT file, as mentioned earlier. And the POT file is generated by your chosen software (again, see the following subsection for links and suggestions), which in turn has parsed your theme looking for your translation strings, the `__()` and `_()`.

WORKING WITH LANGUAGE FILES

There are several ways to work with the portable language files. One of the most popular programs available is Poedit (www.poedit.net), which is available across platforms. You can easily open and edit available .po files in Poedit and then save them as .mo files to be used with your theme or plugin.

Other software and services for working with .po files include GNU's very own `gettext` (www.gnu.org/software/gettext) and Launchpad (https://translations.launchpad.net). However, neither of these is as easy to use as Poedit, and most often, Poedit is recommended. There is also an interesting project called GlotPress (http://glotpress.org) that is in its early stages.

When you release a theme or a plugin with a language file, be sure to also make the original .po file available so that the users can translate it into their own language. It is a good idea to encourage that because others may benefit as well.

THE NAMING ISSUE

Although it may not be entirely within your theme or plugin translation scope, a weird error arises when a widget area gets called and can't be found because the name has been changed by the translation. That is (or hopefully was, by the time you read this) the case with WordPress and the Swedish translation of "Sidebar," being a widget area located in sidebar.php, no less. The translators translated "Sidebar" (to "Sidomeny," which somewhat misses the mark, but still), and by doing so, they made the themes that made direct calls to the "Sidebar" widget area fail because it was translated incorrectly. Of course, themes using the sidebar ID rather than the name wouldn't have this problem, so let that be a lesson to use the ID rather than the name.

Messy? Yes, it is. The point is, be wary so that you don't end up translating things that are used for calling up various features, functions, or whatever. At least not without making sure that the actual call for whatever it is is also altered accordingly. You might want to take a closer look at the functions.php file in either Twenty Ten or Twenty Eleven and examine how the widget areas are internationalized there. By internationalizing both the area name (and description) and the actual call for the area, you're avoiding these issues.

WORKING WITH RSS FEEDS

RSS feeds are a great way both to deliver and to subscribe to content. WordPress supports the 1.0 version and the more up-to-date 2.0 version. There is also legacy support for the 0.91 version, but its 301 redirects to the default version. There is also Atom support, but keep in mind that you need to activate Atom from the Settings page should you want to use it.

To enable feeds all across your site, you want to add support for automatic feed links. Add this to your functions.php file, ideally within a function that hooks on to the `after_setup_ theme` hook, much as you did in Simple Blog's functions.php file in Chapter 4:

```
add_theme_support( 'automatic-feed-links' );
```

Most themes have feed links built in, and although the web browser will tell your visitors discreetly that there is a feed available, you really want to push it a bit harder than that. Take a look at just about any successful professional blogger, and you'll see nice RSS graphics, often incorporating the feed icon (if you need the icon, you can get it from Feed Icons at www. feedicons.com) and pushing the subscription services in premier positions.

You should do the same if you want to gain subscribers. That's lesson one on RSS: Position it well on your site; otherwise, people will neither see nor use it.

Lesson two is to seriously consider full feeds. You can choose whether you want to send out a full feed or one just featuring excerpts. Feeds containing just excerpts *will* have fewer sub-scribers because people using RSS prefer to get the whole story. You'll find that a large number of these readers will click the links and visit your site anyway, but they may just opt out if you're not publishing full feeds. Then again, if you really, truly, definitely have to get people to your site, and having them read the content in a feed reader is a disaster, then fine. Just make sure that you know what you're doing, and why, if you're strapping your feed.

The third and final lesson is to offer alternative subscription methods. The most popular alternative is e-mail subscriptions, usually delivered by FeedBurner (http://feedburner.com), which is owned by Google. It puts together a daily digest from your RSS feed, delivering it to subscribers via e-mail. This is good because RSS feeds are still something mainly used by the technical crowd, so offering other subscription options is a good idea.

THE WORDPRESS FEEDS

WordPress outputs a number of feeds if you let it. You can get them easily enough, using the `bloginfo()` template tag:

```
<?php bloginfo( 'rdf_url' ); ?>
<?php bloginfo( 'rss_url' ); ?>
```

```
<?php bloginfo( 'rss2_url' ); ?>
<?php bloginfo( 'atom_url' ); ?>
```

These are for the deprecated 0.91 RSS feed, which redirects to the default feed; version 1.0 of the RSS feed; the 2.0 RSS feed; and the Atom feed, respectively.

You can also get the feed for your comments, as well as an individual post's comments. Naturally, you'd want to use these tags in your theme:

```
<?php bloginfo( 'comments_rss2_url' ); ?>
<?php comments_rss_link( 'RSS 2.0' ); ?>
```

The second one is for a specific post's comments feed.

However, I personally prefer to keep the PHP calls to a minimum. All these feeds can be found by directly inputting the URL. Because you understand the necessities of permalinks (or will, when you've finished reading this chapter), you've got your blog set up to use these. This means that these URLs will work for you:

- `http://mydomain.com/feed`
- `http://mydomain.com/feed/rss`
- `http://mydomain.com/feed/rss2`
- `http://mydomain.com/feed/rdf`
- `http://mydomain.com/feed/atom`

The first one is the default; you'll even find it in some themes, although that is a bad idea because it requires permalinks to be set up and not all hosts support that. The following, however, will always work but don't look as pretty:

- `http://mydomain.com/?feed=rss`
- `http://mydomain.com/?feed=rss2`
- `http://mydomain.com/?feed=rdf`
- `http://mydomain.com/?feed=atom`

But there's more! These are just for the main feeds, but there are actually feeds for just about everything in WordPress. Author feeds, category feeds, and tag feeds all come in handy sometimes. There's even one for comments to a particular post. Assuming that you've got your permalinks set up, this is how they are built:

- `http://mydomain.com/author/USERNAME/feed`
- `http://mydomain.com/category/SLUG/feed`
- `http://mydomain.com/tag/SLUG/feed`
- `http://mydomain.com/POST-PERMALINK/comments/feed`

So if my username is "superman" on http://tdh.me and I want to pull out all my posts via RSS, this would work: http://tdh.me/author/superman/feed.

BUILD A CUSTOM FEED URL

Sometimes you may want your feed to exclude a category or consist of a couple of tags only, perhaps. You can accomplish this by hacking the feed URL, which actually takes some parameters. Then, if you want to, you can run that feed through a service such as FeedBurner because the URLs tend to be pretty long and ugly.

For example, say you want to exclude the category with ID 47 from your custom feed. Then the URL would look like this: `http://mydomain.com/feed/?cat=-47`.

That would output the full RSS feed but nothing in the category with ID 47. Notice the minus sign in front of the ID; it works here just as it does in most other cases.

How about a feed for a search query? Just as simple: `http://mydomain.com/feed/?s=keyword1+keyword2`.

Or maybe you want to just run category 39 and show the tag with the slug `ninja`. Do it like this: `http://mydomain.com/feed/?cat=39&tag=ninja`.

Basically, you add parameters to the URL and work from there. The accepted parameters are shown in Table 6-1.

Table 6-1: Accepted Parameters

Parameter	Description
author	Author ID
cat	Numeric ID
tag	Tag slug
keyword	Search keywords
year	The year (for example, 2012)
day	The date (for example, 15)
monthnum	The month by number (for example, 3 for March)
hour	The hour (for example, 19)
minute	The minute (for example, 45)
second	The second (for example, 13)
p	The post ID
paged	A specific page relating to the front page post listing

BASIC SEO IMPLEMENTATIONS

Getting the most out of the search engines is a topic for a book in itself. The cold, harsh truth is that the best SEO (search engine optimization) is manually edited on a per-post and per-page basis, rather than automatically generated. However, there are some things you can do in your theme from the start to get better SEO results.

Here are some tips to consider when setting up your theme:

- Validate: Valid code is better. You can check your code using the W3C Markup Validation Service at http://validator.w3.org.

- Permalinks, obviously: Permalinks change those ID-based, ugly URLs to more user-friendly (as well as search-engine-friendly) ones. The earlier keywords in your perma-links get picked up first, so you should really get the post and page title slug in there (not the ID), and possibly the category as well. Some claim that having date-based data in the permalinks helps the search engines as well, and that may very well be true if the site is updated often enough. The big bump, however, will be when you switch to permalinks, so make that a must in every setup.

- Tags and keywords: Tagging your posts not only helps describe the content for your readers, but it is also an opportunity to tell the search engines more about them. You can use a plugin to populate the meta keywords field with your tags (not linked of course) or something similar.

- Generate a site map: One of the most heralded solution for this is the Google XML Sitemaps Generator plugin, available at www.arnebrachhold.de/projects/wordpress-plugins/google-xml-sitemaps-generator.

- The title tag: Your title tag should include both the post name (first) and the site name (last). A divider between the two helps differentiate.

- Headings: On the front page, your blog's name should be in an h1 block. When viewing single posts or Pages, the title of the post or Page should be in the h1 block. On archive listings (search, categories, tags, and so on), I tend to set the listing title as h1 and have the post titles returned as h2.

- Reconsider links: Links are only good when they are relevant, so pushing that massive blogroll in the sidebar all the time may not be good. This is a bit fuzzy, however, so consider it wisely. Relevant links are always good.

- Related posts are relevant links: There are numerous related post plugins out there, and as long as they return relevant links to your posts, they are a good thing.

- Breadcrumbs: Breadcrumbs are links, usually on the top of the page, showing where the page is located — for example, Home → Reviews → Smashing WordPress. They are not only helpful for the user, but they also help the search engine read your page. You need to use a plugin for this functionality. WordPress SEO is popular and easy enough to add: http://yoast.com/wordpress/seo/.

- Load time: It is not only users that appreciate a fast-loading site, but also search engines, so clean up your code. You may even want to consider a caching plugin, although some of these may end up creating duplicate content — so be sure that you read up on it accordingly.

Also, be sure to check out the plugin lists later in the book in Appendix A, "Essential Word-Press Plugins," for links and advice on good SEO plugins that make your WordPress site even more attractive to search engines. Naturally, you'll want your theme to be as search-engine-friendly as possible because a lot of traffic comes that way.

TRIMMING WORDPRESS ON THE THEME SIDE

All sites should be as fast-loading as possible. You can do quite a lot on the theme side of things, but the question is how much you really want to do. If you take it to the extremes, you'll end up with one-line files that will be completely impossible to edit, which means that you'll need a nonoptimized work file that you later optimize. This usually applies to style sheets, which can be smashed together quite a lot, and hence you'll save a few bytes, but it also means that you won't be able to scan them easily when looking for something.

With that in mind, what can you do to speed up your theme? Try these tips:

- Clean out unnecessary code. Most themes can use another going-over or two after they appear to be finished.
- Minimize PHP usage. Don't use dynamic functions and whatnot with PHP if you expect large amounts of traffic; hardcode as much as you can into the theme instead. This will obviously make the theme more tied to your particular site, but sometimes that is what's needed.
- Beware of plugin overload. Plugins are great, but sometimes they aren't all that well coded. At the very least, they represent one or more PHP queries and possibly database processing. You should consider each of them carefully.
- Think about outside services. This is not strictly in your theme, but outside services such as chat widgets or Twitter badges take time to load and will impact the performance of the site in the eyes of your visitors.
- Optimize the server. Your hosting solution of choice may offer PHP accelerators and caching for often-called functionality. They might or might not be running programs such as Varnish, and perhaps there are things in the web server software that could be tweaked or removed to speed up things; it all depends on the setup. Talk to your hosting provider for options and then make sure that they are compatible with WordPress; all may not be.
- Consider WordPress caching. There are caching plugins for WordPress that store static files rather than serve data from the database all the time. This can actually speed up a site, so it may be worth employing.
- Tighten the files. You can Google your way to both HTML and CSS compressors, which tighten your files but make them a whole lot harder to read. Be sure to check the output to ensure that the compressors' scripts haven't added something malicious. You can never be too sure.

In the end, tightening a WordPress theme is more or less the same as tightening any site. Good and tight code, preferably valid, will load faster than clunky and bloated code, so get it right from the start.

And if you're doing everything right but your WordPress site keeps chugging slowly, then maybe you've outgrown your host. After all, when all the PHP calls are minimized, the server is running everything it should and nothing more, the code is tight and valid, and you've got your accelerators and caching plugins working, then there's just not much more that you can do other than crank up the voltage to power your beast. Although you shouldn't look for a new host just because your site is performing poorly, it might be the solution to the problem, especially if your site has grown rapidly.

THEMES VERSUS PLUGINS

The themes are not only the look and feel of a site these days, but they are also simple plugins. You use themes to get everything to be displayed where you want it and to break the normal flow of posts provided by the loop. You can achieve a lot using the template and conditional tags; and by adding extra functionality in functions.php, by using action hooks, and by being crafty overall, you can build just about anything.

As I've hinted at in this chapter, cramming functions.php full isn't always such a great idea. A lot of things you do in that file can just as well be done by a plugin, and although that is unnecessary or even redundant at times, sometimes it truly is the best decision. After all, the whole idea with various skinning concepts in publishing systems is to separate as much design from the code as possible. When it comes to WordPress themes, this means that you'll have to break that rule a bit if you want to do crafty things.

A lot can be handled by plugins rather than code in the themes, which fits better with the whole dividing design and code concept. You'll learn a lot more about plugins in the next couple chapters.

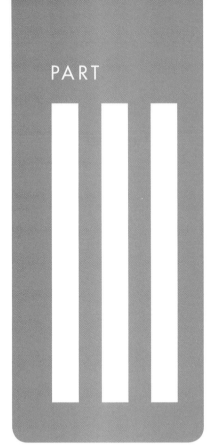

USING PLUGINS WITH WORDPRESS

CHAPTER

THE ANATOMY OF A WORDPRESS PLUGIN

IT GOES WITHOUT saying that plugins are different from themes, but they have a lot in common. You could say that when you're adding functionality to your theme by adding code to the functions.php template file, you're actually writing a plugin.

But there is a huge difference. Themes are there to display the WordPress site, using the tools available. Plugins, on the other hand, are used when you need to extend the WordPress functionality with additional features. You should remember that because bloating your theme's functions.php with features isn't always the best way to go.

In this chapter, you'll look at plugins from a slightly different standpoint than you did in the themes chapters. The reason for this is simple: Your plugin can do anything. It is basically a way for you to add whatever functionality you want; compare that to doing funky stuff with a select few template tags, and you see the difference.

With plugins, it is not a matter of what you *can* do, it is more a question of *why* you would want to do it.

DIFFERENT TYPES OF PLUGINS

There are three primary types of plugins: regular plugins, which you've no doubt used a number of times; drop-in plugins, which are used to replace core functionality; and must-use plugins.

REGULAR PLUGINS

By *regular plugins,* I mean plugins that you are used to. These are the ones you download, install, activate, and just start using. Akismet (http://wordpress.org/extend/plugins/akismet) is what I'd like to call a regular plugin. Basically, it just works when activated, sometimes with some necessary settings, but that's it. Regular plugins reside in the wp-content/plugins/ folder and are activated as usual.

You already know all about how to use this type of plugin, so I'll move along.

DROP-IN PLUGINS

Drop-in plugins, or drop-ins, are plugins meant to overwrite core functionality. You put them directly in the wp-content folder to replace their corresponding core file — for example, advanced-cache.php or db.php.

The following drop-ins are available. Remember, if you use them, you actually need to replace the functionality they represent in the core; otherwise, you'll probably have problems.

- advanced-cache.php for advanced caching
- db.php for a custom database class
- db-error.php for custom database error messages
- install.php for your own install scripts
- maintenance.php for custom maintenance messages
- object-cache.php for an external cache
- sunrise.php for executing things prior to multisite loads
- blog-deleted.php when blogs are deleted in multisite
- blog-inactive.php for messages on inactive blogs for a multisite
- blog-suspended.php for messages on suspended blogs for a multisite

You should be careful with drop-ins. They are very powerful, though; chances are you've seen them in action or perhaps even used them as a part of another plugin, especially drop-ins such as advanced-cache.php for caching. Some are less hazardous to play with, such as adding your own maintenance.php file, which is a nice way to give your readers a more personal maintenance message when you're upgrading your install.

MUST-USE PLUGINS

Must-use plugins differ a bit from regular plugins. They reside in wp-content/mu-plugins/, and you can't deactivate them from within the admin interface; the only way to deactivate a must-use plugin is to remove it from the folder. Must-use plugins don't need to contain plugin headers; they will be executed nonetheless.

You can drop any plugin in the wp-content/mu-plugins/ folder, but you might have problems with it depending on how it is built, especially across multisite networks, so proceed with caution. It is better to use the plugin as it is meant to be used.

Must-use plugins are a great tool when you need to make sure that functionality stays active and won't accidentally be deactivated.

DEVELOPING PLUGINS FOR NETWORKS

As of WordPress 3.0, the multiuser version of WordPress, previously called *WordPress MU,* is a part of the regular version. Now called WordPress *multisite,* this feature is used to power multiple blogs at once, in a Network. Most plugins (and themes for that matter) will work with the multisite feature. The only time you may run into issues is if you add tables to the database or possibly if you play with the core tables. You can activate this feature by adding a few lines of code to your wp-config.php file. To get you started, add the following line above the "That is all, stop editing!" line in the wp-config.php file of your install:

```
define( 'WP_ALLOW_MULTISITE', true );
```

This will enable the Network Admin link in your WordPress admin interface (see Figure 7-1). WordPress will then guide you through the simple steps needed to get your multisite feature up and running. You can read more about that in the Codex at http://codex.wordpress.org/Create_A_Network.

A *multisite* can most easily be described as something of an umbrella that allows admin superusers to manage other blogs created underneath. On WordPress.com, anyone can create a blog, but that isn't necessarily the way a WordPress multisite install works; you can just as well run it to power multiple blogs (such as a blog network) and not let users register and/or create their own blogs.

The process of developing plugins for WordPress using multisite doesn't differ much from that of traditional WordPress plugins. The only differences are in the database and to a minor degree, in the directory structure.

As for the directory structure, almost everything is the same as in the standard version of WordPress. The only real difference is the blogs.dir directory in the wp-content folder, which contains all the created blogs' data, such as images and uploads. You won't be using that folder much because themes and plugins belong in the main wp-content folder, just as you're used to.

Figure 7-1: The Network Admin looks something like this.

If you want to force your plugins across the network, you can choose to activate them sitewide (as an admin superuser). Another option is to use must-use plugins or just drop any plugin in the wp-content/mu-plugins/ folder, although that might end up giving you some problems should the plugin be unsuited for this. Activating sitewide is usually the best solution.

Actual plugin development is just as for standalone WordPress. You do, however, need to be extra careful when creating new tables in the database or relying on content from core tables. Most of the time, you'll be fine, but there are some differences in the database when you're running several sites in a WordPress install, so be watchful.

Another thing to consider when creating plugins for a multisite is how they are intended to be used. Because you can run a multisite install in so many ways, open or closed, with plugins enabled for bloggers, just for admin, and so on, you may have to rethink the way the plugin works.

SITEWIDE WORDPRESS PLUGINS

You can also activate plugins sitewide from within admin. This means that you can activate plugins located in wp-content/plugins/ to be active sitewide. This is of course a lot more user friendly, so you should definitely consider managing sitewide plugin-powered features this way, rather than with must-use plugins. After all, because WordPress supports automatic updates, the more that are available at a click from within the admin interface, the better.

PLUGIN BASICS

A plugin's essentials are similar to a theme's essentials:

- The main plugin file needs to be a PHP file with a unique filename or a unique folder name if your plugin consists of several files inside a folder.
- The PHP file needs an identifying header, just like a theme's style.css does so that Word-Press can recognize it as a plugin.

Then you can expand by adding even more functionality outside of the main plugin PHP file if you want, just like you add template files to the child theme's style.css.

> *Before you move on with plugin basics, you should know that writing plugins is usually a lot more demanding than working with WordPress themes. You need a firm knowledge of PHP, so if you're lacking that, I suggest you brush up on your skills before embarking on any large plugin writing adventure.*

Giving your plugin a unique filename or folder name is very important because plugins reside in wp-content/plugins/, and you don't want any conflicts. Name it appropriately, and in such a way that there is no doubt which plugin it is should someone need to find it using FTP who knows it only by the name it is displayed as in the WordPress admin interface.

The identifying plugin header block will look familiar. The following is a dummy:

```php
<?php
/*
Plugin Name: My Smashing Plugin
Plugin URI: http://my-smashing-plugin-url.com/
Description: This is what my Smashing Plugin actually does.
Version: 1.0
Author: Thord Daniel Hedengren
Author URI: http://tdh.me/
*/
?>
```

Actually, only the plugin name line, the first one within the comment notations, is mandatory. The rest should be there, however, so that the user knows what the plugin is, where to get updates, version numbering, who made it, and so on.

You should include licensing information as well. This is the standard GPL licensing info dummy text that is recommended in the WordPress Codex:

```php
<?php
/*  Copyright YEAR  PLUGIN_AUTHOR_NAME  (e-mail : PLUGIN AUTHOR E-MAIL)

    This program is free software; you can redistribute it and/or modify
    it under the terms of the GNU General Public License as published by
```

```
    the Free Software Foundation; either version 2 of the License, or
    (at your option) any later version.

    This program is distributed in the hope that it will be useful,
    but WITHOUT ANY WARRANTY; without even the implied warranty of
    MERCHANTABILITY or FITNESS FOR A PARTICULAR PURPOSE.  See the
    GNU General Public License for more details.

    You should have received a copy of the GNU General Public License
    along with this program; if not, write to the Free Software
    Foundation, Inc., 51 Franklin St, Fifth Floor, Boston, MA  02110-1301  USA
*/
?>
```

Naturally, you'd want to change YEAR, PLUGIN_AUTHOR_NAME, and PLUGIN AUTHOR E-MAIL to the correct information. You can also include the full license as a text file, aptly named license.txt of course. Obtain the license from www.gnu.org/copyleft/gpl.html.

And that's about it. All you need for WordPress to find the plugin is this, one single file with an identifying header. Dropping it in wp-content/plugins/ will result in it being listed in the Plugins section of WordPress. Activate it from the Plugins admin page, and it will be available to you in your theme and from WordPress's actions themselves.

This is where the fun part begins because now you have to figure out what you need to do and how you'll accomplish it.

Whether you're planning on writing the plugin you think will change the way you use WordPress or just need some extra functionality for your latest project, you should go through the following plugin checklist before getting started. It may just save you some time and headaches.

- Is there a plugin for this already? If there is, consider using that instead or forking/editing it if it nearly does what you want.
- Make sure that you've got a unique name for your plugin. Don't just check the WordPress. org plugin directory; Google it to make sure. One way to ensure a unique name is to add your company's initials to the front of the plugin name, such as acme_pluginname.
- Decide on a unique prefix to all your functions and stick to it. That way, you're doing your part in eliminating any unnecessary conflicts due to a similar naming structure. This is important: Prefix everything!
- Do you want to internationalize your plugin? You really should; it works the same way as with themes and is pretty easy after all.
- Should this plugin have widget support? If it should, what kind of settings should it have?
- Do you need a Settings page within the admin interface? Try to keep settings to a minimum as they tend to confuse users.
- What license should the plugin have? Keep in mind that it has to be GPL-compatible to get hosted by the WordPress.org directory.

- Don't forget the final check. Is the header up to date? Is the version number correct? Do all the links work? Is every necessary file in the package? And last but not least, have you spell-checked your plugin?

METHODS FOR INCORPORATING YOUR PLUGINS

Writing plugins is more like traditional PHP coding than working with WordPress themes. Although you may use both template and conditional tags, most likely, you'll be writing a lot on your own as well, not relying so much on the built-in features that WordPress tags offer you. Of course, it all depends on what your plugin does, but overall plugin development is more you than WordPress.

The usual way you generate WordPress plugins relies on creating functions and then applying them to action and filter hooks. By inserting your function where you need it to be, perhaps when `wp_head` or the comments are getting loaded, you can trigger your plugin code at the appropriate time.

The following subsections describe three ways you can write and work with plugins, starting with the ever-important hooks.

USING HOOKS

Remember the action hooks from the previous chapter, "Advanced Theme Usage"? *Action hooks* are triggered by specific events when a WordPress site is running, such as publishing a post, which would be the `publish_post` hook. A second type of hooks, *filter hooks,* on the other hand, are functions that WordPress passes data through, so you'd use them to do stuff with the data. Useful filter hooks include `the_excerpt` and `the_title`. You ought to recognize them from the template tags.

Hooks come in handy for plugins as well, not just for themes. Thanks to hooks, you can add your cool plugin functionality to the appropriate part of WordPress, such as `wp_head` or `wp_footer`. The web statistics example in Chapter 6, in which you added a function in the theme's functions.php template file and then added it to the `wp_footer` hook using `add_action()`, is very much the way a plugin might work.

Often, you'll end up writing a function in your plugin and then you'll add it to one of the hooks. This is how `add_action()` works:

```
add_action ( $hook_name, $function_name, $priority, $parameters );
```

The `'hook_name'` is of course the name of the hook to which you want to add the action. What happens is that WordPress, when encountering that hook when running the code, will check to see if there are any added functions registered for the hook. If there are, the function will run; if not, it won't. And the function is, of course, the one you've defined in `'function_name'`.

For example, the following code snippet would cause the `'smashingshortcode'` function to run when `wp_head()` is executed:

```
add_action ( 'wp_head', 'smashingshortcode' );
```

`$priority` and `$parameters` are optional integers. The first, `$priority`, is the priority argument (which defaults to 10), used to sort actions when there are several added to a specific action hook. The lower the number is, the earlier the function will be executed, so if you need to make sure that something happens before or after something else, this is where you control that. `$parameters`, on the other hand, is the number of arguments your function can accept (defaulting to 1). If you need the function to handle more than one argument, you can set it by entering another number here.

Most of the time, you won't see the priority or number of arguments in plugins, but they come in handy when needed. As they are optional, you can just leave them out when you don't need them. At other times, you really need the priority because you might clash with other plugins otherwise. If that seems to be the case, it's a good idea to adjust the priority to make sure that your plugin loads first, or last for that matter.

Filters work more or less the same way, but you use `add_filter()` instead of `add_action()`. The parameters are the same, and you pass them the same way as well. The only difference is that you can't use the action hooks with `add_filter()`; you use the filter hooks instead. Other than that, the two behave in the same way.

Adding functions to a hook, whether it is of the action or filter kind, is easy enough, but what about *removing* functionality? Sometimes you don't want an action or filter hook to run, and that means you need to make sure that it gets removed. This is done with `remove_action()` and `remove_filter()` for action and filter hooks, respectively. The syntax is simple:

```
remove_action( $hook_name, $function_name )
```

And the same for `remove_filter()`:

```
remove_filter( $hook_name, $function_name )
```

This is not just used to remove functionality you have added; you can also remove core functionality from within WordPress with these. Any action or filter function can be removed this way, from pinging to deleting attachments, so some plugins may actually be designed only to limit WordPress functionality rather than extend it, all depending on what your goal is.

CREATING YOUR OWN TEMPLATE TAGS

Another way to access your plugin functionality is by creating your own template tags, much like `bloginfo()`, `the_title()`, and so on. This isn't hard at all; in fact, just by creating a function in your plugin (or in functions.php for that matter), you can access that function with a simple little PHP snippet:

```
<?php function_name(); ?>
```

Not very complicated, right? It really isn't, but that doesn't mean that it is the best way to include plugin content, even though it is by far the easiest method. With this method, you don't need to add any hooks, and the function will be executed when the plugin template tag is loaded, which means that you'll just put it where you want it within your theme files. This is especially handy if there is no hook available to execute whatever it is you want to do; then you can just create a template tag and have it do your dirty work. Naturally, it is a better option to use existing hooks whenever possible.

One thing you need to keep in mind before going down this route is usability. Not everybody is comfortable with editing the theme files, and if you intend to release your plugin or deliver it to a client, it may not be a good idea to force template file hacking for usage. If you'll be doing the deployment yourself, it really doesn't matter. However, if the end user will have to fiddle with the plugin's position or perhaps will need to pass parameters to it, then it is probably a better idea to look at other solutions.

At other times, just adding functionality using template tags won't cut it, and you need to overwrite parts of the core WordPress functionality. That's when you turn to the pluggable functions.

THE PLUGGABLE FUNCTIONS

Sometimes you may need to overwrite parts of the WordPress core functionality, perhaps to replace them with your own or just because your particular use of WordPress differs from the intended one. Maybe you don't want localizations to work in WordPress admin, for example, in which case you'd need to get rid of `load_textdomain`, or perhaps you want to replace the admin footer with your own. Just removing a hook won't do it. That's when you turn to pluggable.php, located in wp-includes. Naturally, you won't hack it because that would be a tedious thing to manage with updates; instead you'll write a plugin that does the override. Now this is dangerous stuff. First of all, you can perform an override only once, so if two plugins have different overrides on the same pluggable function, the site will misbehave (at best) or break (at worst). This means that two plugins both relying on overriding the same pluggable function can't be installed at the same time, which is a serious drawback. Therefore, you should probably keep your pluggable functions to sites you are in complete control of.

Also, to avoid unnecessary errors, you may want to wrap any code pertaining to a plugin relying on these things in a check to see if the function exists:

```php
<?php if ( ! function_exists( 'function_name' ) ); ?>
```

There are, naturally, times when the pluggable functions can come in handy. See the most up-to-date list of what functions you can get in this way in the Codex: http://codex.wordpress.org/Pluggable_Functions.

And use with caution, obviously. Just writing the plugin in the correct way, which is covered next, isn't enough when you're nulling out parts of the WordPress core. Don't be surprised when things stop working or conflicts come out of nowhere if you dive into these things. After all, the WordPress functionality you're bypassing is there for a reason.

CUSTOM TAXONOMIES AND CUSTOM POST TYPES

Custom taxonomies and custom post types are powerful tools, especially when you want to use WordPress beyond straightforward blogs. In Chapter 14, "Uncommon WordPress Usage," you'll do some creative stuff with both custom taxonomies and custom post types, in case you need a little bit of inspiration for what you can do with these tools.

Just to recap: Custom taxonomies let you add additional ways to organize your content. The default tags and categories are in fact nonhierarchical and hierarchical taxonomies, respectively, and the actual tags and categories are terms in said taxonomies. Custom post types, on the other hand, are additional post types, much like posts and pages, which are post types themselves.

WHY USE A PLUGIN?

The reason for using a plugin for your custom taxonomies and custom post types is portability. If you put this sort of functionality in your theme's functions.php file (which is possible), you will lose it when using a different theme, although you obviously can copy and paste it to the new theme as well. It makes more sense to put things related to content rather than design in a plugin so that it is portable across themes. Just keep the plugin activated, and you'll be fine.

You can read more about data portability in Chapter 8, "Plugins or functions.php?."

CREATING A CUSTOM TAXONOMY

To create a custom taxonomy, use `register_taxonomy()` within a function and attach it to the `init` hook. The settings for `register_taxonomy()` are all simple enough and control how your taxonomy will be referred to in the admin interface, along with other things such as if it should have its own permalink (the `rewrite` argument) and if it is to be hierarchical or not.

The following example creates a nonhierarchical taxonomy, which is to say that it will behave much like the default tags, called *Smashing Tags* (depicted in Figure 7-2):

```
// Attach function to init hook
add_action( 'init', 'smashing_tax', 0 );

// Taxonomy function
function smashing_tax() {

    // Register the taxonomy
    register_taxonomy( 'smashing_taxonomy', 'post',
        array(
            'hierarchical' => false,
            'labels' => array(
                'name' => 'Smashing Tags',
                'singular_name' => 'Smashing Tags',
                'search_items' => 'Search Smashing Tags',
```

```
                    'popular_items' => 'Popular Smashing Tags',
                    'add_new_item' => 'Add New Smashing Tags'
                ),
            'query_var' => true,
            'rewrite' => true
        )
    );

}
```

Figure 7-2: The Smashing Tags taxonomy.

Not too complicated, right? You can use this code in functions.php, but chances are your taxonomy really isn't theme-related but rather something that belongs with the content, and that means a plugin is more portable. Just putting the code within PHP tags and adding the plugin header will do the trick, so here's the Smashing Taxonomy plugin file:

```php
<?php
/*
Plugin Name: Smashing Taxonomy
Plugin URI: http://tdh.me/wordpress/smashing-taxonomy/
Description: Adding the Smashing Tags taxonomy.
Version: 1.0
Author: Thord Daniel Hedengren
Author URI: http://tdh.me/
*/

// Attach function to init hook
add_action( 'init', 'smashing_tax', 0 );

// Taxonomy function
function smashing_tax() {

    // Register the taxonomy
    register_taxonomy( 'smashing_taxonomy', 'post',
        array(
            'hierarchical' => false,
            'labels' => array(
                'name' => 'Smashing Tags',
                'singular_name' => 'Smashing Tags',
                'search_items' => 'Search Smashing Tags',
                'popular_items' => 'Popular Smashing Tags',
```

```
                         'add_new_item' => 'Add New Smashing Tags'
                ),
                'query_var' => true,
                'rewrite' => true
        )
    );

}
?>
```

CREATING A CUSTOM POST TYPE

Creating a custom post type is simple enough. Although you can do it in a plugin (and there are actually plugins that will act as a UI for creating custom post types), I'll concentrate on how it is done in a theme here. The following code can be used in functions.php, but you are better off putting it in a plugin. The key to everything is `register_post_type()`:

```
// Register post type
register_post_type( 'smashing_post_type',
    array(
        'labels' => array(
            'name' => 'Smashing Post Type'
        ),
        'singular_label' => 'Smashing Post Type',
        'public' => true,
        'show_ui' => true,
        'capability_type' => 'post',
        'has_archive' => true,
        'hierarchical' => false,
        'show_in_menu' => true,
        'supports' => array( 'title', 'editor', 'author', 'revisions', 'comments' )
    )
);
```

This will register a new post type, called `smashing_post_type`, which you'll find just before the array with the settings for the post type. These settings alter how things look and feel — for example, what's on the labels in the admin menu, whether this is something that is public, if there's supposed to be a menu option at all, and what sort of user level is needed to be able to use it. Most of it is pretty self-explanatory, but the `supports` array within `array` is interesting. This is where you decide what the post type supports: In this case, you've got a title, the Write Post Editor box, the author, revisions, and comments. No taxonomies at all, no excerpt, no custom fields — everything is set here.

Just pasting this code into any theme's functions.php will make the custom post type appear in the admin interface, as shown on Figure 7-3. You'll most likely have to rebuild your permalinks when this is done; otherwise, the links to the post and archives might not work.

Figure 7-3: The Smashing Post type.

Content from custom post types won't show up in the regular content flow; you'll have to alter the loop (with `query_post()` or something similar — see Chapter 3 for more about the loop) to get content from custom post types to show up. However, if you have enabled it, there's nothing that stops you from linking to an archive page from a menu, for example.

There are a lot of options available when creating your post type. Consult the Codex for all of them at http://codex.wordpress.org/Function_Reference/register_post_type. You'll use custom post types for projects in Chapter 14, so look for more on what you can do with them there.

So how would a custom post type look in a plugin? Pretty much the same as the custom taxonomy. Here's the Smashing Post Type plugin in all its splendor:

```php
<?php
/*
Plugin Name: Smashing Post Type
Plugin URI: http://tdh.me/wordpress/smashing-post-type/
Description: Adding the Smashing Post Type.
Version: 1.0
Author: Thord Daniel Hedengren
Author URI: http://tdh.me/
*/

// Add to init hook
add_action( 'init', 'smashing_post_types' );

// Add these custom post types
function smashing_post_types() {

    // Register Smashing Post Type
    register_post_type( 'smashing_post_type',
        array(
            'labels' => array(
                'name' => 'Smashing Post Type',
                'menu_name' => 'Smashing Posts'
```

```
        ),
        'singular_label' => 'Smashing Post Type',
        'public' => true,
        'show_ui' => true,
        'menu_position' => 5,
        'capability_type' => 'post',
        'has_archive' => true,
        'hierarchical' => false,
        'show_in_menu' => true,
        'supports' => array( 'title', 'editor', 'author', 'revisions',
                        'comments' )
    }
  );

}

?>
```

MUST-HAVE FUNCTIONALITY FOR PLUGINS

Strictly speaking, the only thing your plugin really must have is a main PHP file containing the identifying header and whatever code is needed to get the job done. However, in reality, you should probably take it a few steps further than that. After all, someone other than you may have to work with your plugin, so it should be as simple and accessible as possible. That means that you should go to great lengths to make the plugin blend in nicely with the WordPress admin interface.

The same goes for whatever parts of the plugin will show to end users. Some plugins add visual functionality, and that should work with as many themes as possible if you intend to release the plugin. Naturally, if you've developed a plugin for use with a particular project only, this won't be an issue. The same goes for localization support; there's no need for that if there won't be any language support other than the default one, is there?

Finally, I think every plugin should come with a license and some sort of instructions as to how the plugin should be used. Readme files are nice and all, but it's better still to build the instructions into the actual plugin because a lot of users are reluctant (or just too impatient) to read the attached readme files. You can also extend the Help tab in WordPress using add_help_tab(), which you can read more about at http://codex.wordpress.org/Function_Reference/add_help_tab.

PLUGIN SETTINGS

Sometimes you want to save things in the database. You've got the freedom of any PHP script here really, which means that you can add full tables and so on to the database should you want to. I won't cover that.

I will, however, tell you how to use the Settings API (more here: http://codex.wordpress.org/Settings_API) to let WordPress take care of your necessary data saving. This not only saves you a lot of time, but it also means you will have a solid base when it comes to security because WordPress takes care of things such as nonces.

Put it to the test by creating a simple settings page under Settings in the left admin menu that stores two values: a text field and check box (which obviously is checked or not).

First, you need to create a plugin; it'll be a single PHP file called smashing-settings.php, starting with this:

```php
<?php
/*
Plugin Name: Smashing Settings
Plugin URI: http://tdh.me/wordpress/smashing-settings/
Description: A simple settings plugin.
Author: Thord Daniel Hedengren
Author URI: http://tdh.me/
*/
```

Moving on, you need to add the Settings page to the menu by hooking a function on to admin_menu. For this example, you'll use add_options_page(), but there are other options as well:

```php
// Add the settings page function to the menu
add_action( 'admin_menu', 'smashings_settingsdemo_add_page' );

// Add to the menu
function smashings_settingsdemo_add_page() {
    add_options_page( 'Smashing Sample Settings',
        'Smashing Settings',
        'manage_options',
        'smashings_settingsdemo',
        'smashings_settingsdemo_do_page' );
}
```

With add_options_page(), you create a page called *Smashing Sample Settings,* shortened to *Smashing Settings* in the left admin menu. This is available only to users that have the manage_options capability, has the unique ID of smashings_settingsdemo, and calls a page with the function smashings_settingsdemo_do_page(). You need to create that last function, so do that next:

```php
// Add the actual settings page
function smashings_settingsdemo_do_page() {
// Leaving PHP for a while ?>

    <h2>Smashing Settings</h2>
    <p>This is our settings page.</p>
    <form action="options.php" method="post">
    <?php settings_fields( 'smashings_settingsdemo' ); ?>
    <?php do_settings_sections( 'smashings_settingsdemo' ); ?>
```

```php
    <?php submit_button(); ?>
    </form>

<?php
} // Back to PHP
```

This is the entire settings page markup — a really simple one that you'll want to expand upon to make it look good. Note `settings_fields()`, which points to a settings field created with `add_settings_field()` called `smashings_settingsdemo`, and `do_settings_sections()`, which calls a section with the same name. There's no need to create your own submit button either to save these settings; `submit_button()` will do that for you.

Next, whitelist your settings and use `add_settings_section()` to add a settings section and `add_settings_field()` to add an input field:

```php
// Whitelist the settings
function smashings_settingsdemo_init(){

    // Add the section
    add_settings_section('smashing_settings_section',
        'Smashing Settings',
        'smashing_settings_section_callback',
        'smashings_settingsdemo');

    // Add settings field
    add_settings_field('smashing_sample_input',
        'Input sample',
        'smashing_sample_input_callback',
        'smashings_settingsdemo',
        'smashing_settings_section');

    // Register settings
    register_setting( 'smashings_settingsdemo', 'smashing_sample_input',
        'smashing_settingsdemo_validate' );

}

// Initiate smashings_settingsdemo_init() in admin
add_action( 'admin_init', 'smashings_settingsdemo_init' );
```

This isn't too complicated, actually. First you create a section, `smashing_settings_section`, with `add_settings_section()`. You'll recognize `smashings_settingsdemo`, which is the `$page` parameter. This is what you called for previously, in your settings page markup, with `do_settings_sections()`. You connect the `smashing_sample_input` settings field to the newly created settings section with the final parameter, `$section`, by passing `smashing_settings_section`. For a full list of parameters for `add_settings_section()` and `add_settings_field()`, refer to the Codex at http://codex.wordpress.org/Function_Reference/add_settings_section and http://codex.wordpress.org/Function_Reference/add_settings_field, respectively.

Then you add the function `smashings_settingsdemo_init()` to the `admin_init` hook.

Next, add a little something to the section just to prove that you can:

```
// Runs at the start of the section
function smashing_settings_section_callback() {
    echo '<p>This is the section intro.</p>';
}
```

You'll recognize the function name, `smashing_settings_section_callback()`, from the earlier `add_settings_section()`. It is the callback function, so this will run at the beginning of the section, echoing a `p` tag with some text.

In a similar fashion, create the callback function for the `add_settings_field()` you created, called `smashing_sample_input_callback()`:

```
// The input sample setting
function smashing_sample_input_callback() {
// Leaving PHP for a while ?>
    <input type="text" name="smashing_sample_input" value="<?php echo
      get_option( 'smashing_sample_input' ); ?>" />
<?php }
// Back to PHP
```

This function contains only an input field with the value of `smashing_sample_input` passed through `get_option()`, which is what you'll be saving. This is obviously the ID of the settings field you created.

Finally, you need to sanitize the form input a bit. For this example, `esc_attr()` will be enough, but you might want other types of sanitation:

```
// Sanitize
function smashing_settingsdemo_validate($input) {

    // Encode
    $newinput = esc_attr($input);
    return $newinput;

}
```

So what just happened here? You created a settings page, which in turn contains `settings_fields()` for all your settings fields (just one in the example — you can have more than that) and `do_settings_section()` for your sections. The following is the complete settings plugin, from start to finish:

```
<?php
/*
```

```
Plugin Name: Smashing Settings
Plugin URI: http://tdh.me/wordpress/smashing-settings/
Description: A simple settings plugin.
Author: Thord Daniel Hedengren
Author URI: http://tdh.me/
*/

// Add the settings page function to the menu
add_action( 'admin_menu', 'smashings_settingsdemo_add_page' );

// Add to the menu
function smashings_settingsdemo_add_page() {
    add_options_page( 'Smashing Sample Settings',
        'Smashing Settings',
        'manage_options',
        'smashings_settingsdemo',
        'smashings_settingsdemo_do_page' );
}

// Add the actual settings page
function smashings_settingsdemo_do_page() {
// Leaving PHP for a while ?>

    <h2>Smashing Settings</h2>
    <p>This is our settings page.</p>
    <form action="options.php" method="post">
    <?php settings_fields( 'smashings_settingsdemo' ); ?>
    <?php do_settings_sections( 'smashings_settingsdemo' ); ?>
    <?php submit_button(); ?>
    </form>

<?php
} // Back to PHP

// Whitelist the settings
function smashings_settingsdemo_init(){

    // Add the section
    add_settings_section('smashing_settings_section',
        'Smashing Settings',
        'smashing_settings_section_callback',
        'smashings_settingsdemo');

    // Add settings field
    add_settings_field('smashing_sample_input',
        'Input sample',
        'smashing_sample_input_callback',
        'smashings_settingsdemo',
        'smashing_settings_section');

    // Register settings
    register_setting( 'smashings_settingsdemo', 'smashing_sample_input',
```

```php
        'smashing_settingsdemo_validate' );

}


// Initiate smashings_settingsdemo_init() in admin
add_action( 'admin_init', 'smashings_settingsdemo_init' );

// Runs at the start of the section
function smashing_settings_section_callback() {
    echo '<p>This is the section intro.</p>';
}

// The input sample setting
function smashing_sample_input_callback() {
// Leaving PHP for a while ?>
    <input type="text" name="smashing_sample_input" value="<?php echo
      get_option( 'smashing_sample_input' ); ?>" />
<?php }
// Back to PHP

// Sanitize
function smashing_settingsdemo_validate($input) {

    // Encode
    $newinput = esc_attr($input);
    return $newinput;

}

?>
```

There you have it — an extremely simple settings page that will save your data in the database, as shown in Figure 7-4.

Figure 7-4: The simple settings page, with some text and a selected check box saved.

DATABASE CONTENT AND UNINSTALLING

When creating a plugin that stores data to the database, you need to consider what happens when someone doesn't want to use it anymore. Do you need to uninstall functionality to clean up after yourself? You usually do if you have saved a bunch of things in the database, which shouldn't be sitting around full of unused data, anyway.

There are a number of ways to remove unwanted functionality. One method is to include an uninstall.php file with your plugin. This file contains the uninstall code to delete the database content you have added:

```
delete_option( 'my-data' );
```

This would delete the my-data field in the option database table. Because a lot of plugins store some option data in that table, it can get cluttered, and that's never a good thing. Naturally, you'd add whatever you need to remove to the uninstall.php file. This also applies for uninstalls made through the WordPress admin interface.

Here's a dummy uninstall.php:

```php
<?php
    // For old versions
    if ( !defined( 'WP_UNINSTALL_PLUGIN' ) ) {
        exit();
    }
    // Delete the option data --
    delete_option( 'myplugindata_post' );
    delete_option( 'myplugindata_feed' );
?>
```

The first part is a check to see if the uninstall feature is present. This feature was not used in earlier versions of WordPress, so if you are not using WordPress 3.0 or later (which you of course should be!), the script will exit, not doing anything. That way, this file is backward compatible. The remaining code deletes the option data stored in the database: 'myplugin-data_post' and 'myplugindata_feed', in this case. This is done when deleting the plugin from within the WordPress admin interface; hence, the user gets a cleaned-up database.

The important thing is that you remember to add uninstall functionality should you have stored anything in the database. You may want to make it optional, however, to remove the data because it may be useful later on. Also, it is probably a good idea to remove the data on deactivation because that is recommended for all plugins when doing manual WordPress upgrades.

AFTER UNINSTALLING

It is easy to forget that when a plugin is uninstalled, it may leave a few things lying around. Database data is one thing, and hopefully the uninstall at least gave the user a chance to clean up after the plugin, but there is one thing that is even more pressing: shortcodes.

What happens when a plugin relying on shortcodes gets uninstalled? *Shortcodes* are snippets of code that output something within the post content. The most common shortcode that WordPress uses is the `[gallery]` shortcode, which you'll see when you include a gallery in a post and switch to HTML view in the Add New Post screen.

So what happens to shortcodes used by a plugin when that plugin is uninstalled? The shortcode won't be parsed; hence it is outputted as regular text. Your `[myshortcode]` shortcode will end up printed just like that, in the middle of your post.

It won't look good.

So although the plugin may not be active, or even present anymore, you still need to maintain some sort of backward compatibility to it. That means that you should offer some sort of solution for the user to make sure the posts aren't littered with unparsed shortcode. One way would be to run a SQL query and simply remove all the shortcode automatically, but that may be a bit drastic, and what happens if something breaks during this process? It may destroy the database. Or, more likely, how do you know that there isn't a human error within the post that for some reason causes the removed shortcode query to cut too much?

How you choose to handle redundant shortcode depends on the kind of usage you have introduced in your plugin. This is covered more in depth in Chapter 8, "Plugins or functions. php?."

Obviously, not all types of plugins will need this treatment. For example, plugins utilizing widgets will just stop displaying the widget when removed.

ADDING WIDGET SUPPORT TO PLUGINS

Widgets make it easy to customize the contents of a blog or site. You can put them in the widget area(s), dragging and dropping them from within the WordPress admin interface. WordPress ships with a few widgets, such as one for outputting RSS, displaying the latest posts, listing the Pages, listing the categories, and so on. These widgets may not be enough, however, and when you create a plugin, you may want to give the user the chance to run it from within a widget area. This is a lot more user friendly than having to put the plugin PHP template tag in the theme's template files, so it may be a good idea to widgetize your plugin if it should be displayed in a widget area.

Thanks to the Widgets API (which you can read more about at the Codex page http://codex. wordpress.org/Widgets_API), creating widgets for your plugins isn't all that complicated. You extend the built-in widget class, called `WP_Widget`, give it some instructions, and then register it so that it will show up, as shown in the following code:

```
class SmashingWidget extends WP_Widget {
    function SmashingWidget() {
        // The actual widget code goes here
    }
    function widget( $args, $instance ) {
```

```
        // Output the widget content
    }
    function update( $new_instance, $old_instance ) {
        // Process and save the widget options
    }
    function form( $instance ) {
        // Output the options form in admin
    }
}
register_widget( 'SmashingWidget' );
```

In this example, you extend the `WP_Widget` class with the `SmashingWidget` widget. The first function, which is just `function SmashingWidget()`, is the actual widget with the functionality you want, so that's where the action is. The `widget()`, `update()`, and `form()` functions are necessary to get the widget to behave the way you want. Obviously, you wrap it up by registering the widget with `register_widget()`. Both the Cancel link and the Submit button are built in to the widget API, so you needn't worry about them when it is time to save whatever changes you'll let your users meddle with.

CREATING A WIDGET

This section walks you through creating a simple widget. This widget will output some text to say hello to the visitor, and you'll also be able to rename the heading from within the admin interface:

1. Remember, all this code is within a plugin file, which is PHP and has the plugin identifying header. Unless you have a plugin you want to add this functionality to, you should create a brand-new one with an appropriate name.

   Start with the widget class:

   ```
   class SmashingHello extends WP_Widget {
   ```

   The widget is named `SmashingHello`, so you can probably tell what's coming.

2. Next, you get the widget function:

   ```
   function SmashingHello() {
       parent::WP_Widget( false, $name = 'Smashing Hello' );
   }
   ```

3. Remember, you need `widget()`, `update()`, and `form()` to make cool things happen. This is the next step, starting with `widget()`:

   ```
   function widget($args, $instance) {
       extract( $args );
       ?>
           <?php echo $before_widget; ?>
               <?php echo $before_title
                   . $instance['title']
                   . $after_title; ?>
               Well hello there! Ain't that just Smashing?
           <?php echo $after_widget; ?>
       <?php
   }
   ```

You take `widget()` and extract the arguments. Notice the `$before_widget`, `$after_widget`, `$before_title`, and `$after_title` settings. These shouldn't be changed unless necessary. They are controlled by the widget API and default theming, so they make things look good.

So what happens? You echo `$before_widget` and then `$before_title`, without telling them to do anything fancy, so they'll just pick up the default code. Then there's the `$instance` title, which is the title you'll use as an input field in the widget interface within admin, so people can write whatever they want there. Then you're done with the title, getting to `$after_title`, and then there's your lovely text that the widget will display: "Well hello there! Ain't that just Smashing?" Not high prose, of course, and you can put just about anything here, a WordPress loop query or whatever. Finally, the widget is all over, and you get `$after_widget`.

Again, these `before` and `after` bits are to make the widget behave the way the theme wants them to. This is something the theme designer can control, so if you want to keep your widget cross-compatible, you can stick to the defaults and worry about how it looks in the design.

4. Moving on, you need to make sure that the widget is saved properly when updated:

```
function update($new_instance, $old_instance) {
    return $new_instance;
}
```

This is easy because `update()` takes only `$new_instance` and `$old_instance`. Naturally, you want to return `$new_instance`, which is whatever you changed. You may want to do some tag stripping with `strip_tags()` here if the kind of widget you're creating may run into some nasty HTML stuff. That's easy; just do something like this for an input field named `'music'`:

```
$instance['music'] = strip_tags( $new_instance['music'] );
```

See `strip_tags()` at work here? It makes sure that no stray HTML code gets through. Very handy.

5. Now add one more setting to change the widget title:

```
function form( $instance ) {
    $title = esc_attr( $instance['title'] );
    ?>
        <p>
            <label for="<?php echo $this->get_field_id( 'title' ); ?>">
                Title: <input class="widefat" id="<?php echo $this->
                get_field_id( 'title' ); ?>" name="<?php echo $this->
                get_field_name( 'title' ); ?>" type="text" value="<?php
                    echo $title; ?>" />
            </label>
        </p>
    <?php
}
```

The keys here are `get_field_name()` and `get_field_id()`. They handle which field does what. And then, when you've built your pretty little widget settings form, just save it (with the Widgets API automatically created Save button), and it does the trick.

6. Finally, you need to close the class with a curly bracket and register the widget:

```
}

function smashing_widget_init() {
    register_widget( 'SmashingHello' );
}

add_action( 'widgets_init', 'smashing_widget_init' ) );
```

Figure 7-5 depicts the widget.

Figure 7-5: The widget you just created, dropped in the sidebar widget area.

There you have it, a widget where you can change the title and output some text. This can just as easily be something else, thanks to the fact that widget output is just PHP spitting something out.

Another thing to remember is that not all widgets need to take options. If you just want to drop an element in a widget area, with the ease it brings, then by all means just create the widget and forget about the settings. It is really all about what you need in terms of functionality.

DASHBOARD WIDGETS

You can create not only regular widgets, but also Dashboard widgets. This means that you can add widgets to the admin area of WordPress, commonly referred to as the *Dashboard*. All those boxes you see on the front page of the Dashboard are in fact widgets, and you can add your own.

To create a Dashboard widget, you need to create a plugin and hence a file in which the code goes. The following one is a simple reminder to the users of a group blog to visit the internal pages, so it only outputs some text and some links. First you need to create the function that does this:

```
function dashboard_reminder() {
    echo '
```

```
        Hey you! Don\'t forget the internal pages for important stuff:<br />
        &larr; <a href="http://domain.com/internal/forum">Forum</a><br />
        &larr; <a href="http://domain.com/internal/docs">Documentation</a><br />
        &larr; <a href="http://domain.com/internal/staff">Staff</a><br />
        OK THX BYE!
    ';
}
```

It's a simple function called `dashboard_reminder()` that echoes some HTML. This is what you want the widget to display. The next step is to add the Dashboard widget itself:

```
function dashboard_reminder_setup() {
    wp_add_dashboard_widget( 'dashboard_reminder_widget', 'Staff Reminder',
      'dashboard_reminder' );
}
```

The key here is `wp_add_dashboard_widget()`, to which you pass first an identifying ID of the widget (`'dashboard_reminder_widget'` in this case), then the text label to describe the widget, and finally the name of the function containing the Dashboard widget's content (obviously, the `dashboard_reminder()` function). It's worth knowing that the Dashboard widget ID, which is the first parameter passed to `wp_add_dashboard_widget()`, is also the class the widget will get should you want some fancy CSS stylings.

Pause for a moment and look at the `wp_add_dashboard_widget()` function. There's a fourth parameter as well called `$control_callback`, which passes a null value by default and is optional. It isn't included in this example, but it may be a good idea to keep in mind that you can pass a fourth parameter for more functionality in your Dashboard widget.

Returning to the example, you need to add the widget action to the `wp_dashboard_setup` hook, using `add_action()`:

```
add_action( 'wp_dashboard_setup', 'dashboard_reminder_setup' );
```

There you have it, a Dashboard widget (see Figure 7-6)! As of now, there is no Dashboard widget order API, so your widget will end up at the bottom in the Dashboard. The user can reorder widgets manually, of course, but you may want to force things to the top. There are some hacks available online, such as the one described in the WordPress Codex (http://codex.wordpress.org/Dashboard_Widgets_API) should you need to achieve this.

Now that you've gotten your hands a little dirty with plugins and widgets, it's time to discuss database usage. It is easy enough to store data in the options tables, but sometimes it is just not the best practice.

Figure 7-6: The Dashboard widget in all its glory.

PLUGIN CONSIDERATIONS WHEN USING THE DATABASE

Storing data in the database is sometimes necessary to make your plugins function the way you want. From storing some simple options to adding full tables with more data for the users to utilize, the database is truly a tool that should be put to good use. Putting data in the database means that you can query for it easily; it is just very convenient.

However, it comes at a price. A cluttered database isn't very nice to maintain, and you have to make sure that the user can uninstall the data stored by the plugin. And if that's not enough, you need to decide where to save this data. Either you use the Settings API to make sure that things end up where they should — a nice solution for smaller settings — or you create your own table within the database for the plugin only. The latter solution is probably better if you need to store a lot of data, but it extends the database in such a way that it may create issues with other plugins interacting with the database, should you want to integrate with them in any way. It also means that there is a part outside WordPress that needs to be backed up, and should you want to move the install, the Export/Import method won't cover the data unless you sort that out, too.

Then there's caching, which is something you might need to consider for your plugin, especially if it pulls data from an external service at regular intervals. You could use files for caching obviously, but another option is the Transients API, which was created for these things. You can read more about that at http://codex.wordpress.org/Transients_API.

So what's best? Data in options or in its own table? Maybe you should even use the meta tables or the posts table? It is entirely up to you, depending on what you need to store. My personal guideline is that settings should go in options, and if it is actual content or larger amounts of data, I consider the external table option.

Just make sure that you inform the user and make sure that it is possible to clean up after uninstallation should it be necessary, and you'll be fine.

BACKWARD COMPATIBILITY FOR PLUGINS

Another aspect to consider when developing plugins is whether you want or need backward compatibility. There are new functions and hooks added to WordPress all the time, and if you rely on the new ones, previous versions not featuring them naturally can't run the plugin. That's why you should be careful when using new features as they may just not work in older versions of WordPress.

However, it is not just WordPress functionality that changes; the system requirements have seen some revamps too. As of this writing, PHP 5.2.4 is required. The basic premise should be to support the software that WordPress runs on, but sometimes that's just not enough, and you want to use more cutting-edge versions of PHP and/or MySQL. If you take that route, be sure to output an error message should someone try to run your plugin using older versions of PHP and/or MySQL.

How far back you want to let your users go with your plugin is up to you. Since the addition of automatic updates, one can only hope that the updating frequency of the end users is higher than it was before auto updates, but a surprisingly large number of blogs still run on older versions of WordPress, which is bad news for developers and for site owners. After all, older versions can lead to security issues as well as compatibility problems.

HOSTING YOUR PLUGINS ON WORDPRESS.ORG

Just as with themes, there is an official plugin directory on WordPress.org where you can host your plugins. You don't have to post your plugins on that site, of course, but doing so allows users to get automatic updates so that they can keep up-to-date with the latest fixes.

However, there are some terms that your plugins needs to fulfill to be hosted on WordPress.org:

- The plugins must be licensed under a GPL-compatible license.
- The plugin can't do anything illegal or be "morally offensive."
- The plugin must be hosted in the WordPress.org subversion repository.
- The plugin must have a valid readme file.

To get access, you need to be a WordPress.org user. Then submit your plugin (http://wordpress.org/extend/plugins/add) and wait for approval. This process can take some time, depending on the workload of the people involved.

When your plugin is approved, you'll get access to the subversion directory, to which you submit the plugin, along with a valid readme file. A readme validator (http://wordpress.org/extend/plugins/about/validator) makes sure that all the data needed for the wordpress.org directory to list the plugin information is there.

You should read the Plugin Directory's Developer FAQ before submitting a plugin to make sure that you have the most up-to-date information on the matter. This will almost certainly speed up the approval process. You can find the FAQ at http://wordpress.org/extend/plugins/about/faq.

The benefits of being hosted in the WordPress.org repository are not only the automatic update functionality from within the actual users' admin interfaces, but also the statistics it adds. You'll see how many people have downloaded the plugin, get ratings, and be able to get comments on it. In addition to that, WordPress.org is also the central point for WordPress, which means chances are good that people will find your plugin, compared to just hosting it on your own site and hoping people come across it. Add the plugin search interface within the WordPress admin interface, and your plugin can be found from within any up-to-date WordPress system out there and installed with just a few clicks.

That is, if you're in the WordPress.org repository. So get in there!

> *Looking for an alternative to WordPress.org for your plugin hosting needs? Check out GitHub (http://github.com), which is free for open source software and pretty sweet to work with, especially if you know Git. If not, then there is always software that will help you out.*

A FINAL WORD OF WARNING ABOUT CREATING PLUGINS

Developing WordPress plugins differs quite a lot from creating WordPress themes. Sure, there are a lot of similarities, but in the end, what you're really doing is writing PHP scripts that tap into the WordPress functionality. This means that whereas just about anyone with a little scripting knowledge can bend WordPress themes to his or her will, the same just doesn't apply when it comes to plugins. You need a working knowledge of PHP, and you need to be wary because you can cause a lot of damage, especially if you're tinkering with the database.

With that caveat noted, if you know a little PHP, developing plugins can be the solution to building the site you want, so knock yourself out.

The next chapter discusses when to use a plugin and when to just rely on your theme's functions.php file.

8

PLUGINS OR FUNCTIONS.PHP?

WORDPRESS THEMES AND plugins typically work separately from each other, coming together only when it comes to implementing features. This cooperation is usually managed by having the correct widget areas available in the theme's template files, so the user can drop the plugin's widget where it should be, or by actually putting plugin PHP code snippets into the theme. Sometimes the plugins will output or activate the functionality by use of the WordPress hooks, which in essence means that the theme only has to comply with WordPress to trigger the plugins. It is all pretty straightforward.

However, there is one case in which themes and plugins collide, and that's when the functions.php file comes into play. The theme file can do more or less anything a plugin can, which means that it can be an optional solution for a publisher that normally would require a plugin. It also means that functions.php can clash with plugins, if not used with caution.

This chapter explains when you should use a plugin and when to use functions.php instead.

WHEN TO USE A PLUGIN

When opting for the plugin solution over the functions.php option, or comparing the use of a plugin with a custom hack in the theme, you need to consider the following questions:

- Is the plugin really needed?
- Does the plugin extend WordPress functionality in a way that is either too complicated or so standalone that it really isn't an option to try and do the same thing in the theme files?
- Does the plugin need to work outside of the chosen theme?

A positive answer to all these means that you should go ahead with your plugin.

EXTENDING FUNCTIONALITY WITH PLUGINS

In short, there is a good basic rule as to when to use a plugin: Everything that extends WordPress functionality should be a plugin. This means that if you add something to WordPress that you wouldn't be able to do otherwise, you should do the actual addition with a plugin. Examples of such functionality range from added data management to integration with third-party apps.

However, there's a big gray area here. A lot of plugins are actually mimicking WordPress and its loop, such as recent post listings and similar solutions that exist so that the user won't have to create a lot of custom loops within the theme's template files. The plugins can handle that for you, and they do it in a more user-friendly fashion, with options pages that set up the custom loop for you and widgets that let you drop them wherever you like. Compare that to having to actually write the loop code and put it in your theme file to be outputted where you want to. That may not seem like a big deal if you are a PHP expert, but for most WordPress users, it is a real hassle. In such cases, plugins aren't really extending functionality but enabling users who might not otherwise be able to access that functionality.

Custom fields are another example of built-in functionality that might be better handled with a plugin. Custom fields are great for a lot of things, but at the same time, they aren't exactly easy to use, with a bulky interface and so on. A plugin can do the same thing, and in fact use custom fields, but with a sleeker interface. That can potentially make updating your site easier.

CAUTION: PLUGINS CAN SLOW DOWN YOUR SITE

Nobody likes a slow-loading site, no matter how flashy it is. How fast your site needs to be depends on the target audience and kind of content being served. After all, intro pages with movies and sound and whatnot are still fairly common, and they should really not exist unless there is an audience for them.

No site should be slower than it needs to be, and a sure way to bloat your WordPress site is to fill it to the brim with plugin-powered functionality. Think about it: Most plugins need to be initialized to work when the visitor encounters their functionality on the site, and that in turn can mean anything from running a PHP function (at the very least) to a full-sized loop with database queries. Say you have ten plugins on a page, and each one initializes a loop and outputs relevant database content. That will not only take time, but it will also put additional strain on the server, possibly making it move sluggishly.

As mentioned earlier, a lot of plugins are really the loop in disguise. If you're displaying posts, comments, tags, or anything that builds around that, you're really querying the database. It is just like putting all those custom loops in your theme and watching them spin.

Now, a decent server won't usually mind the extra burden, but a lot of visitors at the same time can bring it to its knees. Database queries are heavy stuff, so you should be wary of having too many of those on the same page without the hardware to back it up.

The same is true for other types of functionality, from simple PHP functions to inclusion of third-party content. True, the biggest issue with these things comes whenever you fetch something from outside the server, which means that you'll be relying not only on your own host's hardware, but also the speed that the content can be reached (in other words, the speed of the Internet) and how quickly the target server can serve you the content. That is why a bunch of widgets pulling data from various services online will slow down any site out there.

The lesson is to not use too many plugins that put a strain on the server. That way, you'll keep site load times as low as possible. If you do need to use a lot of heavy plugins, make sure that you use whatever cache solutions fit your needs. Ironically, the best ones are plugins themselves, such as W3 Total Cache (http://wordpress.org/extend/plugins/w3-total-cache). By using a cache plugin, you will serve static files instead of dynamic content to most of your visitors. See Appendix A, "Essential WordPress Plugins," for some of the options out there. It is also important to remember that although a lot of plugins can make your site's performance less than stellar, it is not a universal truth. You could have a large number of plugins installed without slowing down your site; it all depends on the plugins themselves.

WHEN TO USE FUNCTIONS.PHP

When is it really a good idea to use functions.php? I have a rule for that too: Only use functions.php when the added functionality is unique to your theme.

The reasoning around this is simple: functions.php is tied to one particular theme, which means that if you switch themes, your added functionality won't be available, forcing you to either re-create it in the new theme or abandon it altogether. This effectively disqualifies functions.php from any kind of use that controls output of content because that would mean when you switch themes, the content would not be outputted or, at worst, it would render the site broken and full of errors.

Many of the things you do to extend your sites will be minor, and to be honest, you would probably be smarter to make those changes within the actual template files, keeping the plugin count to a minimum. However, some features are such big parts of the actual site functionality that they need to be added because you'll probably need them in the long run. And although you may think that you just created the perfect theme, sooner or later you'll end up switching to the next perfect theme, and that means that you'll have to tackle the loss of whatever you've added to functions.php. True, you can just move the code from the old theme's functions.php file to the new one, but why bother with that?

The rule of just putting functionality in functions.php that is unique for the particular theme is a good one, I think. Examples of such functionality include layout settings (obsolete in a different theme) and theme option pages that would change slightly depending on how something is added and/or shown in the theme. Because putting that functionality into a plugin would make the plugin obsolete when you switch themes, functions.php is a better choice.

So, plugins are for extending WordPress functionality, and functions.php is for things unique to the actual theme. That pretty much wraps it up.

THE SHORTCODE DILEMMA

Shortcodes, which you played a bit with in the previous chapter, might sound like a great idea, and sometimes they are. Far from all end users will want to write HTML code, and sometimes a shortcode might be warranted. However, they can be a problem if the code behind them is located in the theme's functions.php. It's really quite simple. Say that you have a shortcode for a fancy pull quote, called [pull]. The functionality came with your theme, and you've been making your posts looking fine and dandy ever since you activated the theme. But time flies and your needs change, so you end up getting a new theme. You activate it, and suddenly all the fancy pull quotes are gone! Instead, you get [pull] wherever the shortcode usually outputted the pull quote. How come?

It's quite simple really. Because the code for making the [pull] shortcode work was located in your old theme's functions.php and that theme isn't active anymore, the [pull] shortcode will be handled as common text. Not too pretty, that.

Luckily, you can solve this problem easily enough. You can copy the [pull] shortcode part from your old theme's functions.php to your new theme's functions.php. An even better solution is using a child theme's functions.php, which you'll get to in a little bit. Another solution is to create a functionality plugin where you keep all your fancy stuff, which makes it theme independent. This obviously goes for other features as well, not just shortcodes, but it is by far the most common problem when switching themes and there are shortcode features involved. You'll read about functionality plugins later in this chapter.

SOLVE IT WITH CHILD THEMES

Another way to solve the features problem is to use child themes. Assuming that you've created or found the perfect theme to build on, you can create child themes for the various iterations of your site. As always when it comes to child themes, keep your core features — which would include any cool functions.php features you've become reliant on — in your parent theme and the design stuff and minor changes in the child theme you're using.

This means that whenever you need to relaunch your site with new modern looks, you can just create a new child theme without losing any of the functionality. No copying and pasting of functions.php code, as that all sits in the parent's functions.php.

You can read more about child themes in Chapter 5, "The Child Theme Concept."

THE BEST OF BOTH WORLDS: A FUNCTIONALITY PLUGIN

A functionality plugin is the best of both words. The idea is to take the parts of your theme's functions.php file that need to be available even after you switch themes and stick them in a plugin instead. This would include shortcodes (obviously) but also declarations for custom taxonomies and custom post types because neither of these are really theme specific; you wouldn't want your custom taxonomies to disappear from the admin area just because you switch themes, right?

Things you wouldn't want in a functionality plugin would include (but not be limited to) sidebars and menus because those all depend on how the theme is built and designed. The same goes for feature images, header images, whether the theme supports a custom background, and such. These things are theme specific.

CREATE YOUR OWN FUNCTIONALITY PLUGIN

Creating a functionality plugin is simple. Because the code in functions.php is plugin-ready by itself, all you need to do is create a plugin and then add the parts from your theme's functions.php file that you want to store in the plugin instead. So why not get started on creating your own functionality plugin? Here's the beginning of smashing-functionality.php, the plugin file that will host all the functionality you want to put in it:

```php
<?php
/*
Plugin Name: Smashing Functionality, Baby!
Description: This plugin keeps my features portable.
Version: 1.0
Author: Thord Daniel Hedengren
Author URI: http://tdh.me
*/
?>
```

You probably recognize this; it's a simple plugin head. The Plugin URI part is cut out because frankly there's no need to have that when this is just something you'll do to keep your features portable between themes. You could add the license information as well, but I'll omit that here for the sake of keeping things simple.

Now, just add something to this plugin, something from functions.php. Say that you do have a [pull] shortcode in your theme's functions.php that you want to keep around. Then you'd just add it after the plugin declaration, like this:

```php
<?php
/*
Plugin Name: Smashing Functionality, Baby!
Description: This plugin keeps my features portable.
Version: 1.0
Author: Thord Daniel Hedengren
Author URI: http://tdh.me
*/


// Pullquote shortcode
function smashing_pullquote( $atts, $content = null ) {
    extract( shortcode_atts( array(
        'float' => '$align',
    ), $atts ) );
  if ($content) {
      return '<blockquote class="pullquote ' . $float . '">' . $content .
        '</blockquote>';
  }
}
add_shortcode( 'pull', 'smashing_pullquote' );
?>
```

Just adding the code from functions.php like that will do the trick. Now, obviously, you will need to remove the code from functions.php because otherwise you'll have a nasty clash between the functionality plugin (when activated) and the theme's functions.php. In the preceding example, you might want to add a style sheet as well, for styling the `pullquote` CSS class, but I'm refraining from that because my pull quote might look and feel different depending on what theme I'll be using. Whether you put the style with the plugin (queuing a style sheet up with `wp_enqueue_style()`) or in your theme's style.css is completely up to you; I'm sticking with the functionality only here.

You can add whatever features you like this way, effectively making the features portable across themes because all you need to do is activate the plugin. Of course, you'll have to make sure that your themes will actually handle the features you add. If you put the code for a custom taxonomy in a functionality plugin, for example, that will just enable the custom taxonomy for you. To actually output it on the posts on your site, you'll have to make sure that your theme does just that.

Functionality plugins work well for other things as well, not just stuff that usually goes in functions.php. Perhaps you don't want to use any of the plugins for Google Analytics, but you don't want to risk forgetting about putting your tracker code in your theme's template files. No problem — just add the code using the `wp_head` and `wp_footer` hooks, via your functionality plugin. That way, you'll keep your Google Analytics code snippets outside of your theme files and make sure that you won't forget to put them in, losing valuable statistics, the next time you activate a new theme for your site. Obviously, this could just as well be a plugin of its own, so perhaps you won't end up with just one functionality plugin, but several.

THE IMPORTANCE OF PORTABILITY

I've already touched on portability several times in this chapter, but it is very important, so I'll devote some more time to the need for it. I'm talking about making features continue to work even after you have switched themes, which you can easily achieve by using a functionality plugin rather than filling your functions.php file with a ton of features.

If any of the following features should continue to function even after you switch themes, they need to be portable and hence should reside in a plugin rather than in a theme's functions.php file:

- Custom post types
- Custom taxonomies
- Anything involving shortcodes
- Admin customizations

Not all of these should always be in a functionality plugin, but they should be most of the time. Perhaps your admin customizations, such as hiding various boxes and features for the end user, are directly tied to your current theme's needs; then those customizations would be useless when you activate a new theme.

Custom post types and custom taxonomies are usually global features that will be just as important when you swap themes. After all, you will probably want to continue to work with the content in your custom post types and keep using the terms from your custom taxonomies even after you have switched themes, right?

Make sure that features not directly tied to a specific theme can make the transition across themes. Doing so means using plugins, not the theme's functions.php file, to avoid a lot of unnecessary copying and pasting.

PLANNING FOR EXTENDED FUNCTIONALITY IN YOUR WORDPRESS SITE

Whenever you feel the need to extend the WordPress functionality on a project, you will have to figure out whether you can tweak the theme to pull off your ideas or if you need to develop a plugin. More often than not, when stepping outside of the typical flow of content, it is a mixture of both, and that's okay. The important thing is that there are solid ideas behind the choices being made. The obvious questions are

- Do I need a plugin for feature X?
- Is it possible to extend feature X without completely overwriting it with new functionality?
- Will feature X work if/when the project gets a new theme?
- Will feature X perhaps become an issue when WordPress is updated?
- How will feature X integrate with the theme and other plugins/features?

The point is to establish a plan on how to build your WordPress site. This is true whether you just want to pimp your blog, publish an online newspaper, or do something completely different with the platform. Naturally, the more extreme things you do, and the further you take WordPress beyond the blog, the more thought you'll need to pour into the project. For examples of what you can do, just look at the solutions in the next part of the book, "Additional Features and Functionality."

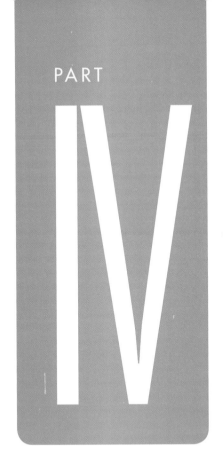

ADDITIONAL FEATURES AND FUNCTIONALITY

CHAPTER

9 USING WORDPRESS AS A CMS

CMS IS SHORT for *content management system* — simply put, a way to manage content. You use a CMS to write, edit, and manage your work online, usually by storing content in a database or in files. This is a lot more convenient than editing files or updating the database directly, which was the way the web used to be managed.

Although WordPress started life as a blogging platform, it has over time become a powerful and versatile CMS in its own right. This chapter tackles the challenges you face and the decisions you need to make when you want to use WordPress as a more traditional CMS, powering nonblog sites with the system. It is not only possible to use WordPress in this way, but it is also a great solution that saves time and money.

IS WORDPRESS THE RIGHT CHOICE FOR YOUR CMS?

By now you've gathered that WordPress is useful for much more than just blogging (if not, just wait until Chapter 14, "Uncommon WordPress Usage"). Basically, you can do just about anything that involves managing written content, along with other media such as images, sound, and video. I often tell newspaper and magazine publishers that there is no newspaper or magazine site that I couldn't rebuild in WordPress. Those sites are usually powered by expensive licensed systems, and whereas it was unlikely that anyone would make that claim a couple of years ago, today it is taken seriously. Larger publishing companies are already putting WordPress to good use for their editorial group blogs, and others are powering opinion sections using the system.

Picking the right CMS is important because your system should excel at what you want it to do. WordPress is the right choice if you want a CMS that is

- Open source and free
- Fast and easy to use
- Easily extendable
- Convenient for designing and developing plugins
- Excellent with text
- Search-engine friendly
- Good enough with images

Basically, if your site is an editorial one with primarily text content, you'll be safe with choosing WordPress. Most image-based sites will work just fine with WordPress as well, as will anything built on embedding video content, for example.

So when should you consider using an alternative to WordPress? Arguments for the potential advantages of other CMSes include

- Community features: Previously, other systems offered better access to community features such as forums, but the release of BuddyPress (http://buddypress.org) and the easy integration with forum options such as bbPress (http://bbpress.org) have really overcome this deficiency.
- Modular structure: Some of the heavier CMSes (such as Drupal) have a more modular structure, which means that you can create pretty much anything you want, wherever you want. This is usually at the expense of usability, so you need to compare features and workflow before deciding which route you should take. Also, a lot of these things are possible with WordPress these days, but they require more advanced knowledge from the theme and/or plugin developer.
- Product support: Another common criticism against open source CMS alternatives such as WordPress is that commercial products offer support as part of the package, making it worthwhile to pay for a CMS. The counterargument to this is that the money allocated to

licensing could be spent on a consultant and/or developer when needed, and not just be the cause of a big hole in the coffers. You can take those licensing fees and build your adaptations, should you not find the solution available already. And after that, it is all free.

WordPress is a great CMS option, especially if you're building an editorial site. Whether you think it is right for your project or not, you should always sit back and figure out what you actually need first. Then find the ideal CMS and consider how you would use it for this particular project.

WORDPRESS CMS CHECKLIST

So you're considering using WordPress as a CMS for a project? That's when the following checklist comes in handy. You need to think about these things first to avoid running into unwanted surprises along the way.

The first questions

- Do you really need a CMS for this project? Sometimes hacking HTML is the way to go, after all.
- Is WordPress the correct CMS for your project? It may be great, but sometimes other things would work better to meet your needs.

The WordPress admin interface

- What additional functionality do you need for the admin interface?
- Should you use plugins (or custom code) to cut down on functionality? The admin interface can be pretty overwhelming to less experienced users.
- If you're going to employ user archives, consider what usernames to give everyone involved.
- Do you need features for menu editing, custom backgrounds, and custom headers?
- Does it matter that the admin interface is branded WordPress? If yes, you need to give it some new style, and don't forget the login form.

Categories and tagging

- What is your strategy with categories and tags? Do you need to add further taxonomies, such as separate tag groups or hierarchical categories, to make the site work? Do these taxonomies need be portable when the site changes themes in the future?
- Which categories should you include, and do you need custom category coding and/or templates?
- How should tags be used, and how will you educate the users in the praxis you've chosen?

Pages and posts

- Do you need custom fields?
- Do you need to create Page templates to make parts of your site behave like you want? If so, make sure that you've got those Pages created from the start.

- How should Pages relate to each other? What should be a top-level Page, and what should be a sub-Page? Make sure that you know the hierarchy and how you will present the various sections.

- How will you present the posts? Do they need any specific treatment to fit in?

- Will you use the new post formats for custom formatting of posts? If so, should the posts keep their custom formatting when viewed as individual posts?

- Do you need additional kinds of content that are separated from posts and Pages? In that case, make sure that you have a plan for your custom post types and consider whether they need to be portable across themes.

- What will be on the front page? A static page, latest news updates, or something else?

Additional considerations

- Figure out your permalink structure right away and stick to it. You may need plugins to tune it the way you want.

- Do you need specific shortcode to speed up the publishing and avoid unnecessary HTML code in the posts (see the "Custom Shortcodes" section in Chapter 13 for more info)? If you do, what is your strategy for keeping this functionality when changing themes in the future?

- Do you need any features that are not built in to WordPress? Can you use plugins to achieve the necessary functionality? Will such plugins cause problems with upgrades in the future?

- If your project requires localization, are the language features you need available? There are plenty of language files for WordPress, but what about themes and plugins? Will you need to do additional work there?

TRIMMING WORDPRESS TO THE ESSENTIALS

When you work for clients or other people within your organization, you'll have to think a little bit differently than if you were going to be the primary user yourself. Remember, you're a savvy user, but that may not be the case for everybody else. That's why you need to trim WordPress to the essentials and make sure that there aren't too many options to confuse the user.

The first and foremost trimming action you can perform is to limit the user privileges. As mentioned in the discussion of security in Chapter 1, "The Anatomy of a WordPress Install," not all users need full admin accounts. Most of the time, the Editor account role will be enough, and sometimes you may want to go below that. For every step down the user level ladder you take, fewer options are displayed for the user, and that is a good thing.

It goes without saying that you should make sure there are no unnecessary plugins activated because these not only potentially slow things down, but they also clutter the admin interface with option pages and related elements. So keep it clean.

TWEAKING THE ADMIN INTERFACE

You can make the WordPress admin interface appear in tune with your needs by using one of the CMS plugins available. There are several, but WP-CMS Post Control (http://wordpress. org/extend/plugins/wp-cms-post-control) is a good choice. With this plugin, you can hide unnecessary elements for your users, disable autosave (which can be a nuisance), control which image uploader should be used, and a bunch of other things. It can really make the WordPress interface a little easier and less scary for new users. I especially like the message box option, which can contain information for the user on how to proceed and links to more help.

There are several plugins that let you hide parts of the admin interface. You may want to consider them if you will be responsible for running a site at your company, or for a client, for a long time. But beware if it is a one-time gig! As you know, new WordPress versions roll out all the time, and that means that plugins may stop working or need to be upgraded. Although that is easy enough in WordPress, it also means that you have to educate the client about how to do it if you're not providing ongoing support.

Still, to use WordPress as a CMS makes a lot more sense if you hide the stuff you don't need. The competition may not be doing it, but if you're using WordPress to power a semistatic corporate website, it certainly sounds like a good idea to remove all the stuff the users don't need to see. Just make sure that you've got the upgrades covered when they roll out.

Another option is to remove parts of the interface yourself. Although most boxes can be hidden using the built-in Screen Options pane at the top right of every page in WordPress admin, sometimes you want to make sure that the boxes just aren't there. How you do it would depend on what you want to remove, but chances are `remove_meta_box()` is what you're looking for. To remove the excerpts box on posts, use this code in functions.php or in a plugin if you feel that this is something that needs to stay portable across themes:

```
function smashing_remove_post_excerpt() {
    remove_meta_box( 'postexcerpt' , 'post' , 'normal' );
}
add_action( 'add_meta_boxes' , 'smashing_remove_post_excerpt' );
```

Here is a function with `remove_meta_box()`, and you're using the `add_meta_boxes` hook, which loads on the Edit screen in WordPress admin.

You can even remove widgets that you just don't want your users to end up littering the site with, also in functions.php or from a plugin:

```
function smashing_unregister_widgets(){
    unregister_widget( 'WP_Widget_Calendar' );
    unregister_widget( 'WP_Widget_Meta' );
}
add_action( 'widgets_init', 'smashing_unregister_widgets' );
```

This function removes the Calendar and Meta widgets. You're adding it to the `widgets_init` hook with `add_action()`.

One more thing. Perhaps you're building a site using a child theme, but said child theme doesn't need all the widget areas of the parent theme. Luckily, you can unregister them, like this, also in functions.php:

```
function smashing_remove_some_sidebars(){
    unregister_sidebar( 'name-of-sidebar' );
    unregister_sidebar( 'name-of-another-sidebar' );
}
add_action( 'widgets_init', 'smashing_remove_some_sidebars', 11 );
```

Handy tools all. You can read more about these things in the WordPress Codex (http://codex.wordpress.org).

UNBLOGGING WORDPRESS

Much of the functionality built in to WordPress may be overkill when you're using it as a CMS to power simple websites. A company website built around static pages containing product information might not need comments or trackbacks, and the only kind of fluid content might be a news or press clippings section. It just makes sense; some functionality just isn't needed, and neither is the blog lingo.

So when you need to build the kind of site that just doesn't require all the bling and the functionality, you won't want to include all that in your theme. The following subsections outline a few changes you should make when using WordPress as a CMS for an unbloggish site.

Template Files

You can stick to just one template file, index.php, for all your listing and search needs, but you can chop this up into several templates if you want to. If you don't need commenting functionality, comment-related tags and code are completely unnecessary. Page templates, on the other hand, are very useful, and you'll most likely end up having a static front page using one of these.

You might also want to remove the traditional postmeta data if your site won't employ it. To a lot of people, showing off timestamps and categories as well as tags and authors will draw the thoughts to blogs. Remove these parts unless you need them or consider using them in a more traditional fashion.

Lingo

There's a lot of bloggish lingo within WordPress by default; "categories" and "tags" are used in the permalinks, for example. You can change these on a URL level in the Permalink Settings. Maybe you want to go with "news" or "updates" instead of the default "category," and perhaps "view" or "topic" rather than the default "tag." Actually, a good way to create a news section for a static corporate site is to use Pages for any serious content, such as company information and product descriptions, whereas you'll use the one category, called *News* with the slug "news," for the news posts. That way, you can set up your permalinks so that `/news/` will be the category listings, or the News section in this case, and then you let all the posts (which of course are just news items) get the `/news/post-slug/` permalink by applying the `/%category%/%postname%/` permalink structure in the settings. Really handy, and no need to build a custom news section or anything.

You would want more control over the content if you need more than one newsy section, though, in which case Page templates listing the latest posts from the category in question is a nice enough solution, as opposed to just linking the category archives. You would go about it by creating a Page per section and then having a Page template for each of these sections. Every Page template would contain a custom loop fetching the necessary posts. It all boils down to what you need to do and how flexible you want the site to be.

This inevitably leads into what you can do with static Pages and how what used to be blog posts can fill the needs of a more traditional website.

THE PERFECT SETUP FOR A SIMPLE STATIC WEBSITE

Using static Pages and categories as a news model is truly a great tool whenever you need to roll out a typical old-school website quickly. Maybe it is a product presentation, a corporate website, or something entirely different that just won't work with the blog format. That's when this setup is so useful.

Pages (as in *WordPress Pages*) were originally meant to be used for static content. The fact that you can create one Page template (recall that template files for Pages are individual) for each Page should you want to means that they can really look like anything. You can break your design completely because you don't even have to call the same header or footer file, you can have different markup, and you can exclude everything WordPress-related and display something entirely different instead, should you want to. It is a really powerful tool that can just as easily contain multiple loops or syndicated RSS content from other sites. Each Page template is a blank slate, and it is your primary weapon when using WordPress as a CMS; this is where you can make the site truly step away from the blog heritage that the system carries.

And don't get me started on the front page! Because you can set WordPress to display a static Page as a front page (under Settings in admin) and pick any other Page (keep it empty, mind you) for your post listings should you need that, you can really do anything. You can even put in one of those nasty Flash preloader thingies with autoplaying sound (but you really shouldn't). The point is that a Page template, along with the front page setting, is just as much a clean slate as a blank PHP or HTML file would be outside WordPress, but with all the benefits of the system!

On the other side of things, you've got traditional blog posts. These need to belong to a category, and each of them will be more or less the same, visually. Sure, if you want to, you can play around a lot with these too, but on a semistatic site, Pages are a much better idea.

Naturally, it is a whole different ball game if you're going to handle tons of content, but that's not really what we're going for here.

Pages for static content, posts for newsy stuff. This is a great model for most corporate websites using WordPress as a CMS, with Pages for all those product descriptions, and posts for news, announcements, and press clippings. Assuming you've already worked out the design, here is the process you should follow:

1. Decide what will be a Page and what will not. Usually, everything except news and announcements are Pages. Create these Pages and make sure that they get the right slug. This includes making sure that the basic permalink structure is there, which means checking that the post and category URLs look good. Chances are you'll use a plugin to further control this, but it all depends on the needs of the site.

2. Start creating the Page templates. The company profile Page will probably have other design needs than the product Pages, so you'll want to put emphasis on different things and construct any possible submenus and information boxes in ways that fit the style.

3. Create the categories needed, one for each newsy section. This is usually just one category, called *News* or *Announcements,* but sometimes you'll need both, or even more. In some cases, you may really want just one category — Announcements, for example — so opt for sorting within it using tags, one for News, one for Press Releases, one for Products, one for Announcements, and so on. Naturally, you need to make sure that the category listings as well as the single post view look good.

4. Tie it all together by creating a menu (using the menu feature for flexibility for the client, but go ahead and populate it yourself to get him or her started) that links to both the various Pages and the categories involved.

That's it — the elements of a static simple website using WordPress as a CMS. You can take this concept as far as you like really because it is WordPress and you can build on it as much as you like.

Want to make a static simple website on steroids? Consider throwing custom post types into the mix, giving you even more options when it comes to managing primarily static material.

DOING MORE THAN THE BASICS

Sometimes you need more than the static site I just described. For example, you might need to add additional post types; perhaps you need a product listing and have to create a custom post type for products with its own taxonomies and everything.

Some websites obviously need more attention: The more advanced the site, the more tweaks and adaptations are needed to make it fit. Sometimes this means that you'll have to write custom loops or use Page templates, and at other times you may want more flexibility without touching the code for every little update. That's when widgets come in, not only because a lot of cool features come as plugins that are widget-ready, but also because widgets offer drag-and-drop functionality, which nontechie users will surely appreciate.

The following sections discuss how you can add this kind of functionality to a pretty basic WordPress CMS setup without too much hassle.

USES FOR CUSTOM POST TYPES AND TAXONOMIES IN A WORDPRESS CMS

Custom post types is the best thing to happen to WordPress since tagging came along. I already covered the technique in Chapter 6, "Advanced Theme Usage," so this section is more about how you can put it to really good use when using WordPress as a CMS.

There are often great benefits of having more than just posts and Pages to play with. Thanks to custom post types, you can create whatever type of post- or Page-like content you like without having to mix it with your regular posts and Pages. Here are a few examples off the top of my head:

- Products: Create a post type called "Products" and let posts residing in it be products, with descriptions, tagging, and everything.
- Persons: Why not create a directory of people, one person per post in this post type?
- Portfolio: Perhaps you have a portfolio part of your site residing in a category. No need for that anymore; should you want to separate it from the rest of the content flow, just create that post type!
- Manual: Need to put up a static manual? No need to mix it with your Pages anymore; just create a new post type to keep it apart.

The list goes on and on. What's really great is that your custom post types each get their own dedicated menu item on the left side of the WordPress admin interface, just like posts or Pages. That makes it really easy for the end user to find and use them, compared to solutions sporting custom fields or similar methods.

The same advantage goes for custom taxonomies, also covered previously. With these, you can have a separate tag group for properly tagging your products, for example. This is a great way to further control how things are sorted and found on your site. WordPress offers a great mix of default tools, such as posts and Pages alongside categories and tags, along with the ones you can create yourself such as custom post types and additional taxonomies. It takes some thought to find the right toolset out of all these possibilities, but it's worth it.

> *Don't forget about portability when using custom post types and creating your own taxonomies! Most of the time, these features are things that needs to keep working even after you switch themes, so be sure to have a plan for that. You can read more about portability in Chapter 8, "Plugins or functions.php?."*

PUTTING WIDGETS TO GOOD USE IN A CMS

Widgets and widget areas are your friends when rolling out WordPress as a CMS. They are perhaps not as important for the small and static company websites primarily discussed so far, but they can be very useful for the larger ones. Take a look around online; there are numerous sites that push out mixed functionality, especially on their front pages, and display teaser images when it is suitable. You can do a lot of this with widgets.

Using Basic Widget Areas

The most straightforward usage is to litter your site with widget areas wherever you may want to output something all of a sudden; just make sure that the area doesn't output anything by default so that it will remain invisible (as in not containing anything) whenever you haven't populated it with a widget. However, a better practice is to think your widget areas through and put the areas where you know you'll need them, not where you think you may need them two years down the road. After all, you will have redesigned the site by then, anyway.

So you've got your widget areas in. Now, how do you use them? Besides the obvious answer of drag-and-drop widgets on the Appearance → Themes page in WordPress admin, you can add widgets that do whatever you need. The ones that ship with WordPress are simple and somewhat crude; the Pages widget (listing your Pages) won't even let you display just the Pages, it forces an h2 title out there, which you may not want. You want control over how your content will be displayed, so if you're moving down this route, be sure to look at the many plugins that offer widget support; there are several available that will list just the Pages without adding that h2 heading, for example.

The most useful widget is by far the text widget. It accepts HTML code, which means that putting text and images in it is a breeze. This is good because if you want to show off that special promotion (or pimp your Facebook fan page) just below the menu in the header, you can just put the necessary HTML code in a text widget and drop it there for the duration of the campaign, and then just remove it, and the area will disappear until you add new content. There are some great plugins that will help you listed in Appendix A, "Essential WordPress Plugins."

Making Widgets a Little More Dynamic

Why not just put empty widget areas where the various elements on the site could go? It will do the job, but you'll have to cram them in wherever they will fit, and you will have to take the rest of the design and content into account. You will have to do that either way, of course, but there is an alternative: Replace parts of the content with a widget area.

If you're running a magazineish site, you may have an opportunity to roll out big so-called *roadblocks,* ads that take over a lot more of the site than just common banners and leaderboards. Roadblocks usually run for a shorter amount of time, and you get paid a lot for them, compared to ads.

Or take another approach: Say you're an Apple blogger and you want to cover the Apple WWDC or MacWorld in a timely manner, making sure that your readers won't miss it. How? Plaster the site in promotional graphics, of course!

Both these examples will typically work poorly if you just add content into widget areas positioned around the site's normal elements. They will, however, work perfectly well if you replace parts of the site's content, meaning any element really, with a widget area. This effect is pretty easy to get working, thanks to the fact that widget areas can come preloaded with content.

The following code is for a widget area called *Teaser,* and it should come preloaded with the content you want in that particular spot on a day-to-day basis:

```php
<?php
    if ( is_active_sidebar( 'Teaser' ) ) {
        dynamic_sidebar( 'Teaser' );
    } else { ?>
        [The normal content would go here. Links, headlines, whatever. . . ]
<?php }; ?>
```

Just put it in there; it can be anything, really: a headline section, a poll, must-read lists, loops, links, images — you name it. Anything.

However, when you drop a widget in the Teaser widget area within the WordPress admin interface, the default content won't show; it will be replaced with the widget you dropped, thanks to the `is_active_sidebar()` check. So dropping a text widget with your big fat promo image for the Apple event, or your new eBook, or whatever, will replace the original content. When you remove the image from the Teaser widget area, the default content will return by default.

Pretty nifty, huh? And actually pretty simple to maintain as well; if something goes wrong, you can just remove the widget you put there, and you'll always revert to the default.

Another great use of widgets is navigational menus, which make sure that users can add menu items themselves without having to rely on the theme designer.

MANAGING MENUS

Menus need to look good and be easy to maintain; that's true for just about every website. When you're using WordPress as a CMS, this is perhaps even more important. Thanks to the great menu feature in WordPress discussed in Chapter 6, it's easy to create the kinds of menus you need. Given their importance, you'll want to give the menus some thought.

There are two primary ways to create menus. First is the menu area, which uses `wp_nav_menu()` to output a predetermined menu area. Using `wp_nav_menu()` limits you to menus, as opposed to the second solution, widget areas, but it also lets you name the menu area appropriately. This makes it easier for the end user when working with the menu.

The second way you can add menus is by using widget areas. You can use the menu widget to insert any created menu anywhere you can drop the widget. This can sometimes be handy but offers less control than the alternative solution. That being said, don't forget about this option as it is a great way to offer menus on specific parts of your site that use a particular widget area. This way, you can let your users create custom menus as the need arises, without having to touch the code and add `wp_nav_menu()` all over the place.

Either way, the important thing here is that you utilize the menu feature because it makes it a whole lot easier for the site administrator to change the menu(s) on the site. If the menu feature is enabled in your theme, you can check it out under Appearance → Menus, as shown in Figure 9-1.

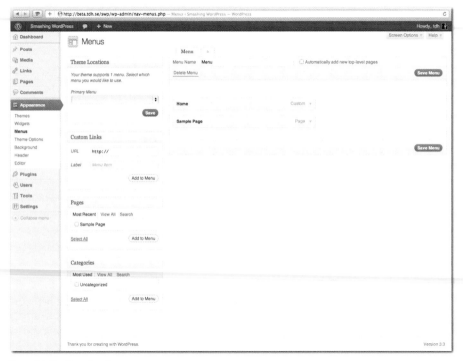

Figure 9-1: The Menus interface.

INTEGRATING NON-WORDPRESS CONTENT

Sometimes you need to get non-WordPress content into your WordPress site. This can be tricky because not all publishing platforms play along nicely. At best, the content you need to expose within your WordPress site can be exported in a widget-like fashion (not the plugin kind, the JavaScript sort), included in whole with PHP, or perhaps even displayed in an iframe if all else fails.

These days, an RSS feed can be a savior if you're looking at text content especially, but also when it comes to video and images. If the outside content is material from the image service Flickr, for example, you can fetch the RSS feed either with a separate plugin (there are Flickr plugins along with RSS variants), or with the built-in WordPress functionality for displaying feeds. Chapter 13 features a few examples of how you can display content fetched from RSS feeds. Another option would be to use a plugin such as FeedWordPress (http://wordpress.org/extend/plugins/feed-wordpress), which queries feeds repeatedly and creates posts in your database — which you can use any way you want, just as you would if the content had been actually written directly in WordPress. There are quite a few similar solutions out there, so if you need to fetch content from external sources using RSS, you have a few plugins to choose from.

Either way, when you've figured out how to display the content you want within your Word-Press site, chances are you'll be creating a Page with its own template containing this code. I suggest putting the code in the template files. This is the easiest way and the technique I recommend before reverting to Exec-PHP or similar plugins that let you put PHP code within posts and Pages, as they can really break things.

At other times, the solution may involve making a plugin that acts as the middle ground. I've done this in the past, when I ran my own CMS and wanted to move to WordPress, but had this huge database of games along with a lot of data. Text and images were easy enough to import into the WordPress databases, but flexible taxonomies and native tagging support didn't exist back then, so I had to be creative with the games database. The solution was to write a plugin that read that part and displayed it using shortcodes. It was a lot more hassle than just displaying something from an RSS feed, but sometimes you just can't get the content into WordPress itself without extending it further.

Finally, if all else fails, just fake it. Make the page look like your WordPress theme but have it outside of the actual theme. I know, that's not as fun, but sometimes systems just clash, and while you can usually sort it out, it may just not be worth the time.

DON'T FORGET TO INCLUDE A MANUAL

For people experienced with web-based systems, WordPress may seem like a breeze to use. The problem is, not everyone sees it that way. In fact, people not used to web-based systems may find WordPress daunting, despite being perfectly comfortable with word processors and other common desktop software. There are user-oriented manuals built in to WordPress, but will they be enough?

Although the WordPress.org website and the WordPress.tv screencast fest may be helpful references for your users, you're probably better off creating a small how-to guide to explain how WordPress works. This is especially important if you're using WordPress as a CMS for a static website rather than blogging; if you point your users of such websites to the Codex, they'll just be confused.

If you're a WordPress developer and/or designer and you do a lot of WordPress sites, I advise you to put together a starter kit that describes the most common tasks of the day-to-day usage. This kit, which can be anything from a simple document to a printable booklet, should be easily updated as new versions of WordPress come along. It should also be constructed in such a manner that you can add to it whatever custom functionality is used for the client sites. Maybe you have a category for video that acts differently from the other ones, or perhaps there's the ever-present issue with custom fields and their usability. Add plugin usage, widgets, and possible settings that you've devised for your client, and you can save yourself a lot of questions if you deliver a simple "Getting Started" manual with your design.

A FINAL WORD ON USING WORDPRESS AS A CMS

It is a common misconception that WordPress isn't a fitting choice as a CMS solution for various projects. Obviously, it is not always the perfect choice — no publishing platform will ever be — but the ease with which you can roll out a site with WordPress is a strong factor in its favor. Add a simple user interface and great expandability thanks to plugins and themes, and you've got a fairly solid case right there.

One of the pros that comes with using WordPress as a CMS is how well it is equipped for search engines. With nicely written code and perhaps with the help of a plugin or two (you'll find some suggestions in Appendix A), you'll have no trouble ranking in the search engines, assuming you've got the proper content for it, of course. That, alongside the social web, is how a lot of traffic is driven these days. So the next chapter, "Integrating the Social Web," shows you how you can integrate the social web into your WordPress sites.

10 INTEGRATING THE SOCIAL WEB

THERE IS NO doubt that the social web is important these days, with Facebook, Twitter, and Google+ being the most prominent examples. When used correctly, services like these can be excellent platforms to promote content, collect stories, and encourage communication. It is only natural that most sites today have some sort of integration with popular social web services, even if it's only a simple Share on Facebook or Send to Twitter button or link.

Before you dig into the various techniques used to display and connect to the social web, it is important not to forget the most obvious integration tool offered: RSS feeds. For the simplest solution, you can use the RSS widget that ships with WordPress, and it easily lets you

show off content from an RSS feed. And today, any social web service, app, community, or whatever has an RSS feed for you to play with, which means that a lot of the integration of these services you may want can be done using RSS. From showing off your latest tweet to mashing up a lifestream, it's all about RSS most of the time.

So when you want to flash your latest finished book saved to aNobii (www.anobii.com), consider the RSS feed (or its widget) before you start looking for plugins or hacking your own solutions. Chances are the service you want to show off your latest actions/saved items/whatever from already transmits this data with RSS.

Enough of that. It's time to get your hands dirty!

INTEGRATING FACEBOOK INTO YOUR SITE

I'm starting with Facebook because this is not only the largest social network as I'm writing this but also by far the easiest to integrate into a site, at least on its most basic level. Facebook has excellent tools to help you integrate its features into your site; just check out the Social Plugins page at http://developers.facebook.com/docs/reference/plugins for a lot of alternatives (see Figure 10-1).

Figure 10-1: Facebook has great tools for adding related features to your site.

Most often, you want to promote two things on your site when it comes to Facebook: having people "like" your content and your Facebook fan page.

THE LIKE BUTTON

The Facebook Like button is incredibly easy to integrate. Just go to this page and build your own button: http://developers.facebook.com/docs/reference/plugins/like.

Don't worry about the URL to Like field as I'll show you how to swap it for `the_perma-link()` template tag anyway. Just put something in there; for this example, I added `http://tdh.me` to this field.

Clicking Get Code will get you three different code snippets; one is for HTML5 (which is the one most of us want to use), one is for XFBML (extended Facebook markup language) users, and the third is a simple iframe that might not always be available for your Facebook needs. In most cases, you'll be using the HTML5 code snippet, so go ahead and copy and paste that one. As you can see, it consists of two parts, one for getting Facebook's JavaScript API onto your site:

```
<div id="fb-root"></div>
<script>(function(d, s, id) {
    var js, fjs = d.getElementsByTagName(s)[0];
    if (d.getElementById(id)) return;
    js = d.createElement(s); js.id = id;
    js.src = "//connect.facebook.net/en_US/all.js#xfbml=1&appId=218861188171083";
    fjs.parentNode.insertBefore(js, fjs);
}(document, 'script', 'facebook-jssdk'));</script>
```

The second part is the code that will actually output the Facebook Like button, and this is the part of the code that carries your specific settings, such as whether the faces of users who liked a post should show up and things like that:

```
<div class="fb-like" data-href="http://tdh.me" data-send="true" data-width="450"
  data-show-faces="true"></div>
```

You'll notice that `"http://tdh.me"` is stored in `data-href` in the preceding code. That's where you want `the_permalink()`, like this:

```
<div class="fb-like" data-href="<?php the_permalink(); ?>" data-send="true" data-
  width="450" data-show-faces="true"></div>
```

Just put this code snippet within the loop in your various theme templates (such as single. php) where you want to let people like things, and you're ready to go.

But what about that XFBML thingy? That code is a bit more versatile and is probably the right way for you to go if you do a lot of things with Facebook on your site. It might be a bit daunting, however, as it doesn't use familiar HTML tags through and through, so if you just want a Like button, you might prefer the HTML5 solution. Either way, all details on how to load the JavaScript SDK so that you can use the XFBML code instead are available here: http://developers.facebook.com/docs/reference/javascript.

Obviously, you need to change the code here as well to get it to work with WordPress. Just as with the HTML5 option, there's a place where you want to use `the_permalink()` instead of `"http://tdh.me"` (or whatever you put in). The code you want to alter is the one for including the button:

```
<fb:like href="http://tdh.me" send="true" width="450" show_faces="true"></fb:like>
```

Just swap out `"http://tdh.me"` for `the_permalink()` in `href` within the loop as well, and you're good to go, like this:

```
<fb:like href="<?php the_permalink(); ?>" send="true" width="450" show_
  faces="true"></fb:like>
```

When using XFBML, you can use the `fb` HTML tag for various Facebook features — `fb:like` here, for example. Don't forget to include the JavaScript SDK; otherwise, this tag won't work.

PROFILE WIDGETS

If you want to promote your Facebook fan page, or perhaps your personal page, there are really simple widgets for that as well. There are simple badges, available at http://www.facebook.com/badges, but chances are you want something cooler. Maybe you want to show off your activity feed or just have people fan you (that is to say, your Facebook page) on your very own site? Then check out the social widgets Facebook offers at http://developers.facebook.com/plugins.

Say that you want to put a Like box for your Facebook page on your website. Facebook is consistent because the Like box builder page works just like the Like button I described earlier but without the need to put in any extra code such as `the_permalink()`. Just style it anyway you like, copy the code, and paste it in a text widget or wherever you want in your theme files.

INTEGRATING TWITTER

There is certainly no doubt that the rise of Twitter has changed things. These days, everyone and their cat tweets, at least among the techie crowd, and the momentum doesn't seem to be slowing down. So although 140 characters is quite a limitation to someone used to punching out 3,000-character blog posts, Twitter can still be quite a tool for online publishers.

If you or your brand are on Twitter, it is likely you'll want to promote your Twitter account on your site. That is easily done with graphics, of course, but you can take it even further. It works the other way as well: By promoting your content with tweets, you can reach an audience that may know you only on Twitter. And that's just scratching the surface; there are a ton of cool mashups and services built around Twitter and its API that you may want to mimic or at least get a piece of.

First things first: Building a cool new Twitter app isn't what this book is about. However, it would most likely be a good idea to take the Twitter promotion one step further than just a small Follow Me on Twitter graphic, right?

ADDING TWITTER BUTTONS AND WIDGETS

These days, it is easy both to show off your tweets, thanks to the Twitter widget, and promote a story on Twitter using the official Tweet button. You can get the latest tweets, get search results, have your tweets marked as favorites, and so on, all using a simple widget that you build and style on Twitter's site: http://twitter.com/about/resources/widgets. What you get, after having styled the widget the way you want, is something like this:

```
<script src="http://widgets.twimg.com/j/2/widget.js"></script>
<script>
new TWTR.Widget({
  version: 2,
  type: 'profile',
  rpp: 4,
  interval: 30000,
  width: 250,
  height: 300,
  theme: {
    shell: {
      background: '#333333',
      color: '#ffffff'
    },
    tweets: {
      background: '#000000',
      color: '#ffffff',
      links: '#4aed05'
    }
  },
  features: {
    scrollbar: false,
    loop: false,
    live: false,
    behavior: 'all'
  }
}).render().setUser('tdh').start();
</script>
```

Paste this in your theme's files, or better yet, in a text widget, and you're good to go. If you want to change something, the easiest way is to just go back to Twitter and redo the whole thing, although a somewhat savvy user can analyze this code and make changes there directly.

Getting a Tweet button is equally simple. Just go to http://twitter.com/about/resources/buttons, pick the look for your button, and add any Twitter account you might want to mention (see Figure 10-2).

Figure 10-2: It's easy to get the code for your own Tweet button.

Again, you'll get a simple code snippet that you can put in your theme's single.php template, for easy twittering of your posts:

```
<a href="https://twitter.com/share" class="twitter-share-button" data-via="tdh"
  data-hashtags="smashing">Tweet</a>
<script>!function(d,s,id){var js,fjs=d.getElementsByTagName(s)[0];if(!d.
  getElementById(id)){js=d.createElement(s);js.id=id;js.src="//platform.twitter.com/
  widgets.js";fjs.parentNode.insertBefore(js,fjs);}}(document,"script","twitter-
  wjs");</script>
```

If you want more control than this, check out the Twitter for Websites documentation at https://dev.twitter.com/docs/twitter-for-websites. There are more advanced options available too, should you want to play with the Twitter API: http://dev.twitter.com.

TWITTER SITE EXTENSIONS

There are numerous widgets, plugins, services, and applications for Twitter. The fairly open ecosystem around the microblogging service makes it easy to build on, and the ever-increasing buzz around the brand isn't exactly slowing things down. The following subsections provide a few handy links to services and URL shorteners that might come in handy.

You won't find any Twitter plugins here, however: They are all in Appendix A, "Essential WordPress Plugins."

Site Enhancers

Some Twitter-related services stand out more than others. The following two add functionality to your site by using Twitter:

- TweetMeme (http://tweetmeme.com) tracks what's hot on Twitter and borrows a lot from Digg while doing so.
- Twitterfeed (http://twitterfeed.com) publishes links from any RSS feed to your Twitter account so that you won't have to. There are competing services that do this as well, but this is the original one with OpenID login and everything.

URL Shorteners

The 140-character limit means that long URLs just won't fit into your tweets. Enter the URL shorteners, a necessary evil according to some, and a great tool according to others. You can roll your own, of course (see Appendix A for cool plugins), but if you can't or don't want to, these shorteners are great options. Remember, you may want to pick one and stick to it so that people get used to seeing you use it. It might also be worth keeping in mind that Twitter uses the t.co URL shortener by default, so you might not need a URL shortener at all. On top of that, WordPress can actually shorten the URLs for you. When logged in, visit the Edit Post page for the post you want a shortlink for and click the Get Shortlink button beneath the title, as shown in Figure 10-3. Services such as YOURLS (http://yourls.org) will help you make your shortlinks even prettier, if you have alternative domains you want to use.

Figure 10-3: The Get Shortlink button is found on the Edit Post screen.

Here are some URL shorteners:

- t.co (http://t.co) is the official Twitter URL shortener, which you get to by using the official Twitter buttons and apps, listed here for reference only.
- TinyURL (http://tinyurl.com) is the original URL shortener used by Twitter before t.co entered the fray, but it doesn't offer much compared to the competition.
- bitly (http://bitly.com) not only shortens your URL but offers statistics as well.
- goo.gl (http://goo.gl) is Google's very own URL shortener.

ADDING GOOGLE+ TO YOUR SITE

Google's latest foray in social networks is called Google+, and it is growing. By adding the +1 button to your website, you'll not only get +1s on your posts in the Google search results for some users, but also encourage your visitors to share your content on Google+.

Adding the +1 button is easy, with more advanced options available should you want them. You get the code from http://www.google.com/webmasters/+1/button, and there is no need to change anything in it, as with the Facebook Like button, for example. Just pick whatever settings you feel work best for your site and then copy and paste the resulting code. Part of the code loads the necessary JavaScript for the +1 button to work, and the other part is the actual button, so you'll want to put that where it belongs.

Google suggests that you put the code for loading the JavaScript before the closing body tag, but there are better ways to manage JavaScript with WordPress. This is the code Google wants you to use:

```
<script type="text/javascript" src="https://apis.google.com/js/plusone.js"></script>
```

Now, you're much better off using wp_enqueue_script() for adding JavaScript to a WordPress theme, so add this to your theme's header.php file:

```
<?php wp_enqueue_script( 'gplus', 'https://apis.google.com/js/plusone.js', '', '',
  TRUE ); ?>
```

This way, the JavaScript will be loaded using WordPress's standards, rather than wedged in there. An even better way to load this script would be to add it to the wp_enqueue_script hook by adding it to your theme's functions.php file. Chances are you have a bunch of scripts loading in your functions.php file already, so if you do, you'll just add this script to them. If not, you could do so like this:

```
function smashing_gplus() {
    wp_enqueue_script( 'gplus', 'https://apis.google.com/js/plusone.js', '', '',
      TRUE );
}
add_action( 'wp_enqueue_scripts', 'smashing_gplus' );
```

I covered wp_enqueue_script() in Chapter 4, "WordPress Theme Essentials," so refer to that if you need a refresher.

The actual code for outputting the button looks something like this:

```
<div class="g-plusone" data-annotation="inline"></div>
```

Just put the code wherever you want your +1 button to appear, and you're all set. No need to specify the_permalink() here; the code knows where your visitors are.

USING A HOSTED COMMENT SOLUTION

With the addition of threaded comments in the WordPress core and the excellent CSS styling options that are now available, as well as the ever-present Gravatar (http://gravatar.com) support, you might wonder how it is possible to enhance the comments. Simple: either by filling them with additional functionality using plugins or by moving them out of WordPress altogether. The former solution can mean anything from user grading of the comments to fetching the buzz from Twitter, whereas the latter means that you'll rely on a third-party service for managing your comments.

See Appendix A for a whole bunch of plugins that make your in-house comments hotter and a few that help you manage logins and the like. This section will deal with the alternative.

Hosted comment solutions mean that you leave the complete comment solution to a third-party service, not relying on the WordPress comment functionality at all. There are two major players in this arena, Disqus (http://disqus.com) and IntenseDebate (www.intensedebate.com). The former has seniority, but the latter is owned by Automattic, which makes it a tempting choice to anyone loving WordPress. Both systems have their pros and cons function-wise, and both are being actively developed, although most would say that Disqus has the upper hand.

To start using either Disqus or IntenseDebate, you simply download a plugin for WordPress and take it from there. Getting started with either Disqus or IntenseDebate is a breeze, although localization has proven to be something of an issue for some, as well as customizing the styling.

> Incidentally, you can add these services to static sites as well, giving any site a commenting functionality. That's pretty cool.

There are some great advantages to using a hosted comment solution. First, spamming is taken care of on a wider scale. Both comment systems also offer various login methods including using Twitter and Facebook credentials, reply by e-mail, and RSS feeds, as well as social web integration and e-mail notifications. The scope of features you'll get out of the box from Disqus or IntenseDebate is something you'd have to supercharge your WordPress comments with plugins to achieve. Finally, it is often said that sites using these systems result in more comments, and that doesn't seem to be just the PR talk of the companies themselves.

My main gripe with the concept of hosted comments, however, is the fact that you're basically giving content to someone else to maintain. That means that if your comment service of choice breaks down or goes out of business, your comments will break in a worst-case scenario or revert to the WordPress default otherwise. The fact that comments degrade somewhat gracefully back to the WordPress default when there's an outage at the hosted comment solution is obviously a good thing, but it might confuse readers. Other possible issues include downtime and added clutter because chances are that the comment solution won't fit seamlessly with your smashing design. Also, problems experienced by the commenting system's host will hit your site as well. That's not good.

With those caveats in mind, if you are to use a service like this, which one should you pick? I've used Disqus for more projects than IntenseDebate (including my own blog http://tdh.me, as you can see in Figure 10-4) and find that it works well, but you should take them both for a spin and make up your own mind.

Figure 10-4: Some social sharing buttons in action, as well as the Disqus commenting form.

USING UNIFIED LOGINS

The idea of a unified login system is a great one. Think about it: Wouldn't one login for everything be great? Not a ton of passwords to mess around with, and no risk of the "one password for too many sites" security hazard. (Except, of course, for the fact that you can access all those sites with one password, anyway.) The idea, however, is that the few providers of these Master Accounts would be so secure that the only risk of users being compromised would be human error, and on your side of things at that. Compared to the risk of some minor site being hacked and your "one password fits all" master password being out there, it sounds pretty good.

That's why OpenID (www.openid.net) is interesting, and that's why the giants such as Yahoo!, Google, and Microsoft are interested in this. For the same reason, Facebook has developed Facebook Connect (https://developers.facebook.com/docs/guides/web), a unified login using your Facebook account. The Sign In with Twitter (https://dev.twitter.com/docs/auth/sign-twitter) solution is something similar, and the list goes on.

You may wonder why you should even consider using your own sign-in procedure if you can lean on these giants. Most WordPress sites don't have their own sign-in procedures for anyone other than the actual writers and administrators, at least not for commenting. It is usually enough to leave a name and an e-mail address. However, if you want sign-ins, one of the unified solutions is worth considering. I would like to point to OpenID, but the truth is that Facebook Connect is way more user-friendly (right now), and Facebook is also an OpenID member.

Soon you'll be using your Google and Live.com accounts to sign in across the web, alongside Facebook and Twitter, all perhaps being connected through the OpenID Foundation. Or not. Either way, you should consider a unified login for your site if you need login functionality for your users. There are plugins that solve this for you (you'll find them in Appendix A), but don't let that stop you from pursuing other options. Read up on the services themselves and make up your mind regarding any potential user registrations in the future.

THE IMPORTANCE OF THE SOCIAL WEB

Today the social web and all the content we publish on services such as Twitter and Facebook are an integral part of the online lives of a lot of people. We interact with each other, choose who to follow or friend, and essentially subscribe to content by "liking" Facebook fan pages and following certain accounts or lists on Twitter. It is only natural that the social web is a part of your sites as well and that you want to promote the content you publish to both your followings on the various social web services you use and the ones your visitors might be using.

It is pretty simple, really. On the social web, you choose who to follow, and chances are that you trust the ones you follow more than you trust the average person. So when a friend on Facebook posts a link, you're more inclined to click it than to follow a random link you come across. Think about it: You're more likely to see a movie recommended by a friend than one that's just advertised.

This has made social web elements, such as Like and Tweet buttons and the various book-marking options available, a reality in designs. When done right, it looks good, but when incorporated poorly, it adds clutter and can make sites perform badly. With that in mind, the next chapter, "Design Trickery," helps you play around with some design elements to make sure that your sites look as good as possible.

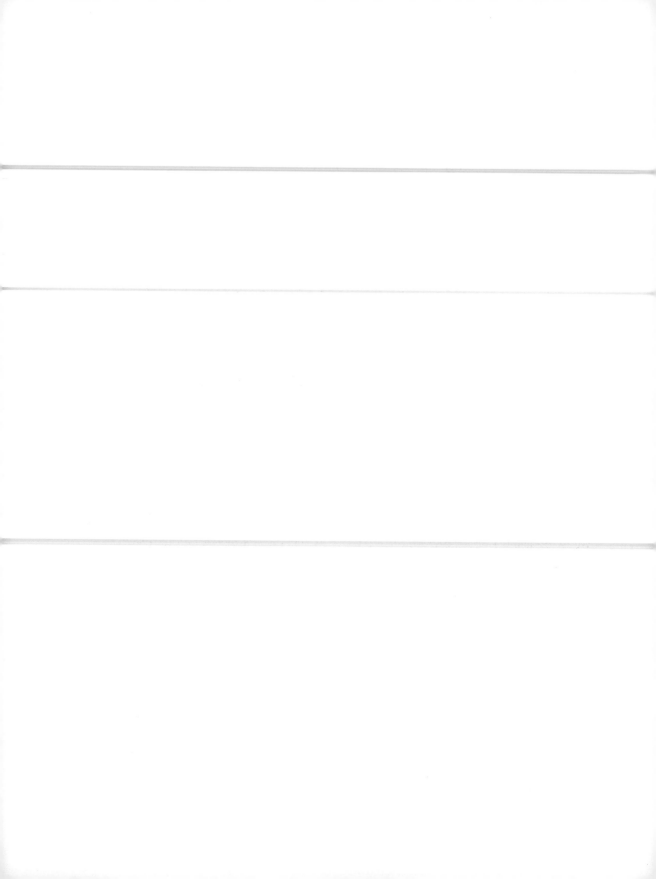

11

DESIGN

TRICKERY

THIS CHAPTER IS all about making your WordPress theme more interesting and giving it that extra functionality that makes it pop. Some of the techniques covered here are directly tied to WordPress and the kind of data you can get out of it, whereas others are adaptations of other techniques and solutions that can come in handy for your projects. This chapter shows you a variety of cool tricks: how to use tag-based design, make the menu do your bidding, include both style sheets and JavaScript libraries the proper way, make your 404s help the lost visitor, and work with ads within the loop.

In other words, get ready for some WordPress design trickery.

ADDING MORE CONTROL OVER YOUR POSTS

WordPress offers various methods for adding more control over your posts. This section covers three such methods: tag-based design, custom fields, and adding your own taxonomies. I won't go over post formats again here, as it is covered in Chapter 6, "Advanced Theme Usage." Otherwise, that is a great way to get more control of your posts.

TAG-BASED DESIGN

The most common setup for a WordPress site revolves around categories and Pages. The former gives individual control of post listings and can be queried by conditional tags such as `in_category()`, which means that you can make them all behave differently. This in turn means that a category archive can easily become a section on a site in a most natural way, and posts belonging to that category can get adequate styling if you want them to. At the very least, this can be a specific set of colors for the category, or perhaps an icon or other kind of graphic, but if you take it further, it could be a completely different style of content presentation.

Tags, on the other hand, are less fixed and generally work best if used to describe only individual posts. This means that they may seem redundant for more static (or other less Web 2.0–bloggish) sites. However, you can still put them to good use should you want to. Tags offer three primary ways of achieving special interactions. The first way is the most obvious: the ability to control the tag archive pages. You may remember that tag.php in your theme can control the display of tags, but you can also use tag-*X*.php, where *X* is the slug of the particular tag. This means that it differs a bit from category-*Y*.php, where *Y* is the category ID and not the slug. It means that you can have your very own properly styled post listing by tag, just as you can with categories. In theory, this means that your tag archives can become sections on your site in the same way as categories.

The second way to control the content based on tags is the conditional tag `is_tag()`. It works more or less just like `is_category()`, and you just pass the tag slug to identify a specific tag, like this:

```php
<?php is_tag( 'pirates' ); ?>
```

Naturally, you need some conditions as well. This kind of usage usually covers it when it comes to categories because most well-planned WordPress theme designs are built using as few categories as possible. Tags, however, are different, so you may want to check for several tags at the same time using an array:

```php
<?php is_tag( array( 'pirates', 'ninjas', 'mushrooms' ) ); ?>
```

This will return `true` whenever the tags `pirates`, `ninjas`, or `mushrooms` are used.

The final way to put tagging to good use is utilizing the fact that `post_class()` returns every tag as a class to a `post` `div`. This means that you can have a lot of potential classes for more in-depth styling.

This, for example, is a post with the ID 129, which you can tell from the `id="post-129"`, as well as the fact that it even has the class `post-129`:

```
<div id="post-129" class="post-129 post hentry category-news tag-pirates
  tag-ninjas tag-mushrooms">
    <!-- The actual post stuff would come here -->
</div>
```

You get a bunch of automatic classes, and finally you get one class per category and one class per tag. In this case, the category used has the slug `news`, so `post_class()` adds the `category-news` class. The same goes for the tags: You've got your `pirates`, `ninjas`, and `mushrooms` tags on the post, and they get added with the prefix `tag-` so that you can see them for what they are. Hence, you get `tag-pirates`, `tag-ninjas`, and `tag-mushrooms`.

The brilliance of this is that it gives you even tighter control of your content. If you want to give some posts more emphasis than others but don't want to tie them to a particular category, then a suitable tag is an excellent solution. Common usage would be featured posts or perhaps sponsor dittos. Say you want to push out a "Thanks to our sponsors" message among the content but don't want the readers to mistake it as an actual post. Then you'd just tag it with something appropriate such as `sponsor` and add some CSS to your style sheet that makes every post with the class `tag-sponsor` look different, using a different font, color, background, border, or image to show that it is something outside the regular content.

As with categories, you can build your sites around tags. My philosophy is that you should be really, really, *really* careful with adding categories; save them for the main sections. Then you can make things happen on a more per-post basis using tags and CSS styling in particular.

USING CUSTOM FIELDS

Say you don't want to use tag-based design. Perhaps you want to push out ads in your content as sponsored posts and style them differently so that you don't risk fooling the readers, but you don't want an ads-only tag to show up in tag clouds. You can just exclude that particular tag from the tag clouds, like this (the excluded tag being `sponsor`):

```
<?php wp_tag_cloud( 'exclude=sponsor' ); ?>
```

Maybe this particular solution just won't do it for you, and you really don't want to use tags in that particular way because of other ways you use them but want the same type of result. A category isn't an option either because you want to control which section of the site the ad posts show up in. That's when you turn to custom fields. The following example creates a custom field called `Poststyle`; you add it just once, on any post, and then save a value for it. This example uses `ad` to keep things apart. (If you don't remember how custom fields work, revisit Chapter 4, "WordPress Theme Essentials," for a refresher.)

Put the class you want in the value for the key `Poststyle`. You can easily get that by checking for the `Poststyle` key on a per-post basis and echoing it. Remember, that last `true` parameter is to make sure that just one value is echoed should more be added. That won't do in this case; you want just the one value that you'll use as a style for the particular post. This in turn means that when you give `Poststyle` the value `ad`, you want that added as a class so that you can style it accordingly. (It also means that you can do even more stuff by adding other classes, but that's a different story.)

The code to echo this is as follows:

```
<?php
    $specialstyle = get_post_meta( get_the_ID(), 'Poststyle', true );
    echo $specialstyle;
?>
```

How do you add that to the list of classes outputted by `post_class()`? This is the code for outputting the ID and classes for the post `div`:

```
<div id="post-<?php the_ID(); ?>" <?php post_class(); ?>>
```

You can just add it to the ID, like this, condensed to one line:

```
<div id="post-<?php the_ID(); ?> <?php $specialstyle = get_post_meta( get_the_ID(),
'Poststyle', true ); echo $specialstyle; ?>" <?php post_class(); ?>>
```

That would add `#ad` to the post should you give `Poststyle` the value `ad`, but it isn't all that pretty doing it in the ID after all, so get it into the `post_class()` template tag instead.

The good thing is that `post_class()` can take parameters, meaning that if you want to add a class — `turtles`, for example — you can do so like this:

```
<?php post_class( 'turtles' ); ?>
```

That would make `post_class()` add `turtles` to the CSS classes outputted, which is what you want to do, but you want to squeeze your custom field value for `Poststyle` in there instead. This means that you have to pass the preceding PHP code to `post_class()`, which luckily is pretty straightforward. However, you can't use it straight out, so you need to alter it a bit. This is the code to use:

```
<?php $specialstyle = get_post_meta( get_the_ID(), 'Poststyle', true ); ?>
```

The `echo` part is removed because `post_class()` will return what you pass to it. And adding it is actually as easy as just removing the PHP declarations from the code and putting it within `post_class()`:

```
<div id="post-<?php the_ID(); ?>" <?php post_class( $specialstyle =
get_post_meta( get_the_ID(), 'Poststyle', true ) ); ?>>
```

This will add the value of the `Poststyle` custom field as a class to the post `div`, just like the `turtles` parameter did.

HOOKING ON TO BODY_CLASS(), POST_CLASS(), AND COMMENT_CLASS()

Staying on the subject of `post_class()` and its output of classes you can get to with CSS, I'll briefly discuss hooking onto it using the `post_class` hook. In fact, this all applies to `body_class()`, used in the `body` tag, and `comment_class()`, used for comments, as well. These three all output the appropriate classes for the situation, and you can pass a parameter to them as you did earlier. Just to clarify — the following code will add the class `solid` to `body`, along with all other classes `body_class()` would normally output:

```
<body <?php body_class( 'solid' ); ?>>
```

You can get to `body_class()`, `post_class()`, and `comment_class()` by using hooks with the same names. Add the `solid` class to `body_class()` using a filter, in functions. php:

```
// Add additional class to body_class()
add_filter( 'body_class', 'smashing_classes' );
function smashing_classes($classes) {
    // Add "solid" to the $classes array
    $classes[] = 'solid';
    return $classes;
}
```

This way, you wouldn't have to add anything to `body_class()` in your theme, keeping the theme code a bit simpler. The same principle works with `post_class()` and `comment_class()` as well, with corresponding hook names. Just replace `body_class` in `add_filter()` with `post_class` for `post_class()` and `comment_class` for `comment_class()`.

You should refer to the Codex for a list of the classes that `body_class()`, `post_class()`, and `comment_class()` will output. See the following pages:

- `body_class()`: http://codex.wordpress.org/Function_Reference/body_class
- `post_class()`: http://codex.wordpress.org/Function_Reference/post_class
- `comment_class()`: http://codex.wordpress.org/Function_Reference/comment_class

ADDING YOUR OWN TAXONOMY

Another way you can get more control over your posts is by adding a custom taxonomy. With this method, you can do conditional checks using `taxonomy_exists()`, which returns `true` should the taxonomy in question be available. (Keep in mind that you need to create your custom taxonomy first, as described in Chapter 6.)

Much like any other conditional tag, this method lets you do a conditional check to see whether a certain taxonomy is present; if so, you do something, and if not, you do something else. Unfortunately, your custom taxonomies won't attach to `post_class()` with custom styles, so you'll have to do that yourself if you want to. You could choose to echo your custom taxonomies with your post `divs` or use them in a similar fashion if you prefer to style your posts that way, mimicking the way tags are added with `post_class()` as described earlier.

You can read more on `taxonomy_exists()` in the Codex at http://codex.wordpress.org/Function_Reference/taxonomy_exists.

> *Post formats, which I've covered previously, are basically a taxonomy that you aren't meant to fiddle with outside of the predetermined formats. If you need something like the post format functionality but don't want to use post formats, you could always replicate it with your own taxonomy.*

Controlling how posts appear, by using tags, custom fields, or taxonomies, is a great way to add more visual appeal to your site, as well as to highlight important content. Making the various elements in a design stand out on their own is important, assuming they fit together in the end. The next section addresses another important part of any design: the menu.

IMPROVING THE MENU

The menu is one of the most important parts of a design. It needs to include enough content to help the visitor dig deeper into a site, but not so much that it becomes cluttered and hard to use. You really need to get the menu right because it is so prominent for the user. That's why there are so many visual approaches used to make menus more interesting, sometimes for the worse because a lot of them tend to ignore utility in favor of a "cool" design.

That being said, a useful and intuitive menu (see Figure 11-1) can also be spiffy looking, and trying out different approaches to how the menu is used is always a good idea. Just don't forget that easy navigation is the main point.

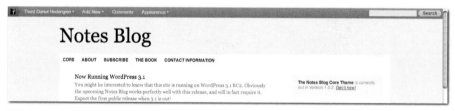

Figure 11-1: A simple menu.

The kind of menu you opt for when using WordPress depends a lot on what kind of site you're working on. Some WordPress sites are built around Pages (static sites in particular), whereas others are more free-flowing and really could do just with a tag cloud and a search field. In the middle, you've got the most common usage with categories (consisting of posts, obviously) for sections and Pages for static information (the boring "About" stuff), and tagging is just a way of describing the post's content better. Whichever it is, you should definitely build the menu using the menu feature that you no doubt remember from previous chapters. That way, populating the menu won't be a problem, and it'll be easy enough to update it. It doesn't solve things such as making everything fit, but it does let you mix categories with Pages with posts with links with . . . whatever.

As if that weren't enough, you still need to decide how the menu should look, what orientation it should have, and if it needs additional bling to make it interesting. One popular technique is called *sliding doors*. The following subsection explains how to implement that method on a WordPress menu.

SLIDING DOORS

The sliding doors CSS technique is a simple yet effective way of using graphics as the background in a horizontal menu, without having to set a fixed width. The idea is to add graphics as a background to your menu items, making them flexible enough to handle any length of text within. The following code is the basis of your menu:

```
<ul id="navigation">
    <li><a href="menu-item-1">First Item</a></li>
    <li><a href="menu-item-2">Second Menu Item</a></li>
    <li><a href="menu-item-3">Third One</a></li>
    <li><a href="menu-item-4">Number Four</a></li>
    <li><a href="menu-item-5">Fifth!</a></li>
</ul>
```

Basically, it's the typical output from most of the WordPress template tags that list categories and Pages, an unordered list that is the proper usage for menus whenever remotely possible. What is a menu if not a list, after all?

Say you want to use a button with rounded corners like the one shown in Figure 11-2 for your menu items; that's pretty and modern, right? Problem is, just applying it to the background of each menu item would require the actual menu item to be of a fixed width, and because you don't want to create a graphic for each of them but rather have the menu item text rendered by the browser with all the freedom that provides, it means that you have to be creative.

Figure 11-2: A button background image with rounded corners.

The solution is to chop up the image into three parts.

First you've got the left side, being the rounded corners on that side. Second, there's everything in the middle, which is the background of your menu link. And the final part is the right side's rounded corners (see Figure 11-3).

Figure 11-3: How to chop a button.

You want to put the middle part in as the background of the link, and because I'm lazy and won't dwell on this subject too long, you'll go for a one-colored middle. Then you want the left side's rounded corners to go to the left of the link and the right side's rounded corners to the right, leaving the colored background to fill out the gap between.

How would you do this in HTML? Easy, just add a span inside each link, like this:

```
<ul id="navigation">
    <li><a href="menu-item-1"><span>First Item</span></a></li>
    <li><a href="menu-item-2"><span>Second Menu Item</span></a></li>
    <li><a href="menu-item-3"><span>Third One</span></a></li>
    <li><a href="menu-item-4"><span>Number Four</span></a></li>
    <li><a href="menu-item-5"><span>Fifth!</span></a></li>
</ul>
```

And then you'd just add the images in the proper way using CSS. The link would get the left side's rounded corners fixed to the left, then it would fill out with the color of choice, and then you'd apply the right side's corners to the span but fixed to the right. What you get in effect is a button that can have any width you want because the actual link background is a filler after the left side's corners are displayed.

Or, to make it even clearer, here's some dummy CSS that you'd want to alter before usage, but it still explains how it works:

```
ul#navigation li {
    float:left;
    padding: 5px;
    list-style:none; }

ul#navigation a:link, ul#navigation a:visited {
    display:block; }

ul#navigation a:hover, ul#navigation a:active {
    background: #888 url(corners-left.gif) no-repeat left;
    float:left; }

ul#navigation a span {
    float:left;
    display:block; }

ul#navigation a:hover span {
    float:left;
    display:block;
    background: url(corners-right.jpg) no-repeat right; }
```

How would you make this work with `wp_nav_menu()`, the template tag for proper output of menus? Easily — just add the necessary `span` HTML with the help of the `before` and `after` parameters, like this:

```php
<?php wp_nav_menu( array(
    'before' => '<span>',
    'after' => '</span>'
) ); ?>
```

THINKING ABOUT HOVER-BASED MENUS

The more content you've got, the more you want to cram into the menu. After all, the purpose of a menu is to help your visitors navigate the site, so it is easy to be tempted to just add and then add some more to the menu. Horizontal menus are popular, but width is a limitation when it comes to expanding these. The solution is usually a hover effect that will drop down a submenu, as shown in Figure 11-4, so that the visitors get easy access to the sections under each menu item.

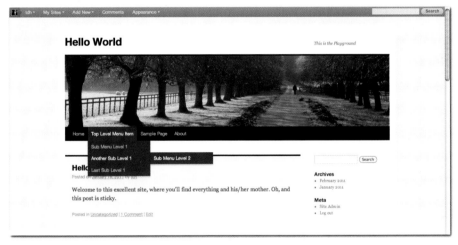

Figure 11-4: The hover menu of the Twenty Ten theme.

With the advent of touch-based devices such as smartphones and tablets, however, you should be careful about relying on hover-based design. Because menus are such an integral part of a site, I recommend that you avoid building them around the hover effect. After all, there is no way to hover on a touchscreen because it is either "press" (meaning that you're touching it, comparable to a click with a mouse-based interface) or not. You can't hover on a touchscreen, so a menu relying on hover effects won't work as intended on tablets. There are already millions of tablets on the market, and this market continues to grow dramatically.

So should you never do hover-based menus, then? Although I recommend caution, I still think there's room for them. If you've got decent fallbacks, such as making the top menu item clickable/tappable and making sure that it is easy to reach the lower items from the target page, then you're pretty much in the clear. It's not as snappy and easy to navigate as it will be with a mouse pointer, but at least it works. Keep this in mind when deciding what kind of menus to use on your future projects.

Now you'll take a sharp turn, from spicing up how the posts and menus are displayed to adding ads within the loop.

PLACING ADS WITHIN THE LOOP

A common question I get is how to insert ads — particularly Google AdSense ads — within the loop. Usually, bloggers want to run an ad after the first, second, or third post and then continue with the loop as if nothing happened.

One way of doing this is to split the loop in two, first querying for a couple of posts (say two) and then displaying the ad. After that, there's a second loop with a post offset corresponding to the number of posts queried in the first loop; hence, it looks like one big thing.

A better way, perhaps, is to just count the number of posts and then output the ad when a certain number has been reached. You can do this with PHP by adding to a variable every time the loop runs, which it does for each post that is to be outputted.

Here's the common way of displaying an ad after the first post, stripped of all the post output code:

```php
<?php
    // Loop
    while (have_posts()) : the_post();
    // Add +1 to $postcount for each loop
    $postcount++; ?>
        <!-- Post output -->
        <?php
            // Check $postcount
            if ($postcount < 2) : ?>
            <!-- Ad code goes here -->
        <?php
            // Done checking
            endif;
    // Loop ends
    endwhile;
?>
```

This code is a basic loop, with some counting added to the mix. You add +1 to `$postcount` every time the loop loops. This is done in the `while (have_posts()) : the_post()` line, which means that the first thing you do after that is add +1 to the `$postcount` value, and you do that with ++, which means just that, add +1.

After that, the code is pretty straightforward. If the `$postcount` value is less than 2, the code will output the post and the ad code, and if not, it will move on to the `else` post output, which is your standard one.

What if you want to insert the ad after each of the first two posts? In that case, just change the `if` query for the `$postcount` value from 2 to 3 instead, which would mean that the ad output would happen on posts one and two in the loop:

```php
<?php if ( $postcount < 3 ) : ?>
```

Beware of the Ad Rules

Inserting ads between posts may sound like a great idea. After all, it is a pretty unobtrusive practice, so it isn't bound to annoy people greatly. It can, of course, but it is a lot better than putting ads in the actual content, which you also can do with some nifty hackery.

However, although it may seem like a great plan to spread out the ads between the posts, you need to observe the rules of the ad network you're using. Google AdSense, widely used, has a limit on how many ads per page you can show, and if you break that limit, you're bound to get in trouble and perhaps get your account suspended. This is bad news for most people, but even worse news for people earning a living on ad revenue.

So although I encourage you to spread out your ads across the site (it is, after all, a lot nicer than having them concentrated at the top of the page), I also feel obliged to remind you to check the ad network's rules for any limitations.

And be careful! Automatic outputs like this one can be dangerous stuff, and a mistake somewhere may land you with a lot of ads all over the place. Neither you, nor your readers, nor the ad network will like that, I'm sure.

Another thing you should be careful with is using 404 Page Not Found error outputs with ads. Sure, you can display ads on these pages, but they won't perform well if they are contextual by nature, and I doubt advertisers paying for ad views would appreciate being on an error page.

CREATING 404S THAT HELP THE VISITOR

Creating useful 404 error pages is important. These are the pages that will show whenever someone reaches a page within your site that doesn't exist, and although you may have everything covered on your end, people linking to you may not, so you need these. The theme template file to manage the 404 Page Not Found errors is aptly named 404.php, and you can do just about anything you want with it because it is served from WordPress.

This section doesn't go into detail on how to build your own 404.php template file (that is covered in Chapter 4). I will, however, tell you what I think a good 404 error page should offer the visitor:

- It should be obvious that the page is not there. In other words, tell the visitor that the page he or she was looking for doesn't exist, and do it in such a way that there is no risk of misunderstanding.

- Offer alternative routes. Because the most likely source of hitting a 404 error page in a WordPress setup is a faulty link from elsewhere, you should offer a different route to the content the visitor was looking for. Encourage searching in particular.

- Open up your site. The visitor may not care enough to search for the content that sparked the 404 error, but maybe you can snag him or her anyway. Add links to your categories and offer a very brief introduction on what they are all about. Turn your 404 error into a sales pitch for your site.

- Show the latest content. It is easy to display a list of links showing the latest updates. Maybe something there will appeal to the visitor.

- Use humor. A bit of light-hearted humor can be a way to make the visitor less annoyed by the fact that the content he or she wanted to see isn't there.

- Offer a means of error reporting. Let the visitor get in touch with you to tell you of the missing content; that sends a positive message as well as helps you find any particular faults in your site.

A useful 404 page says a lot about a site, so spend some time making yours a good one.

USING JAVASCRIPT LIBRARIES WITH WORDPRESS

JavaScript can be a great tool, thanks especially to excellent libraries such as jQuery, MooTools, and Scriptaculous. A ton of these libraries are available, making it easy to add transitions and similar visual bling, as well as more useful stuff. Most cool services online today rely on JavaScript, and the WordPress admin interface isn't particularly fun to work with if you turn off JavaScript in your web browser.

You can bring JavaScript functionality to your WordPress sites as well, whether you're just adding some visual appeal to your theme with smooth animations or something similar or adding some actual new functionality thanks to your brilliant coding. What you need to think about is how you do it, and that is where `wp_enqueue_script()` comes in. With this tag, you can load any of the many JavaScript libraries that ship with WordPress, or you can just attach your own.

The usage is simple. Add JavaScript to the hook where it is needed, using `wp_enqueue_script()`. If you want to load the JavaScript as late as possible because it probably won't be needed before the user does something special anyway, you can use `wp_enqueue_script()` and attach it to the `wp_enqueue_scripts` hook, like this (using jQuery as an example):

```
function smashing_scripts() {
    wp_enqueue_script( 'jquery' );
}
add_action( 'wp_enqueue_scripts', 'smashing_scripts' );
```

This loads the version of jQuery shipped with WordPress. You can find other JavaScript libraries to load this way in the wp-includes/js/ folder. The use of `wp_enqueue_script()` also makes it easy to load the scripts only when you need them, with some clever use of conditional tags. If you just want the script on the home page, use `is_home()` and so on.

You can do a ton of things with JavaScript, and it all depends on the site as well as your own preferences. Some people are more at home in Prototype than in jQuery, and others prefer MooTools or something entirely different. That's why `wp_enqueue_script()` can load anything. You should use it, and you should in particular make sure that you don't slow down your site with scripts if you don't need them or let them load too early. After all, what's the point of waiting for a script when there isn't a page to use it on?

I urge you to read up on `wp_enqueue_script()` in the Codex, where you'll also find information on the various JavaScript libraries that ship with WordPress, how you can pass elements such as dependencies, and how you deregister JavaScript libraries and replace them with your own. Start with the Codex page (http://codex.wordpress.org/Function_Reference/wp_enqueue_script) and then move on to the JavaScript library itself.

REGISTERING SCRIPTS

There is a lot of JavaScript out there that you can use, not to mention extensions to the popular libraries discussed. Be sure to read up on them, though — not only to keep your site clean but also to make sure that they work in all the web browsers you want to support. Barring that, if the extra functionality, flair, or bling does it for your site, this can be a great way to make it more visually appealing.

Another useful tool is `wp_register_script()`, which lets you register a script for easy access, much like the earlier jQuery example. This means that you can register a script that ships with your theme or plugin and access it with `wp_enqueue_script()` just as easily as the scripts that are included with WordPress. You can even set dependencies so that these scripts will be loaded before the script you're registering.

The following code will register a script that ships with your theme:

```
function smashing_scriptloader() {
    // Register your script
    wp_register_script(
        'smashing_script',
        get_template_directory_uri() . '/js/smashing.js'
    );
    // Enqueue the script
    wp_enqueue_script( 'smashing_script' );
}
add_action( 'wp_enqueue_scripts', 'smashing_scriptloader' );
```

If the script were depending on jQuery (for example), you could add that as well to `wp_register_script()`. You can read more about `wp_register_script()` in the Codex at http://codex.wordpress.org/Function_Reference/wp_register_script.

In fact, you could even deregister a script and replace it with your own, so if you want to use a different jQuery version than the one that ships with WordPress, you would do so using `wp_deregister_script()`. You can read more about deregistering scripts at http://codex.wordpress.org/Function_Reference/wp_deregister_script.

MAKING WORDPRESS YOUR OWN

Sometimes, you'll find yourself in a position in which you want to make WordPress carry your brand a bit further than usual. More often than not, this occurs when you're using plugins or features that let the visitors become registered users, with settings and privileges on the administrative side of things. Or, in plain English: They can access the WordPress admin interface.

This means two things. First, visitors get to log in, and that means that they'll use the Word-Press login form, shown in Figure 11-5. The default login form doesn't look the least bit like the carefully designed site you're sporting, so naturally you'll want to do something about that. Second, they get into the WordPress admin interface, and that looks every bit like WordPress and nothing at all like Your Super Brand™. Who would want that?

Figure 11-5: The default login form.

Unfortunately, WordPress doesn't offer the same theming possibilities for the administrative side of things as it does for your site's front end, but there are quite a few things you can do. It all depends on how important it is that the WordPress parts look as little like WordPress as possible and how much time you want to spend making the changes.

A CUSTOM LOGIN FORM

If you need to tweak one thing when it comes to WordPress admin stuff, it is probably the login form. This totally screams WordPress, which in itself is pretty annoying, especially if your site does something totally different from the typical WordPress blog.

You can, of course, just hack the login form by altering the core files in WordPress, but that would mean that you may end up breaking something crucial, and also that you will have to do it all over again with every update because each update will overwrite your hack. A much better choice is to use a plugin. You may have already found a few possibilities in Appendix A, "Essential WordPress Plugins." They are good, so try them out.

However, you may want to keep the login form in line with the theme because it is a design matter after all, and that means that you want the custom stuff with the theme files. Luckily, you can do that by hooking onto the `login_head` action hook and applying some extra style sheet goodness. This means that you can make the login form look just about any way you'd like, as long as you don't need to change the actual layout of the thing. So a black background and your grungy logo is not a problem at all; you just need a bit of CSS.

First, however, you need to create the function to hook onto the `login_head` action hook. You should recognize this type of code from Chapter 6, which covers action hooks in depth. Keep in mind that you should make it easy to build child themes upon your theme, and these child themes may want a custom login of their own. That's why I use `get_stylesheet_directory_uri()` and not `get_template_directory_uri()`in this example. Here's the code:

```
// Custom login stylesheet
function smashing_login() {
    $smashingLoginUrl = get_stylesheet_directory_uri() . '/login.css';
    wp_register_style( 'smashingLoginStyle', $smashingLoginUrl );
    wp_enqueue_style( 'smashingLoginStyle' );
}
add_action( 'login_enqueue_scripts', 'smashing_login', 1 );
```

This code is simple enough; the only thing it does is add the contents of the `nbcustom_login()` function to the `login_head` hook. And that is, of course, the `wp_enqueue_style()` (which works very much like `wp_enqueue_script()`) containing a style sheet located in a folder called `custom` in the theme's directory. You can read up on `wp_enqueue_style()`in the Codex at http://codex.wordpress.org/Function_Reference/wp_enqueue_style.

The rest is up to you: Just hack away at the newly included style sheet (located in custom/login.css in this example). The login page is easy enough to figure out. Some of the elements you may want to change are the background color (using the `body` tag); the WordPress logo, which resides in the `h1` tag; and the whole login box itself, which is in `div#login`. Happy modifying!

> *If you really just want to change the logo, there are several plugins available that you might prefer using rather than having to write code yourself. Then again, you do want to learn, right?*

ADMIN THEMES

Theming the WordPress admin is, unfortunately, a slightly tricky affair. First, the only way to do it without hacking or overwriting the core files (which you don't want to be doing unless you're forking WordPress itself) is by using a plugin. Here's the plugin code:

```php
<?php
/*
Plugin Name: Smashing Admin Colors
Plugin URI: http://tdh.me/wordpress/smashing-admin/
Description: Adds a custom color admin scheme.
Version: 1.0
Author: Thord Daniel Hedengren
Author URI: http://tdh.me/
*/
```

```
function smashing_admin_colors() {
    $file = dirname(__FILE__) . '/smashing-admin';
    wp_admin_css_color(
        'smashingadmin',
        'Smashing Admin',
        plugin_dir_url( $file ) . 'smashing-admin.css',
        array( '#ff4720', '#41b7d8', '#333333', '#a6a6a6' )
    );
}
add_action( 'admin_init', 'smashing_admin_colors' );
?>
```

The smashing_admin_colors() function is added to the admin_init hook; by doing so, you get wp_admin_css_color() to register a new color scheme called *Smashing Admin*. This in turn will get the smashing-admin.css file from the plugin's folder. Finally, the array at the end of wp_admin_css_color() is the colored boxes that represent the color scheme on the user profile screen in the WordPress admin.

Naturally, you also need something in the smashing-admin.css file. This is where the actual styling is happening, so you could have a completely new style sheet there or just alter an existing one. This example imports the style sheet for the classic color scheme and alters a few link colors. Nothing fancy or too pretty, but it shows what is possible. You can view the result when this color scheme is selected in Figure 11-6.

```
@import url(../../../wp-admin/css/colors-classic.css);
.form-table td, .form-table th {
    border-bottom-color: #ffffff; }
#wphead, #footer, #footer-upgrade {
    color: #333; }
#adminmenu a:link, #adminmenu a:visited {
    color:#ff4720; }
#adminmenu a:hover {
    color: #41b7d8; }
```

Figure 11-6: The Smashing Admin color scheme is selected.

There are some pretty impressive admin themes out there, but you should have no illusions. Making the admin interface look the way you want will most likely be hard work. That being said, sometimes all you need to do is to make small changes, such as swapping colors, and that shouldn't be too much of a problem to do this way.

POLISHING YOUR WORDPRESS SITE

Learning the various tricks of the trade when it comes to WordPress is important to lift your site from a mere WordPress theme (no matter how great) to something more complete. Any good site will benefit from the polishing these tricks provide, so you should experiment with techniques and see what you can do.

Although controlling the look and feel of your posts and getting the menu right are all important things, there are limitless possibilities for your site. Excellent blogs such as Smashing Magazine (www.smashingmagazine.com) and A List Apart (www.alistapart.com) will help you find even more interesting techniques for your site. Some you can employ right away, and others need a more hands-on approach. Experiment away!

12

FUN WITH MEDIA

IT'S SAID A picture is worth a thousand words; an image can tell a story a lot faster than text can. The same goes for other kinds of visual media, such as video embeds. These things can be used to illustrate a point and hence drive the text home, or even be standalone content themselves.

If you are using media elements in your site, it's important to give some thought to how you plan to incorporate items such as galleries and illustrations. This chapter is about displaying media in a WordPress site, beyond the traditional inclusion of illustrative points or inspiring scenery in your posts and Pages.

WORKING WITH IMAGE GALLERIES

WordPress has included support for the `[gallery]` shortcode for a long time, with all the possibilities it brings.

> *If you're working in the visual editor, you won't see the gallery button; you'll just see a big box telling you that it is an image area. You can switch to HTML view for a more refined representation.*

What `[gallery]` really does is output uploaded images in a clickable thumbnail grid. Then you can let your visitors see a larger version of the image, either in your theme's design or the original file itself. The former is called the *attachment page* because that's what images are — attachments to blog posts. This built-in functionality should cover most of your needs if you run a text-based site that sometimes publishes images.

To fine-tune it even further, the first stop after installing WordPress and picking the theme of your choice should be the Media page under Settings in the admin interface. Here you can control the circumstances under which the various images are scaled. Each image you upload is saved in up to four different versions, designed for your needs across the site.

Figure 12-1 shows the WordPress Media Settings page, which outlines the various sizes your images can be:

- The thumbnail: A cropped version of an image meant to symbolize the image in question. You can set it to be cropped to exact sizes, which means that it won't actually show the whole image all the time. It's a small image that's meant to be clickable. The default size is 150 x 150 pixels, but you can change that to fit your theme.
- The medium image: The full image downsized, with width and height proportional to the original image you uploaded. You can set a maximum width and height that dictate how the image should be scaled. This is also the image used in the attachment pages.
- The large image: Also your full image but downsized proportionally.
- The original image: Also available, untouched.

There's one caveat: No image version will be created if it is in fact larger than the original image. So if your large image is set to 800 pixels width and height but the image you're uploading is smaller than that, it won't be created and won't be available to include or link to in WordPress. There's just no point.

So what about it then? Why bring this up?

Simple. The thumbnail should be in a size that fits your width and the number of columns you expect to use normally in your image galleries created with the `[gallery]` shortcode. Make it a nice size for your site.

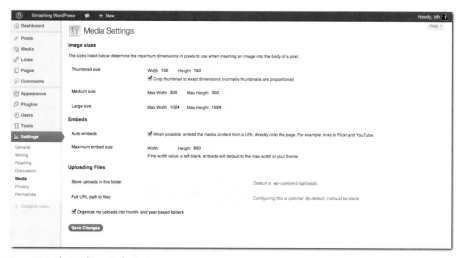

Figure 12-1: The WordPress Media Settings page.

Furthermore, it is my belief that the medium image should be the exact same as the maximum width your design can manage. In other words, if the max width is 580 pixels, set the max width of the medium image to 580 pixels — to ensure that you can include it in your posts whenever you like. Because the medium image is the one used in attachment pages by default, it is a good idea to make it fit well there. Granted, you can just use the large image on attachment pages instead, but perhaps you want to be able to use that for an even larger display of the image — one that is not limited by the page width. No matter how you set up your image sizes and what image size you use for your attachment page, the important thing is to make sure that images look good and fit your needs.

As mentioned, the large image is good for linking a larger variant. It is possible to use the large image on the attachment page by using the attachment.php template, for example, but by default, that's not the case. The large image is usually only interesting if you're uploading a high-resolution photo and don't want to link the original version because it is 15MB and ridiculously large for web view and the large one is substantially smaller and fitted to the screen.

STYLING THE GALLERY

Making the galleries included with the [gallery] shortcode look good is easy, assuming that you've configured your thumbnails according to the number of columns you'll be using. This is something you can choose when you're including the gallery, so you need to pay attention to that.

Actually styling the gallery is also pretty simple. The whole thing resides in a div with a number of identifying classes to use, one of which is actually called gallery. As is the norm in WordPress, there are unique IDs and classes as well, but you'll probably settle with div. gallery for your CSS needs.

Each item in the gallery is enclosed in a `dl.gallery-item`, which in turn contains `dt.gallery-icon`, which has the linked thumbnail image, and possibly also a `dd.gallery-caption` if a caption is provided for the image in question. You get this for as many images you've chosen to display in a row, then it all breaks down to a new row quite unceremoniously with a `br` tag with `style="clear:both"`, and it begins again.

This means that, for the thumbnail gallery listings, you need to style the following (listed hierarchically):

```
div.gallery {}

dl.gallery-item {}

dt.gallery-icon {}

dd.gallery-caption {}
```

The following is the code used by Notes Blog, with a subtle font color and size for the captions and some whitespace in between because that's always pleasant to the eye. Naturally, your design may be a lot flashier than this, adding background images, borders, and so on:

```
div.gallery {
    margin-bottom: 14px; }

img.attachment-thumbnail {
    border:0; }

dd.gallery-caption {
    margin-top: 8px;
    font-size: 12px;
    color: #777;
    font-style: italic; }
```

Now, that's just one half of it. Although you can configure your gallery thumbnails to link to the actual image, you can always choose to link to the attachment page. That's the one showing the image in your theme's design, which probably means that it will revert to either single.php or index.php because most themes lack the attachment.php template file and very few have template files for video.php, image.php, and so on.

To get your theme to be image-friendly, you really should add a link back to the post containing the actual gallery, and you should add Previous/Next links so that the user can browse the gallery from image to image. You can use `previous_post_link()` and `next_post_link()` to output simple navigational links with the previous or next post's title and an arrow by default. These tags also let you limit browsing to a specific category, as well as alter the link:

```
<?php previous_post_link(); ?>
<?php next_post_link(); ?>
```

You can read more about these in the Codex at http://codex.wordpress.org/Function_ Reference/previous_post_link and http://codex.wordpress.org/Template_Tags/next_post_link.

If you need a little more control, you can use the following code to fetch the post's parent (the actual post the attachment is attached to) and link it. Nothing fancy. You can't use the_ permalink(), of course, because that would indicate the attachment itself, while the_ title() naturally is the image title. You probably want to make sure that your attachment template outputs that, too:

```
<p class="attachmentnav">
    &larr; Back to
    <a href="<?php echo get_permalink( $post->post_parent ) ?>" title="<?php echo
    get_the_title( $post->post_parent ) ?>" rev="attachment">
        <?php echo get_the_title( $post->post_parent ) ?>
    </a>
</p>
```

Speaking of outputs, the description you can fill out when uploading or editing an image is in fact outputted by the_content(), which means that you can add decent attachment support to your single.php or index.php template easily enough. Just use the is_ attachment() conditional tag to check for it and output accordingly, and you'll be fine. You could also use dedicated template files such as image.php or attachment.php if you don't want to work with conditional tags.

Back to business: Add those Previous and Next links for navigation within the gallery, in attachment image view. This is done with previous_image_link() and next_image_ link(), both of which by default will output the thumbnail, linked, to the other target image. Here you're using divs to float the Previous and Next links to the left and right:

```
<div class="alignleft">
    <?php next_image_link(); ?>
</div>
<div class="alignright">
    <?php previous_image_link(); ?>
</div>
```

Although the thumbnail output may be cool if tailored to the task, you may want to use text instead. Just pass an empty string to the image size parameters (yes, it takes other sizes as well), and it will output the image post title, being the name you gave it, instead. Or you can add another parameter to pass a custom text link, like this:

```
<div class="alignleft">
    <?php next_image_link( '', 'Next Image' ); ?>
</div>
<div class="alignright">

    <?php previous_image_link( '', 'Previous Image' ); ?>

</div>
```

That's about what you need to know to work with galleries on a WordPress site. The next natural step, after getting it to work with your theme, is pimping the whole affair using plugins.

BETTER BROWSING WITH LIGHTBOX

A *lightbox effect* is a common name for an overlay that displays an image on top of a site, without opening a pop-up (see Figure 12-2). You need to close the image to access the actual site again, which may sound like a bad idea, but compare it to having to open a new page to view the image in full size, and you get the picture. Most decently designed lightbox solutions have accessible browse buttons as well.

Figure 12-2: A lightbox effect in action.

This is pulled off with JavaScript and some design trickery, and there are tons of possible solutions waiting for you. Which solution you choose all depends on how much visual bling you want and what sorts of effects suit you and your site. I do think you should go with one that comes as a WordPress plugin, though, because that means that you won't have to add any classes to your images manually to make sure the lightbox solution recognizes the link as a lightbox one. Consult Appendix A, "Essential WordPress Plugins," for some excellent lightbox plugins, if you don't have a favorite already. The plugins do this for you, and suddenly your image gallery won't have to open those attachment pages at all, and your visitors can browse your photos with ease.

However, there are drawbacks, the most obvious ones being what happens if the visitor has turned off JavaScript or if someone clicks the thumbnail link before the lightbox script is fully loaded. The result is an opening of the image as a whole, outside of the design, just as if the link pointed to the image itself only (which it usually does, but then the script puts it right in the effects it adds). It isn't too pretty when that happens, especially if the visitor expects that nice overlay effect and the easy Previous/Next links it probably sports, but then again, there is a fully functional solution as well, thanks to the web browser's Back button.

Why wouldn't you use a lightbox solution? One main concern is smaller devices. How good does something like this look on a seven-inch low-resolution screen? Is it really useful then? The same can, in all fairness's sake, be said about attachment pages, but it is a bit easier to style those on a per-user agent basis. You should make sure that the lightbox script doesn't override any such solutions.

Finally, if you make your money on page views, don't go the lightbox route unless you think it will bring in more readers. After all, having people load a new page, and hence a new set of ads, whenever they want to view the next image in a gallery can be good business in itself!

USING OUTSIDE SCRIPTS AND SYSTEMS

Finally, I have a few words about using gallery solutions from outside of WordPress, such as standalone gallery software. There are several gallery scripts available, some of which are fully fledged systems in themselves, whereas others just crunch images to various sizes and output content in physical folders on your server as HTML.

I recommend that you think very carefully about using external image galleries, such as Gallery2, before doing so. The foremost concern behind this is flexibility. WordPress can be extended with numerous plugins, and if your images are a part of WordPress, they can sometimes benefit from them. However, if you're running your images in an outside script and just showing them in your theme one way or the other, you won't get these benefits. And what happens if that outside script suddenly stops working or starts clashing with your WordPress install?

The same really goes for plugins that move the gallery functionality from the WordPress core to their own setup. This may mean that they can add new features, better sorting, or whatever, but it also means that whenever the plugin isn't being maintained anymore and stops working because of defunct WordPress functionality or other conflicts, you'll be on your own in a way that wouldn't have happened otherwise. And besides, instead of the flashy gallery functionality that the plugin you were considering offered, why not look for something that adds that to the core image gallery features instead?

That said, sometimes you need more, and then you'll have to move outside of WordPress core features, either by relying on plugins or external systems and/or services. Just make sure that you know what you're doing, and make sure that you know what to do if you need to move back or to something else. Conversion and importing tools can certainly help you feel more secure in such cases.

THE MEDIA POST FORMATS

Post formats offer a bit more control over your post's contents, as discussed previously. With their help, you can style your posts to fit the right type of content, and that is something that is especially useful with media. There are four post formats that spring to mind for these sorts of things: Image, Gallery, Video, and Audio. Figure 12-3 shows how you can use the former two post formats to differentiate between a single image and an image gallery.

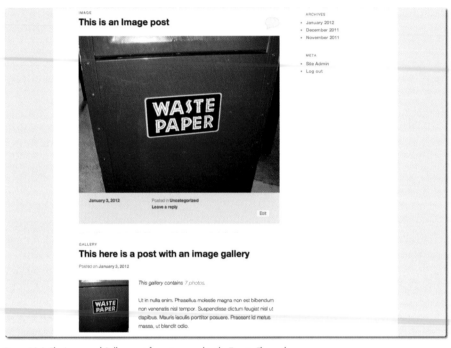

Figure 12-3: The Image and Gallery post formats as used in the Twenty Eleven theme.

I've covered post formats before, so you already know that you can style and manage these in just about any way you like, so let's move on to embedding content, shall we? If you do want to refresh your memory, consult Chapter 6, "Advanced Theme Usage," and onward.

EMBEDDING MEDIA CONTENT

If you're working with video, you're probably using services such as YouTube or Vimeo. This means that you need to embed movies from there to publish them on your site. This is easy enough; just grab the embed code from your video service of choice and paste it into your post. But did you know that you don't need to fiddle with iframe code snippets at all — that you can have WordPress embed it all for you and automatically size it to your media settings at that?

GETTING THE SETTINGS RIGHT

First of all, make sure that you've got your media settings right. Visit the Media Settings page again and look at the options under Embeds. Make sure that the When Possible, Embed the Media Content from a URL Directly onto the Page. For Example: Links to Flickr and YouTube check box is selected, which is what makes WordPress try to embed content in the first place. After that, you want to change the settings for the actual embed size. This is much like the image settings, actually, because WordPress will scale the embed to fit either height or width. Most of us care only about width, so set it to whatever width your theme's content column has (640 pixels, for example) and leave the height blank, as illustrated in Figure 12-4.

Figure 12-4: Get your Embeds settings right.

This will make sure that your embedded content will scale to the right size.

Actually embedding the content is really easy; just paste the URL for the content, and WordPress will try and get it. So if you want to embed the Nyan Cat video on YouTube, found at www.youtube.com/watch?v=QH2-TGUlwu4, you'll just paste that URL on a row of its own and save your post. WordPress pulls the video and embeds it for you. It works just great with the short YouTube sharing URL as well — http://youtu.be/QH2-TGUlwu4 in this case.

You can also use the [embed] shortcode, which will help you embed content. Just put the URL to whatever you want to embed within [embed] and [/embed], like this:

```
[embed]http://www.flickr.com/photos/tdhedengren/4333551150/sizes/o/in/set-
  72157623327077126/[/embed]
```

You can even use [embed] to scale the content. For example, the following code will scale the image down to a width of 250 pixels. Remember that you still load the image itself, so it is scaled by HTML and not actually downsized.

```
[embed width="250"]http://www.flickr.com/photos/tdhedengren/4333551150/sizes/o/in/
  set-72157623327077126/[/embed]
```

THE MAGIC OF OEMBED

Automatic embedding in WordPress is made possible by something called *oEmbed*. This technology makes it possible for WordPress to fetch content from oEmbed-enabled websites, such as YouTube and Vimeo, that there is support for. Unfortunately, this doesn't mean that you can automatically embed any kind of content from any site, or from any site using oEmbed for that matter — WordPress still needs to support the provider in question. More and more sites are added as a core feature, but if you want additional support right now, you need to add it yourself. There are plugins that do that already, such as Twitter Embed (http:// wordpress.org/extend/plugins/twitter-embed), which embeds a specific tweet.

Although I won't delve any deeper than this here, you would be wise to read up on oEmbed should you want to add support for an oEmbed-enabled site yourself at http://oembed.com. When you've got the gist of it, you'll want to start with `wp_oembed_add_provider()` to add your own provider using a plugin (see http://codex.wordpress.org/Function_Reference/ wp_oembed_add_provider).

RANDOMIZING IMAGE ELEMENTS

Setting up your site to randomly display your images and other elements can spice it up and make it feel more alive. In the blogosphere, having a random header image is popular, as well as having random posts promoted. After all, elements that change a bit between visits (without disrupting visitors' ability to navigate) are generally seen as more interesting than a static display.

The most basic way of randomizing is using PHP and any of the randomizing functions it offers, such as `rand()` and `mt_rand()`. There are also several JavaScript solutions you can use. Solutions for both of these techniques are readily available online, so you shouldn't waste time on hacking your own unless you really need to.

It doesn't stop there, however. Several plugins can help as well, a few of which are discussed in Appendix A. Randomized content, especially images, has been done so many times that it is almost ridiculously easy to get going. That is, unless you want to display random images from posts you've uploaded. For some reason, this is a bit harder.

DISPLAYING RANDOM IMAGES FROM YOUR GALLERIES

An even cooler type of random image content would come from your galleries: the images you've uploaded to WordPress. Those are attachments, and you can get to them by doing a little bit of `get_post()` hacking in an additional loop. The idea is to show the thumbnail of any attachment that is an image and link it to that very image. Because you'll have properly styled your gallery (as you learned about in the earlier section "Styling the Gallery"), you know that the visitor can continue clicking and enjoying your photos or whatever from there, so it sounds like a good way to catch the readers, right?

This code shows how to do it, in this case outputting everything in an unordered list because it seems appropriate:

```
<ul class="random-attachments">
    <?php $new_query = new WP_Query( '&showposts=4' ); ?>
    <?php while ( $new_query->have_posts() ) : $new_query->the_post(); ?>
    $args = array(
        'post_type' => 'attachment',
```

```
        'numberposts' => 1,
        'orderby' => rand,
        'status' => 'publish',
        'post_mime_type' => 'image',
        'parent' => $post->ID
    );
    $attachments = get_posts( $args );
    if ( $attachments ) {
        foreach ( $attachments as $attachment ) {
    echo '<li>';
    echo wp_get_attachment_link( $attachment->ID, 'thumbnail', true, '' );
    echo '</li>';
        }
    }
    ?>
<?php endwhile; ?>
</ul>
```

The first two lines are just to get the new WordPress loop started and limit the number of posts to loop out. Next comes an array belonging to the `$args` function. This is a fairly common usage in WordPress; it makes it easier to pass all the parameters and store them in a function. The parameters belong to `get_posts()`, which will control what you'll actually output. You'll get to that in a little bit.

The `$args` array should be pretty self-explanatory, sorting by the attachment post type, showing just one attachment per post (otherwise you'd get several images rather than just one), randomizing the ordering, using only published posts, and limiting things to the `'image'` MIME type. (That could just as well have been `'video'`, for example, so it can come in handy.) Finally, you attach the parent post's ID for good measure; it really isn't needed but can come in handy in other cases, so it is left in here for informational purposes.

You've got all that information in the array stored in `$args` — now to load `get_posts()` with it. This is done with the following line:

```
$attachments = get_posts( $args );
```

Now the whole `get_posts()` with all the parameters from `$args` is stored in `$attachments`, which you'll use in the `foreach` loop. There you'll find the following line, which is what controls how the attachments are outputted:

```
echo wp_get_attachment_link( $attachment->ID, 'thumbnail', true, '' );
```

The `wp_get_attachment_link()` template tag outputs the relevant attachment by default. Here you're giving it the ID from the `foreach`, and then you tell it that it should display the thumbnail rather than the original size (which is the default). The `true` passed after that says whether to link the output to the attachment page, and because that is kind of the point, this needs to be passed. Finally, the last parameter is whether to display a media icon, which defaults to `false`, so you don't need to pass that.

Putting that little code snippet in the sidebar will get you an unordered list of randomized thumbnail images linked to their respective attachment pages.

MORE RANDOM IMAGE OPTIONS

Not good enough for you? Then you should turn to the wonderful world of photo-sharing sites and their various widgets and embed codes, as well as to the plethora of plugins available (see the section "Making the Most of Image-Sharing Services" later in this chapter for more detail). A combination is usually a pretty good recipe for nice image blocks showing off your latest works of art (or just snapped vacation photos), so dig deep into that for more random image goodness. You'll find a bunch of plugins and suggestions in Appendix A, if you haven't seen that already.

A word of advice, though: Beware of clutter, and beware of long load times.

Adding third-party services always adds to the load time, and it doesn't get any better if an image, which may or may not be properly compressed for the web, is served. I know that it's tempting to put in a cool Flash widget from some photo-sharing site, or an Ajax-y plugin that shows off all your best photos in a never-ending slideshow, but you should be careful.

Another consideration is whether you really need the image block. Just because you've got access to a stream of images doesn't mean that you have to use or display it. Will the visitor be interested? If not, forget about it and use that valuable screen real estate to show something else.

Creative Uses of Featured and Header Images

Two special types of images can be used even more creatively in your projects: the header image and featured image. As you know, the header image is often used as a traditional blog header, but there's nothing in the feature that limits you to that. The featured image is a per-post option of setting a specific image as the one that symbolizes the post, most commonly used to headline images or for related purposes.

But you could do other things with these types of images as well! Here are some ideas to get you started:

- Use a header image as a seasonal message. In almost bloggish fashion, you can use the header image feature to display seasonal greetings and other things to your visitors.
- Use a header image for additional branding. As a more traditional take on the preceding idea, use the header image for additional branding, such as highlighting a product, a convention, a service, a person, or something else.
- Use a featured image as a background. Who said you had to have your featured image as a traditional headline image? Use it to set a background for your post instead, further branding it.
- Use a featured image as the header. Did you know that the Twenty Ten theme will swap the custom header for the featured image (if there is one) when you're reading a post? This concept could be refined even further, giving your post a header of its own, perhaps as a site in the site.

MAKING THE MOST OF IMAGE-SHARING SERVICES

For sites running on limited hardware or shared hosting accounts, it may be crucial to save on both space and bandwidth, and what better way than to host the videos on YouTube and the images on Flickr? The same actually applies to larger sites not generating much money, but those tend to be able to afford custom solutions such as stored data in the cloud or static files on servers.

Serving the images from any of the photo-sharing sites out there is a sure way to keep both bandwidth and storage down, especially if the site in question is running a lot of photos. A good example would be a video-game site, pumping screenshots typically over 700KB in size each; plus larger screens and HD resolutions add the need to share them in that resolution as well. Say you shoot out two screenshot galleries every day, each containing ten images. That's 140 images every week, or 600 per month. At around 700KB each, that adds up for sure — to over 420MB per month, actually. You don't need to be a mathematician to understand that such a site will require a lot of megabytes in bandwidth, as well as storage, over the long run.

That's why photo-sharing sites are useful. Pumping images in to Flickr means that you needn't worry about those things, as Flickr will cover your bandwidth. It may be a bit of a stretch to have the big video-game sites running their screenshot library on Flickr, but the same mathematics apply for a photographer's site, for example.

There is money to be saved here, by "doing a YouTube" with images as well. After all, few sites host their own videos these days. Instead, they rely on embedding videos from services such as YouTube or Vimeo, so why not do the same with images?

Naturally, there are drawbacks — most importantly, the fact that if your image host goes out of business, you'll lose all your images. You can sort that out as long as you have backups, of course, but you'd need to put them in again manually. On the other hand, these services are rarely small players, and if you stick to the big ones, it isn't likely that they'll go away. If you can rely on YouTube, you should be able to rely on the likes of Flickr.

Another issue is loading time. If your image host is struggling to serve the images for some reason, your site will suffer for it. In the long run, I believe that images are more of what I like to call "direct content" than video, and that's why I tend to store and serve them locally whenever I can. If I really need to serve them from someplace else to keep a site up, I'll look into file servers and cloud solutions before relying solely on a third-party service.

However, this doesn't mean that I don't think about going the third-party route, and as a dedicated Flickr user, I sometimes use it as an image host. It is convenient and saves time as well as bandwidth and space. Despite all I've said so far, those are hard facts to argue with.

POSTING FROM FLICKR

Flickr (http://flickr.com) is probably the most popular photo-sharing site out there. It lets you upload photos for free, up to a limit, and if you want to upload more photos, you can purchase a pro account. It also works very well with blogs, and you can even share your Flickr photos (and those of others) directly to your blog. This is done in your account settings. WordPress is just one of many types of blogs to which Flickr can let you share photos. Follow these steps to share photos on your blog using Flickr:

1. Sign in to Flickr and go to the Your Account page.

2. Click the Sharing & Extending tab and then click the Edit link to the right of Your Blogs (see Figure 12-5).

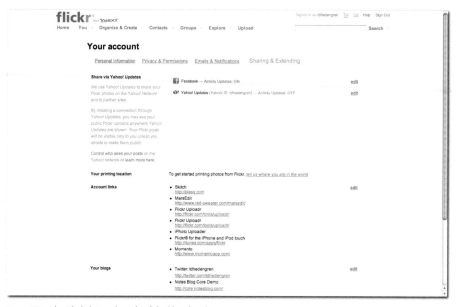

Figure 12-5: The Edit link is to the right of the blogs listed.

3. Add your WordPress blog by filling out the details (see Figure 12-6). You need to activate publishing by XML-RPC in your blog's admin interface, under Settings → Writing. The address you'll fill in on Flickr is the URL to xmlrpc.php, which resides in the root of your WordPress install.

4. Go through the guide and be sure to pick (and possibly edit) a default layout for the posts you'll publish from Flickr.

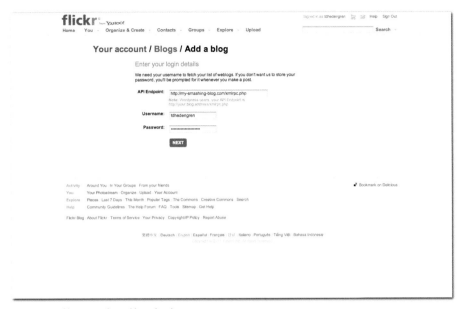

Figure 12-6: Add your WordPress blog's details.

That's it! Now you can send photos from Flickr directly to your blog. Find a photo you want to send, click the Share This link in the top right when viewing it, and then choose your blog under the Blog It tab. Unfortunately, you can't share all photos from Flickr this way; it all depends on the content owner's license as some licenses don't allow sharing.

Flickr is a commonly used tool not only for posting images, but also for saving traffic. By serving the images from Flickr, you won't strain your own server. Of course, it works both ways because if Flickr should go down (or out of business), your images will go down with it, so make sure that you've got backups of everything.

USING THE FLICKR SLIDE SHOW

If you're a dedicated Flickr user, you may be interested in embedding a Flickr slide show. Basically, this is a small Flash widget that you can put wherever you want on your site; you can even alter its size. You can get a slide show of anything grouped on Flickr, be it a full user's photostream or a set of photos. Naturally, the slide show will include only public photos.

Adding the slide show is easy. Just find the set or photostream you want to embed and click the Slideshow link at the top right (see Figure 12-7), next to the Share This link. If the Share This link is present, you can make the content into a slide show; if it's not, you can't — simple as that.

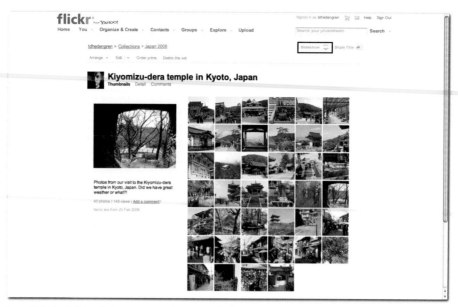

Figure 12-7: The Slideshow link is easy to miss, but it is usually there.

The slide show begins (see Figure 12-8). Click Share at the top right and then click the Customize This HTML link below the embed code. This will bring up a new window in which you can set the width and height that you want or pick a predefined width and height. Copy the embed code and paste it wherever you want.

Figure 12-8: Grab the embed code from the custom page rather than directly from the slide show to get more options.

So when is using a Flickr slide show useful? Sites can use it for coverage when they need to lean on Flickr's weight to get the message (and traffic!) across, but otherwise I'd say you're better off creating cool galleries instead. However, the slide show does indeed fulfill a purpose as an extension to everything else, as in putting a box in the side column showing off your latest exploits and such.

Other than that, the Flickr slide show is more of a novelty. To really put Flickr to good use, other than to serve static images, you have to dig a bit deeper. There is an API to play with (www.flickr.com/services/api), and the numerous plugins available can sometimes take things to a different level, depending on what you need from the service.

BEWARE OF THE CLUTTER

Images and other kinds of visual media are great to spice up a site, especially when you can use services such as Flickr and get nifty little widgets that show off your latest photos. Your visitors will enjoy the living elements you've added, and they all add value to the experience. At least that is the ideal usage; in the real world, a lot of this type of usage means clutter and breaking of the design.

My point is that you need to make sure you put these tools to good use, whether it is a random image element or your latest updates from Flickr. They need to make sense, just like every other element in a good design.

13 EXTRA FUNCTIONALITY

YOU CAN DO a ton of things with WordPress. This chapter is all about showing off some of the cool functionality you may want to use in a project or on a site. You'll take a look at tabbed boxes, login forms, doing stuff with RSS feeds, making WordPress print friendly, and more. Many of the elements described here can be used in myriad ways; because every site is different, your solution may very well vary a lot from the ideas presented here.

For each element described, I also explain when it is a good idea to use the technique and when you should forget about it. Between plugin expandability and the various features you can put in your theme, there are a great deal of options, and it is way too easy to clutter a site with items it just doesn't need. You should question every addition, even if it is hard to resist adding some cool features sometimes.

TABBED BOXES

Tabbed boxes are a great way to save some of that all-important screen real estate. On blogs and somewhat dynamic and living sites, tabbed boxes can be used to show off popular posts, recently commented posts, and similar elements that can be grouped together in a natural way. The key is to make sure that tabbed content that isn't shown by default doesn't always have to be visible. In fact, that's the key thing with tabbed boxes right there: Make sure that you don't hide something crucial on a tab.

Technically, tabbed boxes aren't very hard to create or manage. Some of them may not even look like boxes with tabs on them; it is more a type of functionality than anything else.

SMART USAGE

Creating the actual tabbed box functionality is easy enough, and there are tons of scripts available out there if you don't want to do it yourself. The code in the following example is simple enough for most cases, but it would also work well with some bling. After all, if you've decided to use a tabbed box, why not make it look really good and fit your design?

The following code relies on the jQuery JavaScript library, so you need to load that with `wp_enqueue_script()`, which I've covered previously. In this example, assume that jQuery is loaded. Here is the part that needs to be loaded in the head section of the theme, preferably in its own file and queued using `wp_enqueue_script()` from functions.php:

```
<script>
// Function to view tab
function viewTab(tabId) {
    // Get all child elements of "contents-container"
    var elements = jQuery('#contents-container').children();
    // Loop through them all
    jQuery.each(elements, function(index, value) {
        // Is clicked tab
        if (jQuery(this).attr('id') == tabId) {
            // Show element
            jQuery(this).css({ 'display':'block' });
            // Make sure CSS is correct for tab
            jQuery('#tab-'+ jQuery(this).attr('id')).addClass('active-tab');
        }
        // Is not the clicked tab
        else {
            // Hide tab
            jQuery(this).css({ 'display':'none' });
            // Make sure CSS is correct for tab
            jQuery('#tab-'+ jQuery(this).attr('id')).removeClass('active-tab');
        }
    });
}
</script>
```

If you just want to try this out, you can drop this code snippet in the head section of your header.php file, but please don't use it as such on a live site. JavaScript should be loaded from its own files.

Moving on, here's the basic markup for the actual tabbed box:

```
<ul id="tabs">
    <li id="tab-content-recent" class="active-tab">
        <a href="javascript:viewTab('content-recent');">Recent</a>
    </li>
    <li id="tab-content-popular">
        <a href="javascript:viewTab('content-popular');">Popular</a>
    </li>
    <li id="tab-content-comments">
        <a href="javascript:viewTab('content-comments');">Comments</a>
    </li>
</ul>
<div id="contents-container">
    <div id="content-recent">
        Content for Recent tab.
    </div>
    <div id="content-popular" style="display: none;">
        Content for Popular tab.
    </div>
    <div id="content-comments" style="display: none;">
        Content for Comments tab.
    </div>
</div>
```

You'll need to style this to look like the sort of tabbed box you want, which may not at all be a tabbed box but something entirely different. The key is that the links in the list items open a div container with the contents for the tab (or whatever) in question.

You could stop here, by putting the necessary code for Recent and Popular posts, as well as the latest comments, in the corresponding div. No big deal.

However, if you want to make this a little bit easier to manage, you can create a widget area for each tab's containing div, giving you the freedom to easily swap faulty functionality for a new plugin of your choice. If you want to do it that way, you need to widgetize a bit. Create a widget area by registering a sidebar per container, using register_sidebar() as described in Chapter 4, "WordPress Theme Essentials."

The following adds a fictional sidebar (which you would need to create in functions.php) per tab. The sidebars go in each containing div, respectively:

```
<ul id="tabs">
    <li id="tab-content-recent" class="active-tab">
        <a href="javascript:viewTab('content-recent');">Recent</a>
    </li>
```

```
    <li id="tab-content-popular">
        <a href="javascript:viewTab('content-popular');">Popular</a>
    </li>
    <li id="tab-content-comments">
        <a href="javascript:viewTab('content-comments');">Comments</a>
    </li>
</ul>
<div id="contents-container">
    <div id="content-recent">
        <!-- Recent tab widget area -->
        <?php dynamic_sidebar( 'Recent Posts' ); ?>
    </div>
    <div id="content-popular" style="display: none;">
        <!-- Popular tab widget area -->
        <?php dynamic_sidebar( 'Popular Posts' ); ?>
    </div>
    <div id="content-comments" style="display: none;">
        <!-- Comments tab widget area -->
        <?php dynamic_sidebar( 'Recent Comments' ); ?>
    </div>
</div>
```

Now you can just drop the contents for each tab in the widget area of your choice from within the WordPress admin interface, just like you would with your footer or sidebar widgets. The tabbed box could obviously be used for other features as well — not just for sidebars.

Figure 13-1 shows how a tabbed box can look with a few minor alterations to the preceding code.

TO TAB OR NOT TO TAB

So should you use a tabbed box or not? It all boils down to the kind of site and content you're dealing with. Most importantly, you need to make sure that the usage is intuitive and obvious for every possible kind of user. The content you hide away in tabs can't be crucial because the visitor may not be the clicking kind. Also, content in tabs can be entirely missed when you get an accidental visitor who scans the site briefly and then decides whether to stay and explore or move on elsewhere. You can't hide away your best stuff in tabs, just like you shouldn't make a menu or search box too obnoxious to actually use.

That being said, for a lot of sites, tabbed boxes can make sense. It's all about how much space you want to free up for listings of content, activity, and other things. Is there, for example, any real reason to show your blogroll all the time? Why not put all links in one tabbed box, having a tab for your social web profiles, another for friends' websites, and so on. That takes a lot less space, and anyone looking to delve deeper into your online presence or the friends and partners of a site can easily resort to using a tabbed box. The same user would also most likely appreciate the tabbed box whenever it isn't the focus of attention because it saves space and makes your site a lot easier to deal with.

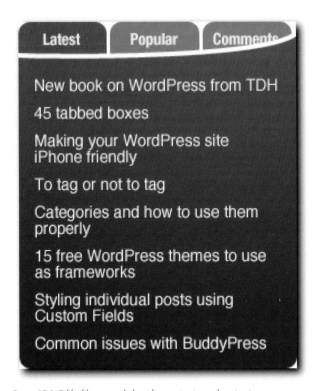

Figure 13-1: Tabbed boxes can help with organization and navigation.

Overall, you should be careful with tabbed boxes, and the same goes with tabbed menus. It is one extra click, and that can be annoying for the visitor. On the other hand, it's not so nice to clutter a site with lists and functions that are rarely used either, so use your best judgment.

DISPLAYING RSS FEEDS

RSS feeds are really useful — not only for subscribing to updates using a feed reader, but also for displaying content from partners or other projects you may be publishing online. You're probably already acquainted with the RSS feed widget that ships with WordPress; it can display updates from just about any working RSS feed.

When you want to work with feeds on your site, you're not limited to just that widget, or even any of the available plugins. You can, in fact, tap into the feed parser directly and hence do more custom stuff with the output from the feed. If you want to output the description, you can do so, just as you can add HTML code around the various elements to get more control and so on. If you want to do more advanced stuff with content from an RSS feed, you either need to rely on a plugin or code it yourself using the built-in functionality (which, incidentally, often is what the plugin you may be considering relies on in the first place!).

One thing worth thinking about, however, is that displaying RSS feeds can slow down your site. If you're fetching the latest updates from several sites (or even just one), you'll find that your site sometimes lags behind. That's because the feed is being queried from your server to the feed host's server, and the PHP needs to get all the data and parse it to be able to produce the output you want. This is true both for hardcoded RSS fetching and if you were putting a ton of RSS widgets on your site. If you rely on a lot of feed content, you should look into caching solutions to make your site as snappy as possible. In fact, ideally you'd let the server run a cron job at regular intervals and cache the content for you to output whenever needed. You could also use caching plugins (see Appendix A, "Essential WordPress Plugins," for some suggestions) or rely on the Transients API, which I'll get to in a little bit.

So, yeah, feeds are great and really useful, but if you browse the blogosphere (in particular) and pay close attention to what it is that slows down sites, you'll find that feed fetching is one of the culprits, along with other functionality that nabs content (be it badges or ads) from external services. Bottom line: Make sure that your site isn't too bogged down by RSS feed content.

THE BUILT-IN PARSER

WordPress includes built-in support for outputting RSS feed content on your site. You can use the feed widget (covered a bit later), but most likely, you want more control than that. Luckily, this is pretty easy to achieve, thanks to the addition of SimplePie in the core. That's right; there's a new feed parser in WordPress as of 2.8, which means that although your old `wp_rss()` calls may still work, they are outdated and should be changed to something more up to date — namely, `fetch_feed()`.

The SimplePie documentation may seem a bit daunting when you first delve into it. However, using SimplePie isn't that complicated at all. Here's a simple inclusion of the latest headlines, linked, from http://tdh.me:

```
<ul>
<li><h2>TDH.me</h2></li>
<?php $feed = fetch_feed( 'http://tdh.me' );
    foreach ( $feed->get_items() as $item ){
        printf( '<li><a href="%s">%s</a></li>', $item->get_permalink(),
            $item->get_title() );
    }
?>
</ul>
```

By including the feed like this, I'm opening it up for SimplePie functions. I'm basically looping the feed here and printing it, fetching the data as I go along. In this case, I'm just pulling the permalink and the title of every post. You can expand on that by adding the description and a date:

```
<ul>
<li><h2>TDH.me</h2></li>
<?php $feed = fetch_feed( 'http://tdh.me' );
    printf( $feed->get_title() );
    foreach ( $feed->get_items() as $item ){
```

```
        printf( '<li><a href="%s">%s</a></li>', $item->get_permalink(),
          $item->get_title() );
        printf( '<p>%s</p>', $item->get_description() );
        printf( '<p><small>%s</small></p>', $item->get_date('j F Y at g:i a') );
    }
?>
</ul>
```

SimplePie is huge — worthy of a book of its own. What you need to know is available in the SimplePie documentation, which unfortunately isn't entirely compatible with WordPress because it is a standalone RSS parser, really. That being said, you should take a look at http://simplepie.org/wiki.

I'll return to SimplePie in a little bit. But first, some words about the Transients API.

CACHING WITH THE TRANSIENTS API

Waiting for RSS feeds to deliver content can make a site feel sluggish, so why not cache the content? There are plugins that can do this, but this is as good a time as any to talk about the Transients API. This is a very useful tool if you need to store temporary data in the database. You can read more about the Transients API in the Codex at http://codex.wordpress.org/Transients_API.

The RSS feed example from the previous subsection is a perfect example of content that could be stored temporarily in the database. Here, you'll use `get_transient()` to first check to see whether there is any stored content you can output and `set_transient()` to save the content when it is appropriate. After all, the cache is supposed to be temporary, so you'll want it to replace the old content every now and then. This is a major difference between the Transients API and the Options API — the ability to set a expiration date to the stored content.

Take a look at how the code from the previous example could utilize the Transients API:

```
<ul>
<li><h2>TDH.me</h2></li>

<?php
// Try to fetch from cache
if ( ! ( $feed = get_transient( 'smashing_feedcache' ) ) ) {
    // No cache - Fetch and store
    $feed_obj = fetch_feed( 'http://tdh.me' );
    $feed = array();
    $feed['title'] = $feed_obj->get_title();
    $feed['items'] = array();
    foreach ( $feed_obj->get_items() as $item ){
        // Store feed contents as an array
        $feed['items'][] = array(
            'permalink' => $item->get_permalink(),
```

```
                'title' => $item->get_title(),
                'description' => $item->get_description(),
                'date' => $item->get_date('j F Y at g:i a')
            );

        }
        // Store for an hour
        set_transient( 'smashing_feedcache', $feed, ( 60*60 ) );
    }
    // Output
    foreach ( $feed['items'] as $item ) {
        printf( '<li><a href="%s">%s</a></li>', $item['permalink'], $item['title'] );
        printf( '<p>%s</p>', $item['description'] );
        printf( '<p><small>%s</small></p>', $item['date'] );
    } ?>
</ul>
```

The first check is to see if there is something stored in the database that you want to return, using `get_transient()` to look for data associated with `smashing_feedcache`. Failing that, you'll fetch the feed data as an array using `fetch_feed()`. Finally, you'll store this data with `set_transient()` and set the expiration time (60 minutes X 60 seconds). The output then takes the data from the array you stored in the database and outputs it.

WHEN TO USE THE WIDGET SOLUTION

So when would you want to use the default built-in RSS widget? The answer is simple: Never! This may sound a bit harsh, especially because what the widget really does is the same as what you did in the preceding section with `fetch_feed()`. That's right; the widget calls SimplePie in the same way.

The problem is, it also slaps on a feed header, linked to the feed URL and everything. That's not really such a good idea, now is it? If you want to display the latest updates from your blog, a news site, Twitter, or whatever, you don't want to link the actual RSS feed at the top of the listing! You may want to link the site itself, but not the feed. I'm hoping this is something that will be changed in WordPress in the future, but it's been around for some time now.

So should you never use a feed widget? That's taking it a bit far because others have realized this problem and released plugins that remedy the situation. Refer to Appendix A for some cool RSS plugins that may achieve what you're after.

In fact, hacking the RSS parsing code yourself should be avoided unless you need to do really funky stuff. It is better to add a widget area and then add an appropriate feed widget. That means you can easily add stuff around it, too, but naturally you have a lot more control if you code the whole thing yourself. As is generally the case, pick the solution that fits your project.

MULTIPLE FEEDS WITH SIMPLEPIE

With the addition of SimplePie, you get the power of multiple feeds, and I'm not talking about the capability to display several feed blocks on the same page. No, I mean the ability to take a bunch of feeds and then mash them together and present the content. In SimplePie, this functionality is often referred to as *multifeeds* (a useful thing to know when looking for solutions in the SimplePie documentation).

In the following example, you'll put SimplePie to a quick test by taking two feeds and listing them depending on date, but limiting the output to show just ten items:

```
<ul>
<Li><h2>Interesting Headlines</h2></li>
<?php $feed = fetch_feed( array( 'http://rss1.smashingmagazine.com/feed/',
  'http://feeds.digg.com/digg/topic/apple/popular.rss' ) );
    $feed->enable_order_by_date( true );
    foreach ( $feed->get_items(0, 9) as $item ){
        printf( '<li><a href="%s">%s</a></li>', $item->get_permalink(),
          $item->get_title() );
        printf( '<p><small>%s</small></p>', $item->get_date('j F Y at g:i a') );
    }
?>
</ul>
```

In this, you're defining the two feeds in an array within `fetch_feed()` rather than just putting the single feed URL in there as you did when you just wanted a single feed output. You can add several more feeds to this in the same spirit if you want to. After that, an `order_by_date` setting is added, acquired from the SimplePie documentation:

```
$feed->enable_order_by_date( true );
```

This could just as well have been in the single feed example, but if you just output a single feed, you can probably rely on the fact that the latest item will come at the top, so it would be a bit redundant.

After that, there's the `foreach` loop again, starting at the first item (`0`) and moving onward to the tenth (`9`), after which the loop is over; hence, you get ten items.

Again, SimplePie is huge, but this is a start at least. At the time of writing, the help section in the WordPress Codex is pretty scarcely populated given that `fetch_feed()` was added in version 2.8, but I'm sure it will be completed with more examples as time goes on. Meanwhile, turn to the SimplePie documentation for an extensive look at what you can do with this RSS parser. You'll most likely want to look at caching solutions here as well.

CUSTOM SHORTCODES

Shortcode is tagged code that you can input in your posts to output something specific. The `[gallery]` tag is shortcode. You can create your own shortcode, which can come in handy when using WordPress, particularly when you're doing nonbloggish things with it.

ADDING SHORTCODES

You can add shortcode functionality through a plugin or by using functions.php:

1. Start by creating a simple shortcode tag that outputs some simple text; you'll put it to more interesting use later.

2. Next, you need a function that does what you want, written within the PHP tags of functions.php, of course:

```
function smashing_text_example() {
    return 'Why, this text was just outputted using the shortcode tag you
        created! Smashing.';
}
```

3. Now you need to assign `smashing_text_example()` to a shortcode. You do that with the `add_shortcode()` function:

```
add_shortcode( 'textftw', 'smashing_text_example' );
```

This creates the `[textftw]` shortcode and loads it with the contents of the `smashing_text_example()` function. So `[textftw]` in your blog post will output in your post, "Why, this text was just outputted using the shortcode tag you created! Smashing."

Simple enough. Now do something useful with it, such as making a shortcode for promoting your RSS feed:

4. Starting with the function, this time you'll use it to output some HTML code as well, which gives you control of how the promotion appears:

```
function smashing_rss_promotion() {
    return '<div class="rsspromo">Never miss a beat - <a href="http://
        tdh.me/feed/">subscribe to the RSS feed!</a></div>';
}
```

5. Next, you need to create the shortcode and add the `smashing_rss_promotion()` function content to it:

```
add_shortcode( 'rsspromo', 'smashing_rss_promotion' );
```

6. Now you've got the `[rsspromo]` shortcode that outputs the `div` container from the `smashing_rss_promotion()` function. All you have to do to wrap this up is add some styling to the style.css style sheet — maybe something like this:

```
div.rsspromo {
    background: #eee;
    Border: 1px solid #bbb;
    color: #444;
    font-size: 16px;
    font-style: italic; }

div.rsspromo a {
    font-weight:bold;
    font-style:normal; }
```

You can use whatever styling fits your design.

Now you can add an RSS promotion box anywhere you like, using the `[rsspromo]` shortcode. Another idea using the same approach would be to add e-mail subscription forms. And why not load a function with your default ad code? That way, you can easily change it should you get a better deal/click ratio somewhere else.

SHORTCODE TIDBITS

You may be wondering if nested shortcode works. It does, and you can put one shortcode tag inside another as long as you open and close them properly, just like HTML. For example, this will work:

```
[shortcode-1]
    [shortcode-2]
    [/shortcode-2]
[/shortcode-1]
```

But the following would probably break and give you funky results:

```
[shortcode-1]
    [shortcode-2]
[/shortcode-1]
    [/shortcode-2]
```

However, for the first snippet to work, you have to allow shortcode within your shortcode by using `do_shortcode()`. So if you have a simple `[pull]` shortcode to create simple pullquotes, you'd have to put `$content` within `do_shortcode()`, like this:

```
function pullquote( $atts, $content = null ) {
    extract(shortcode_atts(array(
        'float' => '$align',
    ), $atts));
   return '<blockquote class="pullquote ' . $float . '">' .
     do_shortcode($content) . '</blockquote>';
}
add_shortcode( 'pull', 'pullquote' );
```

Otherwise, any shortcode placed between `[pull]` and `[/pull]` wouldn't be properly parsed.

Remember, shortcode works only within content, not in headers or even excerpts. It is tied to the `the_content()` template tag. However, you can make it work by using the `do_shortcode()` function and adding a filter. It may be a good idea to at least add shortcode support to widget areas, if you intend to do impressive stuff with them. After all, that text widget can be mighty handy.

The following code in your functions.php file or in a plugin will add shortcode support to the default text widget:

```
add_filter( 'widget_text', 'do_shortcode' );
```

It applies the `do_shortcode()` function to the `widget_text()` function as a filter (with `add_filter()`, obviously). Simple, just the way I like it!

The Shortcode API is actually pretty extensive. You can read up on it in the WordPress Codex at http://codex.wordpress.org/Shortcode_API if you want more information.

Using shortcodes is a great way to let users add both features and functionality to their content. However, sometimes you need to go outside the obvious design elements (be they widgets or loop hacks) and the content itself, especially if the website in question needs to promote other services.

> *Don't forget that shortcode content needs to work when themes are changed as well. Consult Chapter 8, "Plugins or functions.php?," for some options on how to make these features portable across themes.*

SENDING E-MAIL WITH WORDPRESS

If you want to have WordPress send e-mails for you, you can use the `wp_mail()` function. This can be anything from a verification for some action that you want to confirm went through (or didn't) on your site to building a full "My blog has been updated!" notification list.

The `wp_mail()` function is easy enough to use. The following code snippet would, assuming that you activate it with a function of some sort, send an e-mail to smashing@domain.com with the subject "Smashing Party!" and the content (in text format) "Thanks for the smashing party the other night. TTFN!" Figure 13-2 displays the result.

```
wp_mail( 'smashing@domain.com', 'Smashing Party!', 'Thanks for the smashing
party the other night. TTFN!' );
```

You can even attach files and use the HTML format rather than the default plain text. There's more on this in the Codex at http://codex.wordpress.org/Function_Reference/wp_mail.

When working with `wp_email()`, you obviously need to do something. Perhaps you want to send a welcome e-mail to newly registered users, using the `user_register` hook, for example.

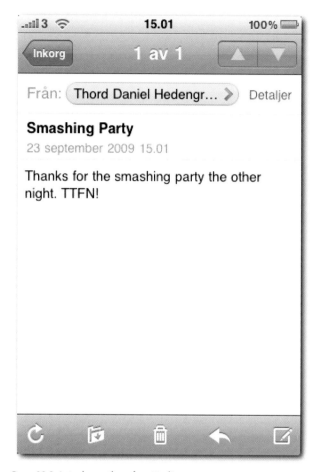

Figure 13-2: A simple e-mail sent from WordPress.

As always when sending e-mail from web pages, there are a few things to observe:

- Don't spam people. That's bad form and evil.
- Beware of e-mailing too much. That can get you blacklisted.
- Make sure that your code works. After all, an unintended hiccup can send hundreds of duplicate messages, bringing your server to its knees and getting you into all kinds of trouble.
- Prevent exploits. Make sure that some nasty person won't be able to spam through your e-mailing solution. This could be anything from just shooting random e-mails to the left and right, to just being a pain by pumping that submit button a thousand times.
- Tell everything. Users like to know what's going on, especially when there are e-mail addresses involved. In other words, be sure to explain how you will use their e-mail address and what they can expect from you. When it comes to e-mail, no surprises is a good thing.

ADDING A LOGIN FORM

Sometimes it can be prudent to have the WordPress login form (see Figure 13-3) a little more handy than just on its own page as it is by default (on wp-login.php, from your WordPress install's point of view). If your site relies on user features that require logins, naturally there is no harm in adding a login form to, say, the sidebar or the header.

Figure 13-3: A simple login form.

The following example assumes that you want to put the login form in the sidebar, which usually is a `ul` itself, so the code would go in an `li` of its own. However, you may want it in the header instead, or someplace else, in which case you probably should put it in a `div` so that you can style it accordingly. All you need for the actual login form is `wp_login_form()`.

```php
<?php if ( !( is_user_logged_in() ) ){ ?>
<h2>Login</h2>
<?php wp_login_form(); ?>
<p>
    Lost your password? <a href="<?php echo home_url( '/wp-login.php?
      action=lostpassword' ); ?>">Recover!</a>
</p>
<?php } else { ?>
<h2>Admin</h2>
<ul>
    <li>
        <a href="<?php echo admin_url(); ?>">Dashboard</a>
    </li>
    <li>
        <a href="<?php echo admin_url( 'post-new.php' ); ?>">Write a
          post</a>
    </li>
    <li>
        <a href="<?php echo wp_logout_url( urlencode( $_SERVER['REQUEST_URI'] ) );
          ?>">Logout</a>
    </li>
</ul>
<?php }?>
```

What you have here is an `if` clause checking first to see if you're logged in, or rather, if you're a user with the role of `contributor` or higher. By echoing `admin_url()`, you get the correct link, appending post-new.php by passing it as a parameter in the second link. The same principle goes for when `home_url()` is not logged in, pointing to the password recovery page.

> *You can read up on roles in the Codex at http://codex.wordpress.org/ Roles_and_Capabilities.*

So the first check is to see if you're a logged-in user, basically, and if you're not, the site will display the login form using `wp_login_form()`. There are some settings for the `wp_login_form()` template tags, for what labels should be called, where the user should end up after login, and things like that. They are straightforward enough, but you can learn more from the Codex at http://codex.wordpress.org/Function_Reference/wp_login_form.

Moving on, the `else` clause is what is displayed when a user is actually logged in. In this example, you output a list with a link to the Dashboard in wp-admin, along with another to the Write Post screen, and finally a logout link. This might be a bit redundant unless you have disabled the WordPress admin bar that shows up on top for logged-in users.

Remember, don't put login forms in your designs unless they serve a purpose. After all, why show off a login form and tease those nasty brute forcers to abuse your WordPress install if you don't have to? Also, there is no point in showing off a login form if the visitor can't put it to good use, as that's just poor use of screen real estate. Make the login forms count.

PRINT THAT BLOG

Sometimes readers prefer to print an article or blog entry on paper for convenience. You should make printing easy, if your site is the kind that would benefit from it.

Start with adding a simple Print This Page link. This is easily done with a little JavaScript; no extra custom stuff or enqueuing of script libraries is needed:

```
<a href="javascript:window.print()" rel="nofollow">Print This Page</a>
```

That's it; the browser will try and print the page. It's simple enough, though your site may not be all that print-friendly, especially if you have a big, fancy header and lots of columns. That's why you need to create a print style sheet. Technically, you don't really have to add another style sheet, but it may be a good idea to separate print-only things from the regular screen stuff.

First, create a style sheet called print.css and look over your theme for what should or should not be included. Most likely, your sidebar and footer will be unnecessary when printing, so remove them:

```
#sidebar, #footer { display: none; }
```

Gone! At least, assuming that the sidebar has the ID `#sidebar`, and the footer has `#footer`, which they usually do.

Now, make sure that the actual content looks decent enough on paper:

```
#content {
    width:100%;
    margin:0;
    padding:0;
    float:none;
    background: #fff;
    color: #222; }

a:link, a:visited { color: #000; }
```

Almost black text, white background, full width, and no floating or weird margins or padding — that will do it. I also added code to make sure that the links are black (no need for the `:active` or `:hover` pseudo-classes, obviously).

I could go on forever on stuff to put in your print style sheet. You may want to make sure that headings look decent, and perhaps you don't want to have those 637 comments you've got on every post printed, either. Just hide the elements you don't want on paper and style the others. It is as simple as that. You may also want to set all font sizes to points (`pt`) rather than pixels or em because that is talk the printer can understand. Also, speaking of printing, consider adding page-break styling to headings, and possibly also elements such as block quotes and lists. It all depends on how you want to present your site in printed form.

The only thing that remains is to include the style sheet, preferably by using `wp_enqueue_style()` and the `wp_enqueue_scripts` hook in functions.php:

```
add_action( 'wp_enqueue_scripts', 'smashing_printstyle' );
function smashing_printstyle() {
    // Register stylesheet
    wp_register_style( 'printstyle', get_template_directory_uri() .
      '/print.css', array(), false, 'print' );
    // Queue the stylesheet
    wp_enqueue_style( 'printstyle' );
}
```

First, you register the style sheet using `wp_register_style()` so that you can get to it easily, and then you queue it up using `wp_enqueue_style()` with the registered handle from `wp_register_style()`. There's no need to add the style sheet to header.php, thanks to the `wp_enqueue_scripts` hook.

There are several solutions for making it even easier to print your pages. One that I've found is pretty nice is PrintFriendly (www.printfriendly.com), which lets you add buttons in a jiffy. There's also a plugin that can help out. If you want to save time, check out PrintFriendly for more info, especially this page: www.printfriendly. com/button.

AND EVEN MORE . . .

Expanding a site with necessary functionality is a natural and obvious step in its development. When it comes to WordPress, expanding a site often means that you want to show off or promote content in some way or add possibilities for interactions, such as the login form.

To top this off, the next chapter, "Uncommon WordPress Usage," shows you some more uncommon stuff that you can do with WordPress. It is not all blogs and traditional websites; after all, WordPress can do so much more. Chapter 14 is all about getting your mind going with the possibilities of this fantastic publishing platform.

14 UNCOMMON WORDPRESS USAGE

YOU ALREADY KNOW that WordPress can power blogs as well as other editorial sites. You can use it for static websites, newspaper or magazine-like sites, and just about anything for which you are publishing text, images, or any kind of multimedia.

But why stop there? WordPress can be used for projects even further from its bloggish roots, as this chapter will show. You can build sites on top of WordPress that the developers definitely didn't have in mind from the start. Hopefully, the adaptations of the platform discussed here will help you see the full potential of the system. You'll see how WordPress can be used to create a job board or as a FAQ and/or knowledge base, how you can add a product directory, how to use WordPress for eCommerce, and a lot more. There are so many things you can do with WordPress, and I hope that this chapter will be an inspiration to you and get your brain started on what you can do with this wonderful publishing platform.

WORKING WITH USER-SUBMITTED CONTENT

Just because WordPress is great as a CMS for sites, big or small, you're not limited to using it for just that. You can have your users submit content beyond comments and then do things with that alongside your regular content. Either you separate the user-submitted content from the rest, or you mix and match with whatever type of content you're producing yourself.

Technically, you need to have your users register to submit content using WordPress's standard features. A popular theme that does that out of the box is the P2 theme, found at http://wordpress.org/extend/themes/p2 and shown in Figure 14-1, which is inspired by Twitter and actually used for internal communication at a number of companies, Automattic included.

Figure 14-1: WPDevel, the official blog of the WordPress core development team, uses the P2 theme.

To demonstrate how you can work with user-submitted content, I'll discuss some possible scenarios in which you can benefit from it and how to manage it. But first, consider the usability factor. Although the WordPress admin area is simple enough to navigate, it still can be a threshold for some users. By adding posting features to the front end, you can get around this problem, at least for contributors of straightforward content.

RECEIVING GUEST POSTS

If you ever wanted to invite guest posters to your blog, and really want it on a regular basis, then it might be a good idea to create a page with a form for submitting guest posts. This is as simple as it gets, thanks to several plugins. For example, you could use the Post From Site (http://wordpress.org/extend/plugins/post-from-site) plugin, which makes it easy to add a simple post form as a widget or using a shortcode. Figure 14-2 shows the Post From Site post form in action on a Page, using the `[post-from-site]` shortcode.

Figure 14-2: Let your users submit guest posts with the Post From Site plugin.

The Post From Site plugin is a pretty good example of how you can receive user content on any WordPress site. Although it is simple in itself, you do have a bunch of options from which to choose. For example, you can choose to have the posts saved as drafts in a specific post type with comments enabled and even let the user upload an image. Ideally, you'll have your users register, obviously, but you could also have all posts attached to a specific user and enable anonymous posting if that fits your needs. Figure 14-3 shows the Settings page so that you'll get an idea of what you're dealing with here. As you can see, it is pretty straightforward stuff.

Figure 14-3: The Post From Site Settings page.

The thing to take from this fairly simple plugin is the possibilities it offers. There are more advanced options, and sometimes you need them; or you might even need to create your own solution, but plugins like this can get you a long way. Way beyond receiving simple guest posts, actually.

HANDLING USER NEWS AND REVIEWS

One of the most obvious uses of user-submitted content is user news and reviews. By letting your visitors submit news posts and reviews, you get additional content and can add another dimension to your site. This might or might not be a good idea, depending on what kind of site you're running. A product-oriented blog might benefit from user reviews, and a celebrity site could really thrive if your users sent in celebrity sightings, for example. There are tons of uses.

Technically, you might be able to get away with the Post From Site plugin mentioned previously, but chances are you need something slightly more advanced. If you intend to receive reviews, you probably need a solution that works with whatever scale you're grading the products in, for example. Serious news sites need a way to credit sources for news submissions, if you intend to let your readers submit actual news copy and not just news tips.

A possible solution would be the One Quick Post plugin (http://wordpress.org/extend/plugins/one-quick-post), which lets you create a widget from which you can have your users write posts. This means that you might need to add a widget area to your theme that is wide enough to work well with this plugin, again depending on your needs. Figure 14-4 shows the plugin in action on the Twenty Eleven theme, looking a bit crowded in the sidebar there.

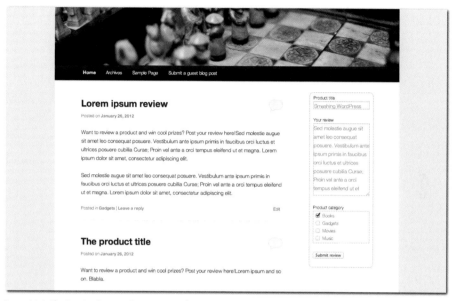

Figure 14-4: The One Quick Post widget in Twenty Eleven.

The One Quick Post plugin has a lot more options than the Post From Site plugin. In fact, it almost gets a bit ridiculous when you configure your widgets because there are so many things to tweak. Everything sits in the widget, which is fine because this means that you can have several widgets on the same site without having to struggle with a Settings page and create the post forms there. It also means that your settings will be saved with the widget in the database, which might be handy. Just so you'll get an idea what I'm talking about, take a look at Figure 14-5, which shows the settings for the same widget seen in Figure 14-4.

Despite the minor nuisance of setting up each widget, which obviously has default values so that you might not need to change a lot if anything, and the lack of a shortcode and such for inclusion on Pages, the One Quick Post plugin is a great tool. You have a lot of options such as what categories should be allowed, if guest posting from unregistered visitors should be allowed or custom fields, and whether a pop-over visual editor should be allowed. That's just a few of the settings available here. You can even easily override the default CSS directly in the widget, enable CAPTCHA to prevent spam, and send e-mails when a post is published. Some of these features are available in the Post From Site plugin as well, but I still find that One Quick Post is a bit more versatile, albeit perhaps overkill at times.

Using One Quick Post, you can easily create a Page containing two columns with a widget area in each (or a full-width column with the widgets at 50% width, floating beside each other, if you prefer) and have your users submit the news or reviews you've been craving.

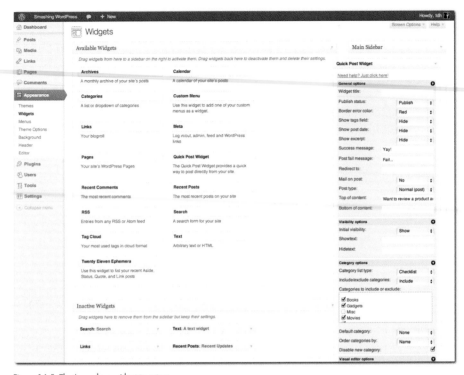

Figure 14-5: That's one long widget to set up.

ROLLING A BOOTSTRAPPED JOB BOARD

So far, this chapter has covered user-submitted content that is some sort of editorial content. But what if you want to do something completely different, such as a job board? We've all seen job boards, and regardless of the shape and size, the core functionality is the same. You post about a job, sometime paying a fee for the exposure. Then people who are looking for work or looking to hire, depending on what you posted, will hopefully see the ad and react to it. Again, possibly for a fee.

You could build this with WordPress. In fact, it isn't even particularly complicated. Theoretically, it could be regular posts, categorized as "Looking for Work" and "Hiring," with a bit of tagging for a more fine-tuned search. Then you add a title, possibly an excerpt, and the actual ad copy, and you're done. List it with regular category archives. The only problem here, for this core functionality, is to get the jobs submitted.

I'm sure that you see where I'm going with this. This whole functionality could be made available to users using either of the two plugins mentioned earlier (but One Quick Post is probably the better choice). All you really need to do is design a site around this, displaying the content in a favorable way.

You could take it a bit further than this, though. If you want to charge for the job ads, you would need to get that part in there. There are some commercial plugins that can help you with that, and there are also some plugins meant for classifieds, such as Your Classified Ads (http://wordpress.org/extend/plugins/your-classified-ads), created by G. Breant, the same person who did One Quick Post. This is where it can get a bit muddy because it all depends on your business idea, but what you could do to just get started — this is a bootstrapped project, after all — is just make sure that jobs received are saved as drafts. Then you'll bill the advertiser using PayPal or something similar, and when paid, you'll manually publish the post. It's not ideal, but it works, especially if you want to make sure that you get quality ads on your site. For sites that process more information, you'll want something more automatic, so in that case you'll either have to search for a plugin that'll help you — again, there are commercial alternatives that might help — or write some code yourself. It all depends on what setup you're after and what sort of site you're building. Maybe you just want to charge for additional exposure of ads; that would mean that you'd sell ads the traditional way instead of charging on a per-ad basis. Lots of possibilities here.

USING WP_EDITOR()

With the help of `wp_editor()`, you can actually get the post editor working on your site. This isn't really something you should be adding to any of the sites previously discussed, but you could use it in a plugin much like the ones mentioned. Outputting `wp_editor()` is easy enough; just throw it in a Page template (or any template you can visit) and take a look for yourself. Here's an example code snippet for you:

```
wp_editor( 'Please write your recipe here!', 'submitrecipe' );
```

This will output an editor box with the default settings. The first parameter is the text that populates the box from the start, and the second is the ID of the box, which has to be in lowercase without any dashes or underscores to make sure that TinyMCE (the visual editor used by WordPress) behaves. Figure 14-6 shows the box you get from this simple code snippet; this should look familiar, as it is just pasted in a simple Page template for Twenty Eleven.

There's not too much you can do here, though — no Save button or anything. You need to add a form and do something with the data to actually put `wp_editor()` to proper use. So if you want to create a really fancy front-end post form, you're better off creating a plugin employing `wp_editor()` well, along with nonces (you can read more about those at http://codex. wordpress.org/Wordpress_Nonce_Implementation) to make it a bit harder to abuse the form.

Most likely, you're better off with any of the aforementioned plugins, but knowing that `wp_editor()` is there to help you create cool stuff using the familiar post editor could come in handy. You can read more about `wp_editor()` and its parameters in the Codex at http:// codex.wordpress.org/Function_Reference/wp_editor.

Figure 14-6: `wp_editor()` in action.

A FINAL WORD ABOUT USER-SUBMITTED CONTENT

User-submitted content isn't all gold and glory. At best, you'll get a lot of great content that will boost your site, but that might not be the case. You might end up with a lot of spam or just plain lousy content. Quite possibly, you will have to approve content before it ends up on your site, which will take time, much like moderating comments does.

User-submitted content can be a great thing. Just make sure that you know how you'll work with it and how you'll keep it under control if your site gets flooded with content in some fashion.

USING WORDPRESS AS A FAQ-LIKE KNOWLEDGE BASE

Companies that want their very own FAQ-like knowledge base can put WordPress to good use. The concept is really quite simple, revolving around user-submitted posts as well as tagging and categories. Thanks to commenting, there can be a conversation around an issue that a user submits, and when it is resolved, the administrator can move it to the knowledge base part of the site.

Here are the key features:

- User-submitted issues using a plugin; each issue is in fact a post.
- Two main categories: the FAQ and the Knowledge Base.
- Tagging of posts (which are the issues, remember) to make keyword searching easier.
- A custom tagging taxonomy for the Knowledge Base.

The site usage flow would be as follows:

1. A user submits an issue using a form on the site. The issue is saved as a post and marked as a draft by using a plugin.
2. An administrator publishes the issue in the FAQ category.
3. The issue can now be commented on. If an administrator answers, his or her comments will be highlighted, but it is possible to let anyone answer should you want that. If you turn off user comments, you need to attach some way for the original submitter of the issue to ask for follow-ups without having to resubmit a new issue each time.
4. When the issue is resolved, an administrator adds the post to the Knowledge Base category.
5. All posts in the Knowledge Base category get proper tagging in the Knowledge Base Tagging custom taxonomy. This means that you can output a tag cloud (or whatever) based only on tags from within the Knowledge Base.

The point of the custom Knowledge Base Tagging taxonomy is so that the users can browse issues that have been resolved to find solutions to their specific problems. It works alongside the standard tagging feature, which also includes FAQ posts and hence unresolved issues. This can also come in handy.

In addition, there's category browsing, which means that it is really easy to create these two sections — the FAQ and the Knowledge Base — of the site.

If you already run your website on WordPress and want to add this type of functionality, you wouldn't want to use the standard `post` post type, but rather create a new post type just for the knowledge base. Custom post types are covered in Chapter 6, "Advanced Theme Usage," and also later in this chapter, and you should have no problem tweaking this example for that should you want to. I'll leave it at that for now.

ADDING THE FUNCTIONALITY

The actual design of the theme in the following example will be simple enough, so I'll stick to the important parts. You can build it on top of just about any theme you like. First, you need to build your new taxonomy. You can read more about that in Chapter 6; this is the code you'll be using. Now, you could put this code in your functions.php file for your theme (no matter if it is a child theme or a parent theme), but ideally it should be in a plugin to make sure that the data stays portable. You can read more about data portability in Chapter 8, "Plugins or functions.php?."

```
add_action( 'init', 'kbase', 0 );

function kbase() {
    register_taxonomy( 'knowledge_base', 'post',
        array(
            'hierarchical' => false,
            'labels' => array(
```

```
                    'name' => 'Knowledge Base Tags',
                    'singular_name' => 'Knowledge Base Tags',
                    'search_items' => 'Search Knowledge Base Tags',
                    'popular_items' => 'Popular Knowledge Base Tags',
                    'add_new_item' => 'Add New Knowledge Base Tags'
            ),
            'query_var' => true,
            'rewrite' => true
        )
    );
}
```

That's it. Now you'll get another tag field in the WordPress admin interface to tag away on any post you like (see Figure 14-7).You will just do this on posts marked with Knowledge Base status, as described previously.

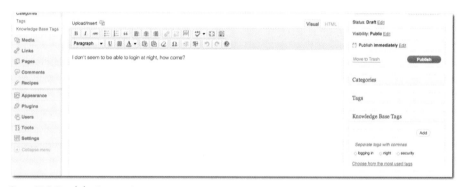

Figure 14-7: Knowledge Base tagging.

With the taxonomy set up, the next step is to start receiving issues. Several solutions on how to receive user-submitted content were covered earlier, so I'll skip that here. You may want to create a home.php template for featuring the most recent submissions and additions to the Knowledge Base (which would just show the latest posts in that particular category) and also either to promote or offer the submit issue form. Personally, I'd add a huge search box as well as a tag cloud showing the hottest tags from the Knowledge Base taxonomy. The latter is done by passing the taxonomy name to `wp_tag_cloud()`, like this:

```php
<?php
    $args = array(
        'taxonomy' => 'knowledge_base'
    )
    wp_tag_cloud( $args );
?>
```

The taxonomy parameter reads the name, not the label, of your custom taxonomy. Style the tag cloud accordingly, and you'll have a series of keywords belonging only to the Knowledge Base taxonomy, which in turn means that only issues that have been resolved will appear.

That's about it, really. After adding the submission part, along with the taxonomy, the rest is just about displaying the latest posts from each respective category and trying to get the users to actually search for an issue before submitting it again.

INCLUDING FURTHER ENHANCEMENTS

Although it is easy to get a FAQ/Knowledge Base site rolling on top of WordPress, there are many ways to make it better. The first step is to make sure that the users understand they should search and browse the site before submitting an issue; otherwise, you'll likely end up with a great deal of duplication. You want your visitors to search, and that means pushing for that functionality. Unfortunately, if WordPress is weak in one area, it is search, so you may want to consider using an external service such as Google Custom Search (http://google.com/cse) or a similar variant that can be easily embedded into your site to add search functionality. There are also a bunch of plugins to enhance search, so you should play with those as well. Consult Appendix A, "Essential WordPress Plugins," if you don't have a favorite already.

Here are some other ideas on enhancements to this setup:

- Registration and editing: Let people register so that they can edit their own questions, get an author archive, and so on. You may even want to force it to make spamming a bit harder.

- A custom post type: If you need to implement this solution into an existing site, you would be well advised to use a custom post type for it instead of relying on regular posts. This method would be just as easy, as you'll see later in this chapter in the section "Building a Product Directory."

- Grading: Let the users grade your answers, in the comments when the post is in FAQ mode and with the actual resolution of the issue when it has moved to the Knowledge Base. In the latter case, you need a plugin that offers grading of the post rather than the comments. Appendix A offers some suggestions.

- Related issues: Expose other issues automatically by using a related posts plugin. The user may find an answer through that route.

- Further search enhancements: With the use of JavaScript, you can make it easier for users to find the answer to common issues. Use the type of search fields that ask you if you meant "XYZ" when you typed "XPT."

- Front page tweaks: The better you can expose issues, the faster users will find them, and because that's what it's all about, you should tweak the front page as much as you possibly can.

- Subscriptions and alerts: Offer ways to subscribe to updates and resolved issues. There are several ways to manage this, and because WordPress has an RSS feed for just about anything, I'm sure the answer is there. Make sure that your users know and understand that, so they can subscribe to things that interest them.

The knowledge base concept is another way you can use WordPress for a nonbloggish site. Another way is using WordPress to power an online store.

WORDPRESS AND ECOMMERCE

It goes without saying that WordPress can be used to sell stuff. Using its simplest form, you'll run a blog or traditional site with WordPress as the back end and use your reach to sell products. You can add *affiliate links,* which basically means that whenever you link to Amazon (for example) using your affiliate URL and someone buys something, you'll get a provision. In fact, if you bought this book by following a link from any of my sites, I made a little extra. Thanks!

However, when most of us are thinking "eCommerce," we've got bigger things than affiliate links in mind — shopping carts, digital distribution, payment received via PayPal accounts — that sort of thing.

You can certainly have all this, and Appendix A includes a bunch of plugin suggestions that can make such things easier to implement, from simple integrations to full shopping carts.

RUNNING A WEB SHOP ON WORDPRESS

You may be wondering if you can run a web shop on WordPress. In short, the answer is yes; you *could* if you wanted to, and if you didn't have too many products.

The long version: It's probably not simple to implement a shopping site, but don't let that stop you; there's really no reason why it shouldn't work perfectly well if you're prepared to extend WordPress with plugins, work with custom fields, and then figure out how to connect your shopping cart with PayPal and other payment solutions.

Kind of disheartening, isn't it? Relax, it's not as bad as it sounds: There are plugins out there that do most of the work for you. However, compared to the other eCommerce systems, most available plugins are on the simple side. You should definitely do a serious assessment of your eCommerce needs and then pick the solution that works for you. This means that you might use WordPress, or you might use one of the dedicated open source eCommerce platforms available. Get all the facts and decide.

One of the strengths of WordPress as an alternative is that chances are you have a site already, and there's nothing stopping you from attaching any of the various shopping cart scripts out there right into your theme. Most will probably work with minor hassle, and that would leave you only with the discomfort of figuring out how to charge for your merchandise. Luckily, companies such as PayPal have made that easy, so you can certainly monetize your blog or WordPress-powered site with a shop selling your goods if you want to. This means that if your needs are of the lighter kind and none of the eCommerce plugins are to your fancy, then there might be a solution that you can implement in your WordPress site without having to install a complex standalone eCommerce system.

If you take just one thing with you from this, make sure it is that you know what you're getting yourself into. This is sales, after all, and not the content business anymore.

SELLING DIGITAL PRODUCTS

Digital merchandise such as eBooks are a completely different matter. Absolutely nothing is stopping you from implementing a payment solution for a digital file, and when paid, you serve the file. In fact, it has almost nothing at all to do with WordPress because it is all about verifying that you got paid and then directing the customer to the file in question. Adding that sort of solution to your blog is really easy if you rely on a third-party service such as E-junkie (www.e-junkie.com) (which will take a chunk of your processed money) to both manage payment and delivery of the files. It's just a matter of setting up a link, and then your provider will handle the rest, much like an affiliate program — but with the benefit of your getting a larger chunk of the money, it being your product and all.

You can do the same on your own as well with the necessary plugins or scripts. However, it is really hard to sidestep the fact that you need to actually charge for your products, which means handling payments. You can, theoretically, handle payments yourself as well. I advise against it, if for no other reason than the fact that people feel more secure when they recognize the party handling their money.

Digital products fit any site perfectly. Although WordPress may be no Magento when it comes to eCommerce, it is fine for selling eBooks, MP3s, design files, or whatever you want to make money on.

BUILDING FOR ECOMMERCE

So you've decided to use WordPress as a basis to sell products, big or small, a lot or a few — doesn't matter. Now you need to figure out how you can set it up to make it as powerful and easy to manage as possible.

Although you could rely on either posts or Pages for your website, you should consider the use of custom post types. Separating the products you want to sell from the rest of the site's infrastructure might not always be necessary, but if it is or could be in the future, then custom post types is the best solution. The next section is all about using custom post types for product-like content on just about any site.

BUILDING A PRODUCT DIRECTORY

Adding a product directory (or any kind of directory really — this could just as well be real estate listings, persons, or whatever) to a WordPress site is a breeze thanks to custom post types. You want to create a new post type for your products to keep them separate from the rest of the content, whether you have just 10 products or over 500.

The kind of information you need to store per product is obviously something unique to your offerings, so this example just shows you the basics:

- Create a custom post type called *Books*.
- Each individual product is actually a book of sorts and is stored in a post-like fashion in the Books post type.

- The example includes support for categories, which in fact will be Books categories for better sorting.
- It does not support tagging (although you could).

The reason for leaving tags out is just to simplify the example. In most cases, it is probably a good idea to enable tagging because it could be used to sort by manufacturer or something like that.

Why Books, by the way? Well, I figured I might as well put this code to good use and create a Books product listing on http://tdh.me. It's always nice to use a live example. You can adapt this code for your own use, just like everything else in this book and most of the stuff I write.

CREATING THE BOOKS POST TYPE

Chapters 6 and 9 in particular cover custom post types, so if you feel uncertain what they are and how they work, you should jump back and read up.

To create the Books post type, add this code either to the functions.php template file of your theme of choice or to a plugin. The latter is a much better idea because it is better for data portability. If you need additional help, refer to Chapters 6 and 7.

```php
register_post_type( 'books', array(
    'label' => 'Books',
    'labels' => array(
        'singular_name' => 'Book',
        'add_new_item' => 'Add New Book',
        'edit_item' => 'Edit Book',
        'new_item' => 'New Book',
        'view_item' => 'View Book',
        'search_items' => 'Search Books',
        'not_found' => 'No books found',
        'not_found_in_trash' => 'No books found in Trash',
    ),
    'public' => true,
    'show_ui' => true,
    'capability_type' => 'post',
    'taxonomies' => array( 'category' ),
    'has_archive' => true,
    'rewrite' => array(
        'slug' => 'books'
    ),
    'query_var' => false,
    'supports' => array(
        'title',
        'editor',
        'author',
        'thumbnail',
        'excerpt',
        'custom-fields',
```

```
        'comments'
    )
) );
```

The code is pretty straightforward, registering the post type as `'books'` and setting appropriate labels to make it look nice in the admin interface, as shown in Figure 14-8. The array in labels tells WordPress how to phrase itself in various situations in the admin area. There are default outputs here, obviously, but things will look a bit better if you adjust them accordingly. Make the post type `public`, make it behave as a post with the `capability_type` setting, and make sure that it has support for categories, supports archive pages, and has a proper rewrite for nice permalinks. (That last one is the default settings, but I tend to put it in anyway.) Finally, the `supports` parameter contains an array of features this post type will offer in the admin interface, usually various kinds of boxes. The rest is default values; again, if you need a refresher, see Chapter 9.

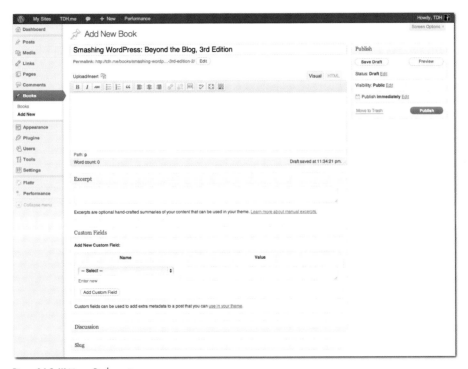

Figure 14-8: Writing a Books post.

Now all that's needed is to add posts to the Books post type, and you have a working post type!

CREATING THE BOOKS PAGE

There are two ways to create a page containing all the products of your custom post type (`'books'` in this example). One way is to create a Page in WordPress and use a Page template to add a custom loop to display the Books posts the way you want. The second method is to rely on the appropriate template file for listings. In this example, I do the latter, which means I want to use archive-books.php. (The archive-[post type].php file takes precedence over archive.php.) I could just add a few conditional tags to archive.php or even index.php to do the same thing, but this way it's a bit cleaner.

I'll take a moment to talk about a common issue with custom post types, especially if you create them using any of the excellent plugins (see Appendix A for some suggestions). The custom post type posts might not be showing up in your theme's content flow. That's because WordPress by default won't include custom post types in the loop. If you want to output posts from a particular post type, say 'books', in a template, you need to use query_posts('post_type=books') to tell WordPress to fetch it. Obviously, you can add several post types together by using an array instead, so if you want 'books' and regular posts it would be this:

```
query_posts( 'post_type => array( 'post', 'books' ) ' )
```

Of course, you could use WP_Query as well (shown in an upcoming example) because that behaves like query_posts(). You can consult the Codex for more on query_posts() at http://codex.wordpress.org/Function_Reference/query_posts.

Back to the books archive page. Say that you don't have a ton of books (like me), so you want to give each book (being a post in the Books custom post type) ample space on your listings page. This means that you want a cover image on the left and some descriptive text about the book to the right. Use the post thumbnail feature to grab the book cover and then query for it. First of all, the post thumbnail feature needs to be enabled, so add this to the theme's functions.php:

```
// Add support for post thumbnails
add_theme_support( 'post-thumbnails' );

// Add image sizes
add_image_size( 'books-small', 150, 0 );
```

First, this adds support for post thumbnails to the theme with add_theme_support(). You could limit this to the custom post type if you wanted to, but chances are you want to use post thumbnails in another fashion on some pages on your site, so enable it globally for now. Second, this code adds a new image size with add_image_size(). The code calls it books-small and resizes it to a width of 150 pixels but doesn't enforce any height and doesn't do any hard crops.

With that in place, you can tackle archive-books.php and put it to good use. You'll notice that this code is internationalized, which is why all the text is in _e() with the tdh7 text domain. You can read up on internationalization in Chapter 6.

```
<?php get_header(); ?>

    <div id="inner-site">
```

```php
<div id="content" class="entry-list">
    <ul id="above-listings">
    <?php dynamic_sidebar('listings'); ?>
    </ul>
    <div id="section-head">
        <p><?php _e('I\'m a published author, and these are my books.
          Just the English ones though, no Swedish works here I\'m
          afraid.', 'tdh7');?></p>
    </div>
    <?php
        // The basic loop
        while ( have_posts() ) : the_post(); ?>

        <div id="post-<?php the_ID(); ?>" <?php post_class('books-
          archive'); ?>>
            <div class="books-cover">
                <a href="<?php the_permalink(); ?>"
                  class="books-cover-link">
                <?php
                    // Is there a featured image?
                    if ( has_post_thumbnail() ) {
                        // Yes, let's use the right one
                        the_post_thumbnail( 'books-small' );
                    }
                    // No? Then we'll use this one
                    else { ?>
                        <img src="<?php echo
                          get_template_directory_uri(); ?>/img/books-
                          nocoveryet.png" width="150" height="190"
                          alt="No cover available" />
                    <?php }
                    // All done
                ?>
                </a>
            </div>
            <div class="books-content">
                <h2 class="entry-title books-title">
                    <a href="<?php the_permalink(); ?>" title="<?php
                      the_title_attribute(); ?>" rel="bookmark">
                        <?php the_title(); ?>
                    </a>
                </h2>
                <div class="entry-summary entry-summary-books">
                    <?php the_excerpt(); ?>
                </div>
            </div>
        </div>

    <?php
        // End the loop
        endwhile; ?>
</div>
```

```php
<?php
    // Right column
    get_sidebar();

    // When possible, display navigation at the bottom
    if ( $wp_query->max_num_pages > 1 ) :
?>
    <div class="navigate">
        <div class="nav-left">
            <?php
                next_posts_link(__ ('&larr; Browse older content',
                    'tdh7') );
            ?>
        </div>
        <div class="nav-right">
            <?php
                previous_posts_link(__ ('Browse more recent content
                    &rarr;', 'tdh7') );
            ?>
        </div>
    </div>
    <?php endif; ?>
</div>

<?php get_footer(); ?>
```

This is a pretty ordinary loop, which you should know pretty much by heart now (but by all means backtrack to Chapter 3 and 4 if you want a refresher). There are just two differences worth mentioning. The first one is `post_class()`, which has gotten the parameter `books-archive`. This is used for styling; you'll see it in the style sheet, and the only thing the parameter does is add the class `books-archive` to the output from `post_class()`.

The second thing is the check for a book cover. The code makes a check to see if there is a post thumbnail for the post, and if there is, that is what will be shown. However, should there be no post thumbnail selected, you'll show a default image because it would look a bit weird without covers for all entries. Even though not all books have final covers until the publication closes in, you want this page to look decent right away.

The styling is pretty obvious, with `div.books` acting much like `div.post` and `div`s for both the cover image and the book description. It's worth noting that custom post types won't get the typical post or page classes from `post_class()`; they'll get one named after the post type instead. So in this case you've got `books` from `post_class()`, which means that you have to style that just like the post class if you want the Books posts to behave like your regular posts. In this case, that just means some margins and stuff like that.

That's really all there is to it. The Books page has been added to the site, as shown in Figure 14-9, and contains each book as a post in a custom post type. Now this page can be easily updated with new books without having to go through the hassle of editing Pages — just adding a new post to the Books post type will take care of it.

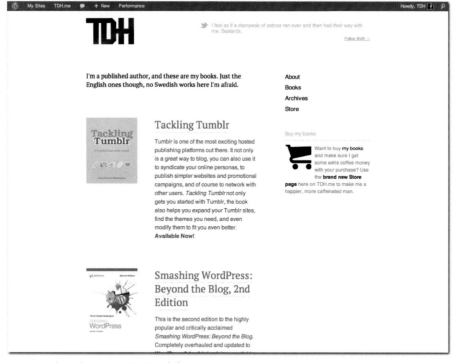

Figure 14-9: The Books page, simple and ready for some TLC.

SHOWING OFF THE PRODUCTS

Posts belonging to a custom post type won't show up in the regular stream of updates by default. You can easily make it so, using `query_posts()` or `WP_Query` (which, you might recall, behaves just like `query_posts()` does), but in the case of having a products directory, it doesn't make much sense. However, you still need to show off your products, which you could do in a number of ways. The following subsections provide a few suggestions, which can be combined.

Add a Loop

The most versatile solution for showing off your products is to add a loop outputting the content from the custom post type to your theme. It could be something like this:

```
<ul>
<?php
    $args = array(
        'post_type' => 'books',
        'post_status' => 'publish',
        'posts_per_page' => -1
    )
    // Let's loop
    $my_query = new WP_Query( $args );
```

```
    while ( $my_query->have_posts() ) : $my_query->the_post(); ?>
    <li>
        <a href="<?php the_permalink(); ?>" title="<?php
          the_title_attribute();?>">
            <?php the_title();?>
        </a>
    </li>
<?php endwhile; ?>
</ul>
```

You'll recognize the loop, I'm sure. This one just outputs every post in the post type `books` as a link in a list item (yes, every one — that's why `posts_per_page` is set to `-1` in `WP_Query`).

Want it to be a bit more impressive? Then why not utilize some fancy JavaScript to make a nice slider to show off your products? There are a few featured post plugins that could be used as well, if you can get them to work with a custom post type, and most likely a few plugins that just rely on whatever you put into them. Just like every other loop out there, the only limitations are your own imagination and your skills with making it look great.

Use Graphics and Links

If you have decent product images or cool promotional material, it is probably a good idea to put them to use to get your visitors to check out your products. The easiest way to gain attention to products on most sites is to just add some linked graphics to whatever widget areas you've got (usually a sidebar), pointing your visitors to the various product pages that way.

The Books example relies on this primarily from posts, but also from widget areas. This solution is most likely best suited for smaller product directories with few updates and additions, meaning that you won't need to expose so many products at the same time. If you have greater needs than this, the loop option shown previously is probably a better option.

A Simple Menu Entry

Sometimes the best solution is the most obvious one. A menu entry pointing to your products page might not be as visual as a graphic or as lively as a loop showing off the latest products, but it is efficient and probably something your visitors would expect. Don't forget to link your products page in your menu, if you have one!

TASTY BLOGGING: USING WORDPRESS FOR RECIPES

Whether you want to keep track of your personal recipes, share them with a select few friends, or launch your very own commercial recipe site, WordPress is the platform you should consider. So why not build just that and see where it takes you?

First of all, you should figure out what the basic features of the site are. Don't worry too much about visual design here; the solution in this example will be portable enough to move across themes. The setup is really pretty simple. You need a separate post type for your recipes to keep them apart from the regular posts and Pages. You also need custom taxonomies for different kinds of recipes and for ingredients. That's basically it, so go ahead and get started then!

STARTERS: THE THEME

You have two ways you can tackle the theme for this project. Either you create a brand-new theme (using a framework or just a theme you like and altering it), or you pick a theme and create a child theme for it. To keep things simple, you'll create a child theme for Twenty Eleven in this example.

Call the child theme *Tasty Eleven* and create the style.css:

```
/*
Theme Name: Tasty Eleven
Theme URI: http://tdh.me/wordpress/tasty-eleven/
Author: Thord Daniel Hedengren
Author URI: http://tdh.me
Description: A child theme for adding recipe features to Twenty Eleven.
Version: 1.0
License: GNU General Public License
License URI: license.txt
Template: twentyeleven
*/
@import url('../twentyeleven/style.css');
```

Nothing weird here at all. Note the import of the style sheet from Twenty Eleven. If you want, you can continue to style the child theme below the import, but you won't be bothering with design in this example.

You'll also need a functions.php. Create that as well and get on with the fun stuff.

MAIN COURSE: THE RECIPE POST TYPE

Creating a custom post type is, as you might remember, easy enough. The whole idea of a custom post type for recipes is to be able to keep the recipes separate from whatever other type of content you have on the site. By doing this, you can easily maintain a blog or news section using the default posts and have static content as default Pages. Naturally, you could build this whole thing without a custom post type for recipes, just using posts for the recipes and adding custom taxonomies, but that limits you a bit in terms of extensibility.

Start by creating the custom post type for recipes. For this example, call it *Recipes,* give its content appropriate permalinks, and make it look good in the admin area with proper naming. You'll recognize this code from the earlier product example, so I won't delve deeper into it for now. Again, this could be either in a plugin for portability or in your theme's functions.php:

```
// Recipes post type
register_post_type( 'recipes', array(
    'label' => 'Recipes',
    'labels' => array(
        'singular_name' => 'Recipe',
        'add_new_item' => 'Add New Recipe',
        'edit_item' => 'Edit Recipe',
        'new_item' => 'New Recipe',
        'view_item' => 'View Recipe',
        'search_items' => 'Search Recipes',
        'not_found' => 'No recipes found',
        'not_found_in_trash' => 'No recipes found in Trash',
    ),
    'public' => true,
    'show_ui' => true,
    'capability_type' => 'post',
    'has_archive' => true,
    'rewrite' => array(
        'slug' => 'recipes'
    ),
    'query_var' => false,
    'supports' => array(
        'title',
        'editor',
        'author',
        'thumbnail',
        'excerpt',
        'comments'
    )
) );
```

You might notice the absence of taxonomies. You could add support for taxonomies here, but you don't have to because you can define where the custom taxonomies are to show up. You'll get to that in a little bit. Now you've got your Recipes post type up and running, as shown in Figures 14-10.

Because custom post types won't show up in the regular content flow, you need to do something about that. First of all, create the archive-recipes.php for your archive needs. This, you'll remember, is the template file that will be used when the Recipe archive is needed. Or, to put it simply, archive-recipe.php will control the Recipes section of your site. What it contains depends on your theme, but all you need is a regular WordPress loop, so I'll skip repeating that here.

Figure 14-10: The Recipes post type, created and ready to go.

DESSERT: CUSTOM TAXONOMIES

Although you could go a long way with just using regular categories and tags, custom taxonomies do offer more options. The idea is to create a custom taxonomy that works just like tags but for ingredients. This way, you can easily tag every recipe with whatever ingredients you're using, from tomatoes to potatoes and whatnot. This in turn will give you ingredient archives automatically, so if you want to cook something involving tomatoes, you can just check that archive out. This also means that you could build solutions that combine several ingredients, giving you a refined archive tailored to the ingredients the user wants to use. Whenever you can, you should think ahead because even if you won't build that feature right away, by having the infrastructure right from the start, you know that you can extend it later on.

A custom taxonomy for ingredients isn't the only one you need in this example. Because being able to sort recipes by type probably would be a good idea, you'll add a category-like, or hierarchical, custom taxonomy for the recipe type. This way, you can attach your recipes to your very own Baking category, for example, hence making it easy for the user to check out all your Baking recipes. Again, this will give you automatic archives, which always is a good thing. You're going with a hierarchical taxonomy here because you want to be a bit more restrictive with the amount of types of recipes, whereas ingredients are more or less limitless and hence fit perfectly well as a nonhierarchical taxonomy.

Start by creating the ingredients taxonomy:

```
// The Ingredients taxonomy
register_taxonomy( 'ingredients', 'recipes', array(
    'hierarchical' => false,
    'labels' => array(
        'name' => 'Ingredients',
        'singular_name' => 'Ingredient',
        'search_items' => 'Search Ingredients',
        'popular_items' => 'Popular Ingredients',
        'all_items' => 'All Ingredients',
        'parent_item' => null,
        'parent_item_colon' => null,
        'edit_item' => 'Edit Ingredient',
        'update_item' => 'Update Ingredient',
        'add_new_item' => 'Add New Ingredient',
        'new_item_name' => 'New Ingredient',
        'separate_items_with_commas' => 'Separate ingredients with commas',
        'add_or_remove_items' => 'Add or remove ingredients',
        'choose_from_most_used' => 'Choose from the most used ingredients',
        'menu_name' => 'Ingredients'
    ),
    'show_ui' => true,
    'query_var' => true,
    'rewrite' => array(
        'slug' => 'ingredient'
    ),
) );
```

Most of this code is pretty self explanatory, and it definitely has a lot in common with the code for custom post types, so you should have no problem reading it. At the start, just after you register the `ingredients` taxonomy, you also attach it to the post type called `recipes`, which you created previously. This could actually be an array if you need to add the taxonomy to several post types, like this:

```
register_taxonomy( 'ingredients', array(
    'recipes',
    'page'
)
```

Worth noting are the two parameters with `null` as a value, which are interesting for hierarchical taxonomies only. You could just leave them out, but because they do have a place for your other taxonomy, go ahead and leave them in.

Moving on, you also need to create the taxonomy for the type of recipes. This one won't be tag-based but rather will behave like regular categories; other than that, it is pretty much the same thing. You'll call it *dishes* because most of the recipes will be a dish of some sorts in the example:

```
// The Dishes taxonomy
register_taxonomy( 'dishes', 'recipes', array(
    'hierarchical' => true,
    'labels' => array(
        'name' => 'Dishes',
        'singular_name' => 'Dish',
        'search_items' =>  'Search Dishes',
        'all_items' => 'All Dishes',
        'parent_item' => 'Parent Dishes',
        'parent_item_colon' => 'Parent Dish:',
        'edit_item' => 'Edit Dish',
        'update_item' => 'Update Dish',
        'add_new_item' => 'Add New Dish',
        'new_item_name' => 'New Dish Name',
        'menu_name' => 'Dishes'
    ),
    'show_ui' => true,
    'query_var' => true,
    'rewrite' => array(
        'slug' => 'dish'
    ),
) );
```

This looks pretty much the same as the Ingredients taxonomy. You'll notice that the `parent_item` and `parent_item_colon` both have values, rather than being set to `null`. The `hierarchical` parameter set to `true` is what tells WordPress that this isn't a tag-based taxonomy but a hierarchical one, much like categories. That's it. Your taxonomies are up and running, only on the Recipes post type, as show in Figure 14-11.

Figure 14-11: You're ready to tag and categorize that recipe.

Now you have automatic archives for both recipes and ingredients. They need some work to be really impressive, of course, but I'll leave that be in terms of this example. If you want to delve deeper, create archive-ingredients.php and archive-type.php to get more precise control of these archives' look and feel.

DIGESTIF: WHAT YOU HAVE SO FAR

This is actually all you need to get started. You've got a custom post type for recipes and the necessary taxonomies so that you can tag and categorize your recipes the way you want and need for proper archives.

Obviously, there are tons of things you could do to further improve this concept. One would be to create the functionality as a plugin rather than a child theme, which would make it a lot more portable across themes. Another improvement might be to add additional form fields to recipes for cooking time and such. That could be done with custom fields, for example, which would let you output the contents using `the_meta()` or `get_post_meta()` in your theme. You could also choose to rely on a plugin such as More Fields (read more about it in Appendix A) for a more user-friendly take on custom fields or just create your own adaptation.

BUILDING A LINKS SITE

A links site can be used for many purposes, so the examples in this section are a bit more generic than the previous ones. The idea is to use posts as link items, making them sortable with both categories and tags. However, you're not just going to put a link in the post field, but rather use the title field as the actual link title and then store the target URL in a custom field. Then you can use the excerpt of the content field to display descriptions, details, or whatever may fit your project.

But you need to start at the beginning. These are your premises:

- Every blog post is a link in your link database.
- You use the title field to save the link title (for example, Google).
- You store the destination URL in a custom field called `'URL'` (for example, `www.google.com`).
- You categorize your links in any number of categories (for example, Search Engines or Web Mail).
- You tag your links with appropriate tags (for example, `free`, `USA`, or `fonts`).
- You use `the_excerpt()` rather than `the_content()` for link descriptions, mostly to keep your doors open for the future.

Now you can get started. First, you store the URL in a custom field. To do so, just create a new custom field on the Write Post screen in the WordPress admin interface and name it `'URL'`. The idea is to put the URL in the value field for each post and then link the title with it.

Next, you need to alter your loop a bit. (For a project like this, you'll probably want to design a new theme that fits the bill, but the default theme is used as an example here.)

You use the following code inside the loop:

```php
<div <?php post_class(); ?> id="post-<?php the_ID(); ?>">
<?php
    // The custom field with the URL
    $CustomField = get_post_meta( get_the_ID(), 'URL', true );
    if ( !empty( $CustomField ) ) {
?>
    <h2>
        <a href="<?php echo esc_url( $CustomField ) ?>"
          rel="bookmark" title="<?php the_title_attribute(); ?>">
            <?php the_title(); ?>
        </a>
        <?php echo $CustomField; ?>
    </h2>
    <div class="entry">
        <?php the_excerpt(); ?>
    </div>
    <p class="postmetadata">
        Filed in <?php the_category( ', ' ) ?> <?php the_tags( 'and tagged ',
        ', ', '' ); ?> <small><?php the_time( 'F jS, Y' ) ?></small>
    </p>
<?php
    // No link
    } else {
?>
    <h2><del><?php the_title(); ?></del></h2>
    <div class="entry">
        <p>Sorry, this link is broken. Please tell an administrator!</p>
    </div>
    <p class="postmetadata">
        It's broken: <?php edit_post_link( 'Fix it!', '', ' | ' ); ?>
        Filed in <?php the_category( ', ' ); ?> <?php the_tags( 'and
        tagged ', ', ', '' ); ?> <small><?php the_time( 'F jS, Y' );
        ?></small>
    </p>
<?php } ?>
</div>
```

I know it's an ugly hack, but the concept is simple enough. Make sure that there is a URL submitted in the 'URL' custom field. That's what these lines do:

```php
<?php
    // The custom field with the URL
    $CustomField = get_post_meta( get_the_ID(), 'URL', true );
    if ( !empty( $CustomField ) ) {
?>
```

If the `$CustomField` variable isn't empty, it'll output the code you want, which contains the linked title and everything.

Next is the actual link title heading, linked to the source, obviously. That was the whole point, after all.

```
<h2>
    <a href="<?php echo esc_url( $CustomField ) ?>"
      rel="bookmark" title="<?php the_title_attribute(); ?>">
        <?php the_title(); ?>
    </a>
</h2>
```

By passing `$CustomField`, which has the URL in it from before, to `esc_url()`, you clean up the output and then just echo it. That's really all there is to it.

That is, unless you forget to add a URL to the custom field. Then the check mentioned earlier will skip to the `else` clause, which just outputs a struck-through post title and a message telling anyone who cares that the URL is broken. There's also an edit link added for good measure; you may want that in the successful results as well.

The rest is pretty basic, with `the_excerpt()` outputting whatever you put in the excerpt field (or the actual content should you have done this wrong), as well as categories, tags, and a date.

There you have it — the basis of using WordPress as a links manager. Sure, you can refine it a bit, but mostly it is cosmetic stuff that you can tackle in your theme.

THE ALTERNATIVE: THE LINK POST FORMAT

Another option would be to use the link post format. This would be a less advanced solution than the previous one perhaps, but it might be a better choice depending on what your goals are with the link directory site. The link post format fetches the first link from your post for you to play with.

To use the link post format, you must enable it first, in functions.php:

```
add_theme_support( 'post-formats', array( 'link' ) );
```

You can obviously extend that array with more post formats should you want to. The beauty of post formats is that they are easy to check for. You can use the conditional tag `has_post_format()` to check for the link post format, which could be a way for alternative post stylings, of course:

```
if ( has_post_format( 'link' ) {
    echo 'Hey look, this is a link!';
}
```

If you want to use post formats, you can update the code in the first example accordingly. For more on post formats, see Chapter 4, "WordPress Theme Essentials."

SOME THOUGHTS ABOUT USAGE

Why should you use WordPress to power what at first looks like a simple links directory? The ease of WordPress management as well as the various feeds and sorting capabilities make the platform an excellent choice for this usage. Add the capability to let users submit their own links using plugins or by having them register, and you've got a solid basis to start from. You can even let other sites include the latest links from a certain category or tag using RSS feeds, although you'd probably want to alter the feed output so that the titles in such cases also lead to the destinations specified in the `'URL'` custom fields.

How can you put this to good use? There are obviously tons of possibilities. Niche link sites are popular, but you can take it up a notch with plugins. Why not let people vote or comment on the links, for example? That way, you can spark user-contributed material and in turn put it to good use with top link lists and similar features. For a closed group, this can be a great way to share resources and stories online, and it is a nice enough option for all those link directory scripts out there. After all, few platforms offer the simplicity of WordPress, and with the ever-present option of building new features into the site with the ease of theming and the addition of plugins, there is no telling where you may end up taking a site like this.

Or you can just use the links directory to share and save links you like, categorizing them and tagging for good measure. That's what several bookmarking services do, after all, so you can certainly put this sort of solution to good use yourself.

MIXING LINK POSTS WITH TRADITIONAL CONTENT

Maybe you want to mix this sort of linked title with your traditional content. You know the kind of site where the post title leads to the actual post, and not elsewhere? What you're looking at, then, is something of a linking aside. This is really easy to pull off. You just reuse the code and let the custom fields' content check do all the work. Something like the following code would do the trick:

```
<div <?php post_class(); ?> id="post-<?php the_ID(); ?>">
    <?php $CustomField = get_post_meta( get_the_ID(), 'URL', true );
    if ( !empty( $CustomField ) ) {
        <div class="linkage">
            <h2>
                <a href="<?php echo esc_url( $CustomField ) ?>"
                  rel="bookmark" title="<?php the_title_attribute(); ?>">
                    <?php the_title(); ?>
                </a>
            </h2>
            <div class="entry">
                <?php the_excerpt(); ?>
            </div>
        </div>
```

```php
<?php // Nope, nothing there - regular post!
} else { ?>
    <h2>
        <a href="<?php the_permalink(); ?>" rel="bookmark" title="Permanent
            Link to <?php the_title_attribute(); ?>">
            <?php the_title(); ?>
        </a>
    </h2>
    <small><?php the_time( 'F jS, Y' ); ?> by <?php the_author(); ?></small>
    <div class="entry">
        <?php the_content( 'Read the rest of this entry &raquo;' ); ?>
    </div>
    <p class="postmetadata">
        <?php the_tags( 'Tags: ', ', ', '<br />' ); ?> Posted in <?php
            the_category( ', ' ); ?> | <?php edit_post_link( 'Edit', '', ' |
            '); ?>  <?php comments_popup_link('No Comments &#187;',
            '1 Comment &#187;', '% Comments &#187;'); ?>
    </p>
<?php } ?>
</div>
```

There are some minor changes compared to the code used in the original example. That's because you want to actually output the posts with linked titles when there is no custom field value in `'URL'`, but when there is, you do it the way you did before. This version omits some categories and stuff, and the added `div.linkage` makes it easier to style (although you can use the `post_class()` styles for most of it).

This code will make every post with content in the `'URL'` custom field have a title linked to that URL, rather than the post itself. It is simple enough to add to any theme.

Of course, this would be a lot cleaner if you used post formats because you could simply use `has_post_format()` and check for the link post format, as explained earlier.

SHORT AND SWEET: OTHER USES FOR WORDPRESS

You can do just about anything with WordPress if you put your mind to it. Here are some final sparks to keep those gears grinding.

AN EVENT PAGE AND A CALENDAR

Because it is so easy to roll out a WordPress website, it has become a popular platform for building event websites. You can easily sort out details such as speakers and workshops with custom post types, while keeping the informational pages as Pages, and the blog is obviously just your regular posts. This kind of setup is really easy to work with, making it a popular choice.

The big decision with an event site comes with the schedule and the sign-up functionality. A schedule could be managed by a hosted calendar service, but there are also several calendar plugins available that might fit your needs. As for the sign-up, there are numerous web services that offer all-in-one solutions, from the initial sign-up to payment, which is handy. If you need to sell tickets and other things for your event, take look at plugins such as WP e-Commerce and the various shopping carts available; they have been used for everything from WordCamps to smaller happenings and might suit you better.

INTRANETS AND COLLABORATION

WordPress is easy to work with as an author, as you no doubt know. That makes it well suited for intranets in which teams need to communicate across the organization as well as with each other. Whether it is just an informal blog to keep everyone within the company in the loop or a major collaborative source of information during projects, the ease of use that WordPress offers makes it a great choice. To get the full power of larger intranets, you might need to push WordPress a bit further with additional plugins and other tools to make it speak to all the other systems on the intranet.

If you need a more collaborative group blog, take a look at the P2 theme (http://wordpress.org/extend/themes/p2), a Twitter-like theme in which the users can post both short and long updates from the front end. Some companies rely on this type of setup for internal communication, either within a closed intranet or by using a plugin to keep everything private.

Although WordPress isn't a wiki, there are some plugins that can add that type of functionality as well. Whether WordPress is the best fit for your intranet all depends on your needs; for blog-like communication, it is obviously a no-brainer, but for other uses you should assess the needs of the company and take it from there.

Some of the community-focused plugins can help here as well, depending on your need for communication within the intranet.

COMMUNITIES AND FORUMS

With the advent of the BuddyPress plugin (http://buddypress.org), WordPress has become a viable option for communities. Thanks to BuddyPress, it is now easier than ever to create a members-driven website, to get users to communicate in groups, and even extend WordPress to blog hosting and forums should you choose to. What's even better is that just about any WordPress site can be extended with the BuddyPress functionality thanks to the BuddyPress template pack (http://wordpress.org/extend/plugins/bp-template-pack), a plugin that helps you BuddyPress-ify your theme.

For forums, BuddyPress ships with a version of bbPress (http://bbpress.org), but there is also a standalone plugin. You might remember that bbPress started out as a standalone project, but as of version 2.0 and onwards, it is a plugin for WordPress that is very convenient to work with because the forums are built using a custom post type. This means that it is very easy to start theming for a forum if you have an existing site. There are other forum plugins as well, but you should definitely look into how well they handle traffic and heavy load. Should those solutions not fit your needs, you can always turn to external forum systems such as Vanilla (http://vanillaforums.org), which integrates nicely with the WordPress user database.

There is no doubt that a lot is going on with the WordPress platform when it comes to extended membership functionality (there are tons of plugins just for membership) and community features.

DATABASES

Everything changed with custom post types. The fact that you can add several new top layers of content management with a few lines of code makes WordPress extremely versatile. That also means that you can build extensive databases with whatever information you choose with WordPress in the middle, possibly just acting as a user interface. Add the fact that you've got RSS feeds for just about everything in WordPress, and you've got a platform that can distribute its updates to other systems easily enough.

It's daring to say so, but custom post types really make the possibilities seem almost endless. You've come a long way from posts and Pages, haven't you?

STATIC SITES

There are still static websites out there, sites that don't feature news or frequent updates. Why should you use WordPress to power such a site? Isn't it easier to just hack the HTML files and be done with it? A bit, perhaps, but if you're doing this static site for a friend or client, then it can certainly save you a lot of headache if you build it on WordPress. Maybe it is all Pages, no posts or categories or custom stuff — just a handful of simple pages telling the visitor whatever message it is that the site wants to deliver. If you use WordPress for this, anyone with half a brain can update these pages. No need to call you just because that corner shop has new holiday hours or to bother you with adding another simple page about the new office in the town down the road.

Simple static sites powered by WordPress might take a little bit longer to develop, but they can save you a lot of annoying edits in the long run. Perhaps that's not what you want if you bill your clients by the hour, but do them (and yourself) the favor of delivering the best possible product from the start. You'll feel better about it, I'm sure.

JOURNALS AND NOTES

Sometimes it is hard to see the forest for the trees. WordPress is great for journals, which makes a lot of sense because the original blogs were little more than online journals. You could choose to set up a journal detailing your life and times and keep it hidden from search engines using the default privacy settings. You could also add another layer of privacy by installing a plugin such as Private WordPress (http://wordpress.org/extend/plugins/private-wordpress), which hides the site for anyone not logged in. This means that you could share your journal with friends and family but leave the rest of the scary world out, which might be nice.

Journals are not just for your private pleasures; you could also keep notes of your work, of studies and lectures, and of your projects in a WordPress site. Because WordPress supports categorization and tagging from the start, you can easily make your content simple to find and group together. If you need additional layers of categorization, there are always custom taxonomies and even custom post types should you want them. In fact, this is a solution we're employing at my web agency — sharing code snippets for projects internally in a closed WordPress site.

YOU CAN BUILD ANYTHING YOU WANT

Well, maybe not anything — even WordPress has limits — but just about. WordPress is an extremely versatile platform, and most content-based sites online will work perfectly well with minimal customization work to the system. Thanks to the flexibility of themes and the extensibility offered by plugins, you can really do just about anything with WordPress. The whole idea behind this chapter is to get you thinking along those lines. Whenever I start thinking about a new project, be it a personal site or something for a client, I turn and twist the concept in my head to figure out how to make it happen in as short a time as possible. More often than not, WordPress is the solution for achieving this.

Although you may not be able to build everything with WordPress, you'll find that most of your ideas are realizable. This is the true strength of the platform — that you can take it so far beyond its original blogging roots. Thanks to the open-source mentality, we have a wonderful tool in WordPress and all its plugins and themes — something we should be thankful for and consider contributing to whenever we can.

PART

V

APPENDIXES

A

ESSENTIAL WORDPRESS PLUGINS

THE NUMBER OF plugins available for the WordPress platform is staggering; there is just no way to try them all or even to keep up with all the changes taking place. This chapter is dedicated to just a smattering of the marvelous plugins that are available for WordPress. Each of the plugins covered here has reached the users, has been thoroughly tested, and clearly fills a need. Still, these represent only a drop in the ocean compared to what's available.

Do keep in mind that plugins are always changing, just as WordPress is. This means that what works great today may not be so useful in the future. Along with using the information in this chapter, you need to continue researching and keep up with updates to make sure that you find the right plugin to fill your needs.

Be advised: Sometimes you'll get warnings when trying out a plugin, telling you that the plugin has been tested only up to this or that version of WordPress, and maybe not on the version that you're running. This doesn't necessarily mean that it won't work for you — just that the plugin hasn't been tested with your particular version or the plugin author hasn't updated the plugin files. So don't be put off just because a plugin isn't tested with your version yet; set up a test blog and give it a go for yourself. Most plugins will work across versions, after all.

CONTENT-FOCUSED PLUGINS

It's all about the content; you want people to find it, get hooked, and then spend an afternoon enjoying your site. Wikipedia does it with links, and so can you. It's just a matter of making them interesting enough and making it easy to dig into the archives. These plugins will help visitors get caught up in your content:

- WP Greet Box (http://wordpress.org/extend/plugins/wp-greet-box): Whenever you get a new visitor from a social bookmarking site, it's a good idea to introduce yourself, or rather your site, to this person. That's what WP Greet Box does: It checks the referring URL and then outputs a message to the visitor. It can be something like, "Hi, welcome, please subscribe!" or something more tailored, like, "Welcome Digg visitor. Did you know I wrote a book on Digg? Get it here!" Very useful.

- Yet Another Related Posts Plugin (http://wordpress.org/extend/plugins/yet-another-related-posts-plugin): The "Yet Another" part of this plugin's name is not only a flirt with code lovers out there; the number of related posts plugins is staggering, and that makes it hard to find the gold nuggets hidden among the rubbish. In my opinion, this is a strong contender to the throne of related posts plugins because it offers so many options and serves relevant links as well. For example, you can set the relevance threshold limits so that a site with a lot of content can be stricter about what is considered to be related content. Other features include related posts in RSS feeds, support for Pages, caching, and also a template system that could be easier to use but still offers nice customization options if you want to take things a step further.

- WordPress Popular Posts (http://wordpress.org/extend/plugins/wordpress-popular-posts): Do you want to promote the most popular posts on your site? Of course you do, and this is a great way to get people to dig deeper into your site. There are numerous plugins available, but WordPress Popular Posts is a nice widgetized solution.

- WP-PostRatings (http://wordpress.org/extend/plugins/wp-postratings): WP-PostRatings is an excellent plugin for rating posts. There are several different grade images included, and you can choose where you want to output it by using the [ratings] shortcode or by adding the plugin's template tags to your theme. It also lets you get the highest and lowest rated posts, sorting by time or overall, as well as category and so on.

- GD Star Rating (http://wordpress.org/extend/plugins/gd-star-rating): Another ratings plugin is GD Star Rating, which stands out with its support for several kinds of ratings per post (stars and thumbs up/down for example), as well as ratings for comments. It also features one of the flashier settings pages I've seen and a bunch of advanced settings. Well worth a look if you need ratings functionality.

- Polldaddy (http://wordpress.org/extend/plugins/polldaddy): It should come as no surprise that the Polldaddy plugin fully integrates the hosted poll and service manager into WordPress, with the option of creating polls without having to leave the admin interface. Automattic owns Polldaddy, which is why it's so integrated, and that's at least one reason to consider this service as well because it has the backing infrastructure needed. If you want to get rid of all the Polldaddy links in your polls, however, you'll have to buy a pro account, so if that's an issue, you may want to consider one of the native poll plugins instead.

- WP-Polls (http://wordpress.org/extend/plugins/wp-polls): WP-Polls is a flexible poll plugin with archive support. You can either add it to your theme templates or use the widget to get the poll where you want it. It may take a while to set it up to fit your design, but it is a good alternative to the hosted Polldaddy solution.

MEDIA PLUGINS

Media most often means *images* when it comes to WordPress sites, and that's the case on the plugin side of things as well. It's not so strange when you think about it. After all, if you want to share a video, you put it on YouTube, right? That way, it gets exposure, and you won't have to worry about bandwidth costs for your HD masterpiece.

- Lightbox Gallery (http://wordpress.org/extend/plugins/lightbox-gallery): Lightbox Gallery adds the popular overlay lightbox effect to your gallery images and makes it possible to open any image by adding the `rel="lightbox"` tag to the link. You can do the same by implementing any of the available scripts out there, but this does it for you. Be aware that there are some hardcoded links in this plugin at the moment, so if you have moved your WordPress install to a subfolder but run the actual site in the root folder, you may run into broken navigational images. Hopefully, this will be remedied in the future; otherwise, you might prefer another option.

- Slimbox (http://wordpress.org/extend/plugins/slimbox): If you want to keep your lightbox overlay effects light, check out Slimbox. It checks for any link leading to an image file and then gives it the lightbox treatment. Granted, it's not as flashy as many of the other options out there but is still cool enough.

- Podcasting (http://wordpress.org/extend/plugins/podcasting): There was a time when podcasting with WordPress was synonymous with the PodPress plugin. Unfortunately, it isn't really maintained anymore, which makes it even sweeter that there's a migration tool for PodPress users so that they can move to the Podcasting plugin. This plugin offers iTunes support, and you can have both audio and video podcasts.

Here are a couple short and sweet media plugins to take a look at:

- Thickbox Announcement (http://wordpress.org/extend/plugins/fsthickboxannounce-ment): This plugin uses the Thickbox lightbox variant to overlay an announcement.

- Featured Content Gallery (http://wordpress.org/extend/plugins/featured-content-gallery): Featured Content Gallery adds an image carousel meant to be used to promote featured content on a front page.

ADMINISTRATIVE PLUGINS

By far the biggest section in this plugin compilation is the one for administrative plugins. That's probably because they range from backup solutions to statistics tools and WordPress admin fixes, as well as CMS-like functionality:

■ No Self Pings (http://wordpress.org/extend/plugins/no-self-ping): If you're tired of seeing your own pings ending up on your own posts just because you're linking internally, this is a must-have plugin. In my opinion, it should be in every WordPress install out there. If you want to crosslink internally, other than by using the actual link in your post or Page, use a related posts plugin.

■ WP No Category Base (http://wordpress.org/extend/plugins/wp-no-category-base): WP No Category Base gets rid of the default "category" in permalinks. You can customize it to say other things in the permalinks settings, such as "topics" or "products," but you can't do away with it altogether. This plugin fixes that, making `http://domain.com/category/my-category` become `http://domain.com/my-category` instead.

■ WP-DB-Backup (http://wordpress.org/extend/plugins/wp-db-backup): You can never have too many backup solutions. This one uses the built-in WordPress pseudo-cron to e-mail you backups of the database or stores them on the server for you in case something goes wrong. No matter what other backup solutions you may be running already, I encourage you to add this one as well. Remember, it just backs up the database, and only the default tables and any others you tell it to. Your uploaded files, plugins, and themes will need a different backup solution. Hopefully, this plugin will be shipped with WordPress in the future, as I'm sure it would help a lot of people.

■ Maintenance Mode (http://wordpress.org/extend/plugins/maintenance-mode): This is a simple plugin that locks down your blog, displaying a message saying that the site is undergoing maintenance to every visitor except logged-in administrators. Remember that WordPress will put your site in its own maintenance mode when you're upgrading it, so this is for other stuff.

■ Shockingly Big IE6 Warning (http://wordpress.org/extend/plugins/shockingly-big-ie6-warning): Microsoft's Internet Explorer 6 is a scourge, and the only reason to run it is if your operating system is forcing you to. That would be Windows 2000, among others, because that particular OS won't run newer versions of Internet Explorer. However, there's nothing that stops users of these systems from installing any of the other web browsers out there; it is just the newer versions of Internet Explorer that don't work. With this plugin, you can educate your visitors to that fact and make the web a better place. Also, it will surely mean a better experience of your site for the user as well.

■ Custom Admin Branding (http://wordpress.org/extend/plugins/custom-admin-branding): Custom Admin Branding lets you customize the admin experience for your users. You can swap out the logo both when logging in and within the admin interface, change colors, and so on. The plugin also supports custom CSS if you want to alter something particular in the WordPress admin.

■ Theme My Login (http://wordpress.org/extend/plugins/theme-my-login): The Theme My Login plugin replaces the traditional login page (wp-login.php) with a page in your theme instead. In other words, you get the login page integrated and therefore stylable, which can be a good idea if you want to give your users a login. You can also control where they'll end up after login and add a login form to any widgetized area. Pretty useful.

- Fast Secure Contact Form (http://wordpress.org/extend/plugins/si-contact-form): There are numerous contact form plugins out there. Unfortunately, many of them are prone to be plagued by spambots, so you should go with a plugin that addresses that problem. Fast Secure Contact Form has a good track record and is easy enough to work with, but there are tons of other options as well.

- Google Analyticator (http://wordpress.org/extend/plugins/google-analyticator): Google Analyticator makes it easy to get Google Analytics (http://google.com/analytics) running on your blog without having to hack the theme's template files. It even offers some stats in the admin interface, which is nice for those of you not addicted to checking the Analytics page ten times a day.

- Google Analytics for WordPress (http://wordpress.org/extend/plugins/google-analytics-for-wordpress): Another plugin for adding Google Analytics to your WordPress site without editing the theme files. Simple enough, with exclusions to make your statistics tracking more accurate.

- WordPress.com Stats (http://wordpress.org/extend/plugins/stats): If you're used to the statistics served within the WordPress admin interface on WordPress.com, you'll love WordPress.com Stats. It's the same but is for your standalone WordPress install. It's nice and simple but doesn't offer as much information as Google Analytics or any of the other "real" web statistics options out there. It needs a (free) WordPress.com API key to work.

- Broken Link Checker (http://wordpress.org/extend/plugins/broken-link-checker): This nifty little tool keeps track of your links. When installed, it will browse through your blogroll, Pages, and posts, looking for links that are broken. Then it lets you do stuff with them. Very handy, but I'm not sure I'd trust it to be running all the time. It rechecks every 72 hours by default, but you can have it check manually as well.

- WP e-Commerce (http://wordpress.org/extend/plugins/wp-e-commerce): If you want to turn your WordPress site into a web shop or perhaps just enhance it to sell some merchandise, WP e-Commerce will most likely be your first stop. The learning curve is a bit steep, but with some tweaking, both designwise and settingswise, you can get it to work the way you like. There is a lot of advanced functionality here, such as cross promotions and categorized products. And if you want more, you can always pay for the extensions, although the plugin will stand well enough on its own.

  Another nice full-scale eCommerce solution is called *Jigoshop* (http://wordpress.org/extend/plugins/jigoshop), and you should really take some time comparing it with WP e-Commerce. Both of these plugins offer advanced features for your online store, so you should take some time finding the one that fits your needs the best.

- Redirection (http://wordpress.org/extend/plugins/redirection): Redirection lets you set up redirects from your blog, so `http://domain.com/smashing-company/` does a "301 moved" redirect to `http://smashing-company.com` instead, or whatever it is you need to do.

- Pretty Link Lite (http://wordpress.org/extend/plugins/pretty-link): If you want to shorten your URLs for use on Twitter or just hide your affiliated links (that's naughty!), Pretty

Link is something to look into. Especially if you intend to roll things out on Twitter and have a short domain name because it even has the option to attach a "Pretty Bar," in a manner similar to what Digg and others are doing. Pretty Link is your own URL shortener with options, basically. There's a paid pro version as well.

■ Pods (http://wordpress.org/extend/plugins/pods): Pods is a plugin aiming to make WordPress even more of a CMS. The developers call it a *CMS framework,* and that's not too far from the truth. You can create content types, create data structures, set up relationships, and so on. Building a site relying on Pods is sure to give you a lot of freedom. The only problem is it may be a bit daunting to get started, especially if you're used to the straightforwardness of WordPress itself. Worth a look if you need WordPress to be more CMS-like.

■ Download Monitor (http://github.com/mikejolley/download-monitor): If you're interested in how many times a certain file has been downloaded, say a WordPress theme you've released or an eBook you're giving away, you can monitor it with the Download Monitor plugin. It offers upload of files (but you don't need to use that — you can just input the file URL), localization, categories, and easy addition of the downloads to posts and Pages. And statistics, of course.

■ More Fields (http://wordpress.org/extend/plugins/more-fields): More Fields is an excellent plugin that makes custom fields easy to work with not only for you as the developer, but also for the editorial team working with the site. You can create custom fields with WYSIWYG functionality, radio or check boxes, and so on. It's especially handy when you're building something for a client. This is how custom fields should work in WordPress out of the box.

You might also want to check out the other plugins from the same developer: More Taxonomies (http://wordpress.org/extend/plugins/more-taxonomies) lets you add new taxonomies to WordPress quickly, and More Types (http://wordpress.org/extend/plugins/more-types) lets you add new post types. Great stuff, all.

Another option for nicer custom fields is WP-Custom (http://wordpress.org/extend/plugins/wp-custom), although More Fields is the better choice, in my opinion.

■ WP Bannerize (http://wordpress.org/extend/plugins/wp-bannerize): For simple advertising needs, WP Bannerize is a great option. It lets you hardcode ad spots into your theme or, even better, put them in widgets. Ads can be bulked together in pools, and WP Bannerize keeps an eye on the number of ad impressions and clicks, as well as makes sure that the campaign ends when set numbers are met, including dates. There are alternatives out there, but chances are that if you want something more advanced than WP Bannerize, you should look into Google's DoubleClick for Publishers (http://google.com/admanager) or OpenX (http://openx.com).

■ FeedWordPress (http://wordpress.org/extend/plugins/feedwordpress): FeedWordPress lets you syndicate feeds into your WordPress database and publish them as posts. That sounds like an RSS scrapers dream, of course, but it can also fulfill other purposes. Among other things, it can power a "planet" website, which exists to pull together relevant content and then expose it to the visitors.

The plugin can be used for a lot of things. Theoretically, you can transform your WordPress install into a lifestreaming monster by sorting posts into appropriate categories and such.

Just so you're clear, scraping other people's content is bad mojo and may be illegal. Don't do it; write your own or obtain permission.

- Members Only (http://wordpress.org/extend/plugins/members-only): Members Only restricts viewing to registered users only; everyone else will be asked to log in. When logged in, you can redirect the user anywhere you like, so this works perfectly with the P2 theme (http://wordpress.org/extend/themes/p2) if you need internal collaboration running on WordPress. There is even a setting for private RSS feeds.

- BuddyPress (http://buddypress.org): BuddyPress is a community plugin for WordPress. The plugin is huge and adds Facebook-like features to your WordPress site, including profile pages with a wall, groups, and so on. There are even plugins that extend Buddy-Press and make it a really powerful tool.

- bbPress (http://bbpress.org): Although there is some great forum software out there, such as Vanilla (http://vanillaforums.org), sometimes you might not want another install to worry about. That's where bbPress comes in, the same forum software that WordPress.org runs, now available as a plugin for WordPress. Besides being really easy to install and set up, bbPress is easily extended with plugins much like BuddyPress, and the two work perfectly well together as well. Styling your forum is a breeze; all you need to do is add the appropriate template files to your theme because bbPress uses custom post types. Very convenient.

Here is a mixed bag of administrative plugins:

- Woopra Analytics Plugin (http://wordpress.org/extend/plugins/woopra): This is perfect for Woopra users, just as the Google Analytics plugins are for Analytics users.

- Random Redirect (http://wordpress.org/extend/plugins/random-redirect): If you want a link that will send the user to a random post on your site, this is the plugin for you.

- Post Editor Buttons (http://wordpress.org/extend/plugins/post-editor-buttons): This cool little plugin lets you add your own buttons to the HTML part of the Write Post editor.

- TinyMCE Advanced (http://wordpress.org/extend/plugins/tinymce-advanced): TinyMCE Advanced adds more features to the visual editor in WordPress.

- Viper's Video Quicktags (http://wordpress.org/extend/plugins/vipers-video-quicktags): This makes it easier to add videos from a number of sites, as well as to upload your own.

- Custom Post Type UI (http://wordpress.org/extend/plugins/custom-post-type-ui): Custom Post Type UI lets you create custom post types and your own taxonomies in admin, without writing any code.

- Revision Control (http://wordpress.org/extend/plugins/revision-control): Revision Control limits the number of post revisions WordPress can save in the database.

- Widget Context (http://wordpress.org/extend/plugins/widget-context): If you want more control over widgets, you can use Widget Context to set rules for where each widget should be shown (perhaps as an alternative to having a ton of sidebars?).

- WP Mail SMTP (http://wordpress.org/extend/plugins/wp-mail-smtp): Should you not want to use your host's mail servers for your WordPress e-mailing needs, this is the solution. It works great with Google Apps, too.

- Editorial Calendar (http://wordpress.org/extend/plugins/editorial-calendar): With Editorial Calendar, it is easier to manage content with a drag-and-drop schedule interface.

- Members (http://wordpress.org/extend/plugins/members): This plugin offers more control over which users can do what, what content should be shown to whom, and so on. It's a pretty cool tool, worth checking out.

- Capability Manager (http://wordpress.org/extend/plugins/capsman): Sometimes you need additional control over what your users are allowed to do. Capability Manager is a great tool if you need more than just the basic roles and capabilities of the user levels in WordPress.

- WP Event Ticketing (http://wordpress.org/extend/plugins/wpeventticketing): WP Event Ticketing is a way to manage and sell tickets for an event, with a bunch of nice options. It includes support for payment via PayPal and might be just what your need for your WordCamp, right?

- Activate Update Services (http://wordpress.org/extend/plugins/activate-update-services): This adds the Update Services setting for all sites in multisite installs.

- Unfiltered MU (http://wordpress.org/extend/plugins/unfiltered-mu): Unfiltered MU makes WordPress more lenient on potentially harmful HTML tags in multisite installs. This means that more embeds work and so on. Use with caution, especially if you're running a blog hosting service — you never know what malicious people can do if they get too much leeway!

SPAM AND COMMENT MANAGEMENT PLUGINS

Battling spam is important, and managing comments in itself is important, too. The following plugins will hopefully help:

- Akismet (http://wordpress.org/extend/plugins/akismet): Akismet is joined at the hip with WordPress and is one of those plugins that tackles the ever-present issue of comment spam. To use it, you'll need an API key from WordPress.com, which means you'll have to be a user there. There are also some commercial licenses available; see http://akismet.com for more. You may also want to complement it with other spam-stopping plugins or at least try out a few others if you find that a lot of spam is getting through.

- TypePad AntiSpam (http://antispam.typepad.com): TypePad AntiSpam is Six Apart's answer to the Akismet plugin, and it works in a similar way. Just like Akismet, it works against a server that logs and analyzes all spam, including the comments you mark as spam, and hence it "learns" all the time. Both the plugin and the necessary API key for your TypePad profile are free, so should Akismet fail for you, this is worth a shot.

- Really Simple CAPTCHA (http://wordpress.org/extend/plugins/really-simple-captcha): CAPTCHA is one of those annoying "fill out what it says in the box to prove that you are human" things, and although you can argue that they aren't really user-friendly, sometimes you need to adopt desperate measures to stop spammers and other exploiters. This plugin really isn't about just slapping a CAPTCHA on your comments, for example, but rather it is meant to be utilized when you need a really simple CAPTCHA check. Works well enough in most cases.

- Get Recent Comments (http://wordpress.org/extend/plugins/get-recent-comments): The recent comments widget that ships with WordPress isn't exactly exciting, and besides it tends to fill up with trackbacks. The Get Recent Comments plugin is an excellent replacement, with adjustable layout, Gravatar support, cached output, order options, no internal pingbacks, and a lot more. If you're going to display the most recent comments, this is an excellent solution.

- Disqus Comment System (http://wordpress.org/extend/plugins/disqus-comment-system): The leading hosted comment service is Disqus (http://disqus.com), and it is easy enough to get it running on your WordPress site using a plugin. If you're running Disqus, you may also be interested in the (unofficial) Disqus Widget plugin (http://wordpress.org/extend/plugins/disqus-widget), which shows off statistics for your Disqus comments.

- IntenseDebate Comments (http://wordpress.org/extend/plugins/intensedebate): Two hosted comments solutions are competing for serving your reader's opinions, and IntenseDebate (www.intensedebate.com) is the one owned by Automattic. If you want to use IntenseDebate for your hosted comments, this is your tool.

- CommentLuv (http://wordpress.org/extend/plugins/commentluv): CommentLuv is a plugin that checks the applied URL for an RSS feed and shows the latest update with the commenter's comment. It also connects to the ComLuv website (http://comluv.com) for more features such as link tracking. Luckily, the whole thing is pretty customizable because the default solution isn't very pretty, including bug buttons and such.

- BackType Connect (http://wordpress.org/extend/plugins/backtype-connect): The BackType Connect plugin checks the social web for talk that is related to your blog posts and publishes it as comments on your post. So if your mammoth article garnered a lot a buzz on Twitter, this will show up on your post as well. Pretty cool, but it can also be really messy when mixing both traditional comments and comments from microblogging systems due to the 140-character limit. Use with care and make sure that your readership is savvy enough to understand what's going on.

Here are a few more short and sweet ones:

- Cookie for Comments (http://wordpress.org/extend/plugins/cookies-for-comments): This plugin is a viable option when you're hit with a lot of comment spam, using cookies to make it harder for those nasty spambots to get through.

- WP-Hashcash (http://wordpress.org/extend/plugins/wp-hashcash): WP-Hashcash is another spam-fighting plugin that you should try if you're overrun by comment spam.

- ReplyMe (http://wordpress.org/extend/plugins/replyme): ReplyMe will e-mail the comment author when someone replies to him or her directly. It will only work if you have threaded comments enabled, of course.

SOCIAL NETWORKING PLUGINS

The social web is a concept, and you've got a ton of profiles to the left and right. Each social bookmarking tool has its own submit link, and although you can just add them all to your theme (which is covered in Chapter 10, "Integrating the Social Web"), you can also rely on a plugin. It's all connected these days, after all. So why not add a little bit of the social web to your site? Show off your Twitter and let your visitors submit your content to Digg. You can do most of that directly in your theme with some custom code (usually found on the various social networking sites' tools pages), but if you want to take a shortcut or add some extra social web flair, these plugins may help:

- Lifestream (http://wordpress.org/extend/plugins/lifestream): The Lifestream plugin easily adds lifestreaming features to your WordPress site. Just install it and tell it what online accounts and RSS feeds it should fetch data from, and then you can include it using a shortcode on a Page, for example. You can also customize each element thanks to the addition of CSS classes, and there is built-in support for several of the largest social media properties out there, although just about anything with an RSS feed will work. And, of course, it is ready for localization as well as being constantly updated, which makes it an interesting option.

- Twitter Tools (http://wordpress.org/extend/plugins/twitter-tools): Twitter Tools connects your WordPress blog with Twitter and lets you send tweets from the blog to your account. A simple settings page makes this a breeze to set up, and you can even control how the tweets you've sent should be tagged and handled on your own site. This means that you can have an asides category and send everything posted in it to Twitter, or the other way around.

- ShareThis (http://wordpress.org/extend/plugins/share-this): Sending posts to social bookmarking sites is popular, and this tool adds that functionality to every post on a site. ShareThis is more than just a plugin; it is a service that hosts your submit form, which means that you can get stats and everything if you sign up for an account.

  The only thing to keep in mind here is that using any third-party element means relying on that party's ability to serve the data. In other words, if the ShareThis server is slow or even unavailable, then so is some or all of your sharing functionality.

- Add to Any: Share/Bookmark/E-mail Button (http://wordpress.org/extend/plugins/add-to-any): This plugin integrates the hosted Lockerz Share (formerly AddToAny) sharing button. You may also want to look at the Subscribe button as well, if you like this service: http://wordpress.org/extend/plugins/add-to-any-subscribe.

You can find more social stuff:

- Wickett Twitter Widget (http://wordpress.org/extend/plugins/wickett-twitter-widget): This is a simple widget that shows your tweets.

- Twitter for WordPress (http://wordpress.org/extend/plugins/twitter-for-wordpress): Twitter for WordPress is another widget used to show off your tweets.

- Sociable (http://wordpress.org/extend/plugins/sociable): This plugin is a popular social bookmarking plugin that adds links to your site.

- Tweet Old Post (http://wordpress.org/extend/plugins/tweet-old-post): If you want to tweet random old posts at an interval you can set, you can use this tool. This might be a great way to get some more traction to your archive content if you have diehard Twitter followers.

- Simple Social Bookmarks (http://wordpress.org/extend/plugins/simple-social-bookmarks): Another social bookmarking option, Simple Social Bookmarks features over 200 networks.
- SexyBookmarks (http://wordpress.org/extend/plugins/sexybookmarks): SexyBookmarks is a popular plugin to show off social sharing icons in a visually appealing way.

SUBSCRIPTION AND MOBILE PLUGINS

Most smartphones have had RSS support for quite some time, and a few high-end "regular" mobile phones as well. The natural next step is that we now consume more and more content through mobile devices, with customized versions of your site for the latest mobile phone from Apple, Google, or whatever the current craze is. The following plugins will help keep you mobile:

- Align RSS Images (http://wordpress.org/extend/plugins/align-rss-images): Images floating to the left and right on your site may be pretty to look at right there, but for RSS subscribers, that same image will be in the midst of everything. You can just skip floating images, but that's a shame. It's better to use Align RSS Images to parse the WordPress default align code (being `alignleft` and `alignright`) and swap for HTML equivalents to make things look good. No settings needed, just install it and forget about it.
- RSS Footer (http://wordpress.org/extend/plugins/rss-footer): RSS Footer adds a line at the beginning or at the end of every item in your RSS feed. This means that you can insert a copyright notice to make things harder on the scrapers or promote your site or other products to readers that prefer the feed to the original site. Very handy and easily customized.
- Disable RSS (http://wordpress.org/extend/plugins/disable-rss): This plugin does just what its name says: It disables the RSS feeds from a WordPress install. This can come in handy for static sites where RSS doesn't fulfill any purpose whatsoever.
- Subscribe2 (http://wordpress.org/extend/plugins/subscribe2): Subscribe2 is a really powerful plugin. It lets your users subscribe to your updates and hence get notifications via e-mail according to the settings you have. Perhaps you want to send a digest on a per-post basis, daily, or weekly. You can also send an e-mail to registered users, much like a traditional newsletter. The settings are easy enough to manage, as are the e-mail templates, so you can get started early on. As always, when it comes to sending e-mails, all hosts may not play nicely, so you should pay attention and do some tests to make sure that everything is being sent the way it is supposed to be. Also, there is the risk of being branded as a spammer in the eyes of ISPs, so use with caution.
- MobilePress (http://wordpress.org/extend/plugins/mobilepress): MobilePress is a cool plugin that serves a mobile theme rather than your regular one when the user is visiting from a mobile device. You can tell the plugin in which cases to serve the mobile theme and when not to, and there's even a theme interface similar to the standard one in WordPress so that you can create a mobile theme that fits your brand.

You also might like these mobile plugins:

- WordPress Mobile Edition (http://wordpress.org/extend/plugins/wordpress-mobile-edition): This is another plugin that gives your site a mobile interface when the visitor is using a mobile device.

- WordPress Mobile Pack (http://wordpress.org/extend/plugins/wordpress-mobile-pack): WordPress Mobile Pack is yet another solution for mobile visitors.

- WPtouch (http://wordpress.org/extend/plugins/wptouch): WPtouch adapts your site to mobile touch devices such as the iPhone or Android phones. There's a pro version if you need more than just the basic functionality.

SEO AND SEARCH PLUGINS

SEO stands for *search engine optimization,* and the whole idea is to get people to find your content. Luckily, you don't need to hire an SEO expert to get ahead in the game; there are plugins that will help you get started:

- All in One SEO Pack (http://wordpress.org/extend/plugins/all-in-one-seo-pack): This plugin adds more settings for your posts so that they'll be better optimized for search engines. A lot of people swear by it, and there's no doubt that it will help, even if you just leave it doing its thing automatically. To really push it, though, you should fine-tune each post all the time.

- WordPress SEO by Yoast (http://wordpress.org/extend/plugins/wordpress-seo): There are a lot of SEO plugins available, but Joost de Valk's WordPress SEO by Yoast is surely one of the more beloved ones. This plugin is really easy to get started with but offers a lot of options and data for the more dedicated user. Well worth a closer look if you feel you need an SEO plugin.

- Google XML Sitemaps (http://wordpress.org/extend/plugins/google-sitemap-generator): Google XML Sitemaps will create a compliant XML site map for your WordPress install and then update it whenever you publish something new or edit something old. This will help search engines crawl your content, which is a good thing. The plugin will even attempt to tell them that your site map is updated.

- Better Search (http://wordpress.org/extend/plugins/better-search): The built-in search functionality in WordPress is lacking, to say the least, which is why many users turn to plugins or Google Custom Search (http://google.com/cse). Better Search tries to change things by tuning the search, as well as adding popular searches and heat maps. Because it automatically replaces the built-in search, it is easy enough to give it a go.

- Search Unleashed (http://wordpress.org/extend/plugins/search-unleashed): Search Unleashed adds a bunch of settings and options for WordPress search functionality, such as keyword highlighting and extendable search engines. It also highlights incoming traffic search queries from sites such as Google, so if someone searches for "Apples" on Google and visits your site as a result, Search Unleashed will highlight "Apples." The plugin is localized, and you can even give priority to various parts of posts and Pages, as well as getting all those shortcodes properly searched should you rely on that. And best of all, no database changes! Check it out; this is one of the better search plugins out there.

■ HeadSpace2 SEO (http://wordpress.org/extend/plugins/headspace2): One of the more user-friendly SEO plugins out there is called *HeadSpace2 SEO*. It features great setup pages and does more than just tweak the metadata and descriptions. You can, for example, have it manage your Google Analytics settings, which is nice. Whether this is a better choice than any of the other SEO options out there probably depends on what you want to achieve and how you go about it, but it is certainly the most user-friendly one.

■ Robots Meta (http://wordpress.org/extend/plugins/robots-meta): Having a robots.txt for the search engines to crawl is a good thing, and Robots Meta helps you set one up by giving you simple settings for categories and other types of archives. Handy for SEO-knowledgeable people, for sure.

■ Global Translator (http://wordpress.org/extend/plugins/global-translator): Global Translator adds flags to your site using a widget, and then the user can get the site translated into his or her language — that is, if you enabled it and the translation engine used (Google Translate, BabelFish, and so on) supports it. Caching and permalinks for better SEO are among the features.

Here are a few more:

■ Search Everything (http://wordpress.org/extend/plugins/search-everything): Another search plugin, Search Everything has keyword highlighting and heavily expanded search parameters.

■ GD Press Tools (http://wordpress.org/extend/plugins/gd-press-tools): This plugin is not for the faint of heart. It adds a lot of customizing to everything from meta tags to custom fields and cron, so use with caution.

■ Breadcrumb Trail (http://wordpress.org/extend/plugins/breadcrumb-trail): Breadcrumb Trail is a breadcrumb script that lets you insert a breadcrumb link by adding the plugin's template tag. Similar to Yoast Breadcrumbs (http://wordpress.org/extend/plugins/breadcrumbs).

CODE AND OUTPUT PLUGINS

There are literally thousands of plugins to choose from in this category, and although a lot of them overlap and quite a few fulfill almost no purpose whatsoever, there are some that don't fit in anywhere in the preceding sections but are still worth mentioning. Most of those are related to custom code or are just small quirky things that can spice up a site by outputting the content differently. In other words, this is quite a mix:

■ SyntaxHighlighter Evolved (http://wordpress.org/extend/plugins/syntaxhighlighter): If you ever need to post chunks of programming code in your posts and on your Pages, from simple HTML to massive chunks of PHP, you know that the built-in parsing will get you in trouble. Sure, there are pastebins and the like, but why not solve this problem by adding the SyntaxHighlighter Evolved plugin, which not only takes care of your precious code, but also highlights it accordingly? It is stylable as well, so you can make the code boxes fit your content. Very neat. There are a bunch of other plugins that do similar things, but this one always performs.

- Blog Time (http://coffee2code.com/wp-plugins/blog-time): Blog Time outputs the time of the server in timestamp mode, either via a widget or the custom `blog_time()` template tag. It's not a clock; it's just the timestamp, which can be pretty handy sometimes.
- WP-Cumulus (http://wordpress.org/extend/plugins/wp-cumulus): Tired of your slack 2D tag cloud? Get one in 3D with WP-Cumulus and its rotating Flash rendition of the tag cloud. Flashy and fun, if nothing else, but I wouldn't recommend using it as the main navigation tool.
- wp-Typography (http://wordpress.org/extend/plugins/wp-typography): The wp-Typography plugin will improve your typography, obviously, which means that it will fix things such as not line-breaking unit values, and it will give you prettier quote marks, dashes, and things like that.
- Widget Logic (http://wordpress.org/extend/plugins/widget-logic): This plugin is as simple as it is brilliant. It adds one tiny little field to every widget, and that field takes conditional tags. This means that you can add checks such as `is_single()` to any widget, which makes it really simple to make a site dynamic.
- WP Super Cache (http://wordpress.org/extend/plugins/wp-super-cache): This is the must-have plugin for any WordPress site experiencing a lot of traffic but not wanting to go all haywire with the hardware. It lets you set up caching of your site, which means that it will serve static files rather than query the database all the time. If you plan on hitting the front page on Digg with your techblog and are on a share-hosting account, WP Super Cache will keep you online. It also is better maintained than its predecessor, WP-Cache. The only caveat with WP Super Cache is that it will cache dynamic output as well, which means that your most recent comments may not actually *be* the most recent ones anymore. You can handle that by controlling what should and shouldn't be cached.

    There's also W3 Total Cache (http://wordpress.org/extend/plugins/w3-total-cache), a great alternative to WP Super Cache. Try them both and figure out which one works best for your setup.
- Query Posts (http://wordpress.org/extend/plugins/query-posts): Query Posts is a really cool widget that lets you build your very own WordPress loop in the sidebar, without even having to know any PHP! It can be a very handy way to get custom output in the sidebar or any other widgetized area. It integrates nicely with the Get the Image plugin (http://wordpress.org/extend/plugins/get-the-image), which lets you grab an image from the post's content, a custom field, or even an attachment.

This list is short and sweet:

- WP-DBManager (http://wordpress.org/extend/plugins/wp-dbmanager): This helps to keep your database up to speed, with repairs as well as backup.
- Exec-PHP (http://wordpress.org/extend/plugins/exec-php): Exec-PHP lets you execute PHP code in posts, Pages, and text widgets. Make sure that you don't let anyone who doesn't know what they're doing loose with this tool!
- WP-PageNavi (http://wordpress.org/extend/plugins/wp-pagenavi): This plugin enhances the page navigation feature. It includes several styling settings, but you need to add the plugin's template tag to your theme files for it to work.

A FINAL CAVEAT: DO YOU REALLY NEED THAT PLUGIN?

It's easy to get carried away with plugins and additional functionality overall when working with WordPress. There is so much you can add and so many possibilities, and with the plugin install a mere click away now that you can do it from your admin interface, it's even harder to resist.

But resist you should. For every feature and every plugin you add, you'll bloat your install some more. Plugins can really slow down your site. It's not just the puny files sitting in the plugins folder; the problem is what they do to your database and the number of access requests and extra queries performed when you use them.

Don't get me wrong — plugins are nice. Some of the coolest WordPress sites just wouldn't be possible without plugins, and the extensive nature of the platform is one of the reasons it is so powerful and widely used. The fact that there's a whole appendix just talking about what plugins you should look closer at, and teasing you with what you can do with them, certainly counts for something!

Just don't go overboard; that's all I'm saying. Use plugins when you need them, but keep it as simple and as clean as you possibly can.

B STARTER THEMES

THERE IS AN abundance of themes for WordPress out there, of varying quality. Chances are most of these themes won't interest you, either because you don't like the look and feel of them or because they just aren't good enough for your needs. By now you know a thing or two about working with themes as well and how they are built, and you are capable of creating your own themes tailored to your needs. That means that you'll most likely want to create or modify a theme.

This appendix lists a select few themes that might save you time or inspire you to create better themes for your needs.

This appendix covers only free themes. There is a huge market for commercial themes out there, some good and some bad, just as with the free ones. If you go the commercial route, be sure to read up on the terms for using the theme and make sure that the theme is GPL compatible.

HOW TO PICK THE RIGHT THEME

Picking the right theme isn't easy. What you need to figure out is what you actually want and need. For example, if you're just looking to launch a site really quickly, maybe an existing theme is good enough for you, perhaps with some minor tweaks. On the other hand, if you want to build a theme framework, you might be looking for something completely different, something that matches the needs you have for this particular framework's use. Different situations call for different themes, so that is something you need to take into account.

If you want to build your own theme framework but want to kick-start the development, you want to look for a theme that is pretty close to what you want. This might mean that you go with something completely devoid of design, or maybe you pick a theme that looks okay out of the box, tweak it to your needs, and then continue development on your own. No matter which of those is true for you or if you end up in between, the thing to take away from this is that you're essentially forking a theme and creating your own. This means that when the theme you've chosen to use as a base for your theme framework is updated, you need to apply those updates to your theme yourself.

On the other hand, if you choose to use a theme framework as a basis, to save time and to get the benefits of the free updates of said theme, then you can get to work on your project much sooner. If you do go down this route, make sure that you pick a theme that stays up to date with WordPress and web technology in general. It is a good idea to pick a theme utilizing HTML5 because that is part of the web's future.

No matter what you choose, it is a good idea to keep an eye on the cutting edge stuff released because you might learn something.

THE TERM *FRAMEWORK*

Throughout this book, I've used the term *framework* pretty loosely. This is on purpose because there is certainly some confusion as to what is a framework, what is a starter theme, and what is a suitable parent theme. If you want to split hairs, most themes using the *framework* moniker aren't really frameworks — they are starter themes. Frameworks are generally functions and features you pull from to easily build whatever you want to be building.

This isn't the place to be nitpicking, though, or to upset theme developers who feel that their theme is a framework and not a starter theme. Pick whatever theme works for you, use it, and don't worry too much about the semantics.

A SELECTION OF THEMES

The following selection of themes is meant to inspire you in some fashion. Whether you want to create your own starter theme, just launch a site quickly, or want to find out how awesome a theme can be, this is where you start. The idea isn't to dazzle you with a beautiful design here, but rather to help you find good starting points for your own projects. Take from it what you need and figure out how to best put it to use for your projects.

TWENTY TEN AND TWENTY ELEVEN

It is pretty obvious, but the default themes for WordPress are a great way to learn about WordPress theming. Both Twenty Ten (http://wordpress.org/extend/themes/twentyten) and Twenty Eleven (http://wordpress.org/extend/themes/twentyeleven) are nice themes so you should make sure that you check them out (see Figure B-1). Also be sure to check out the HTML5-isation of Twenty Ten called *TwentyTen Five* (www.twentytenfive.com), which is a great example of how you can take an existing theme and make it something new and possibly better.

Figure B-1: The Twenty Eleven theme.

STARKERS

Starkers (http://starkerstheme.com) is a great theme to kick off your theme development (see Figure B-2). It is entirely devoid of any design whatsoever; basically it looks as if you are loading a site without a style sheet. The markup is good, so even if you don't want to use the actual theme, it might be a good idea to look through it to learn something. Or why not fork it and create your own theme framework? Starting out with Starkers is certainly a good idea; that's for sure.

Figure B-2: The Starkers theme is pretty, well, stark.

ROOTS

Roots (www.rootstheme.com) is built using the HTML5 Boilerplate (http://html5boilerplate.com) and several different grid systems that might be right up your alley (see Figure B-3). The theme itself does a lot with WordPress in terms of altering what `wp_head()` does, as well as rewrites URLs. You might not like that, but then again, you just might. There are also several settings for the Roots theme that give you further control of the theme. If nothing else, it is a great theme to learn from, even if you don't want to like it.

TOOLBOX

Toolbox (http://wordpress.org/extend/themes/toolbox) is a simple theme using HTML5 and is meant to be styled using CSS particularly (see Figure B-4). The purpose of the Toolbox theme isn't to be pretty out of the box (pun intended); you need to add your own graphics, colors, fonts, and so on to this one. This theme is worth checking out when you need to get that good-looking site up really quickly but want a pretty straightforward content flow. In those cases, you'll get pretty far by just adding some CSS and graphics to the Toolbox theme.

Smashing WordPress

-
-
-

Lorem Ipsum

Lorem ipsum dolor sit amet, consectetur adipiscing elit. Nullam in dui mauris. Vivamus hendrerit arcu sed erat molestie vehicula. Sed auctor neque eu tellus rhoncus ut eleifend nibh porttitor. Ut in nulla enim. Phasellus molestie magna non est.

Bibendum non venenatis nisl tempor. Suspendisse dictum feugiat nisl ut dapibus. Mauris iaculis porttitor posuere. Praesent id metus massa, ut blandit odio. Proin quis tortor orci. Etiam at risus et justo dignissim congue. Donec congue lacinia dui, a porttitor lectus condimentum laoreet. Nunc eu ullamcorper orci. Quisque eget odio ac lectus vestibulum faucibus eget in metus. In pellentesque faucibus vestibulum. Nulla at nulla justo, eget luctus tortor. Nulla facilisi. Duis aliquet egestas purus in blandit. Curabitur vulputate, ligula lacinia scelerisque.

Tempor, lacus lacus ornare ante, ac egestas est urna sit amet arcu. Class aptent taciti sociosqu ad litora torquent per conubia nostra, per inceptos himenaeos. Sed molestie augue sit amet leo consequat posuere. Vestibulum ante ipsum.

Primis in faucibus orci luctus et ultrices posuere cubilia Curae; Proin vel ante a orci tempus eleifend ut et magna. Lorem ipsum dolor sit amet, consectetur adipiscing elit. Vivamus luctus urna sed urna ultricies ac tempor dui sagittis. In condimentum facilisis porta. Sed nec diam eu diam mattis viverra. Nulla fringilla, orci ac euismod semper, magna diam porttitor mauris, quis sollicitudin sapien justo.

In libero. Vestibulum mollis mauris enim. Morbi euismod magna ac lorem rutrum elementum. Donec viverra auctor lobortis. Pellentesque eu est a nulla placerat dignissim. Morbi a enim in magna semper bibendum. Etiam scelerisque, nunc ac egestas consequat, odio nibh euismod nulla, eget auctor orci nibh vel nisi. Aliquam erat volutpat. Mauris vel neque sit amet nunc gravida congue sed sit amet purus. Quisque lacus quam, egestas ac tincidunt a, lacinia vel velit. Aenean facilisis nulla vitae urna tincidunt congue.

Sed ut dui. Morbi malesuada nulla nec purus convallis consequat. Vivamus id mollis quam. Morbi ac commodo nulla. In condimentum orci id nisl volutpat bibendum.

Quisque commodo hendrerit lorem quis egestas. Maecenas quis tortor arcu. Vivamus rutrum nunc non neque consectetur quis placerat neque lobortis. Nam vestibulum, arcu sodales feugiat consectetur, nisl orci bibendum elit, eu euismod magna sapien ut nibh. Donec semper quam scelerisque tortor.

Dictum gravida. In hac habitasse platea dictumst. Nam pulvinar, odio sed rhoncus suscipit, sem diam ultrices mauris, eu consequat purus metus eu velit. Proin metus odio, aliquam eget molestie nec, gravida ut sapien. Phasellus quis est sed turpis sollicitudin venenatis sed eu odio. Praesent eget neque eu eros interdum malesuada.

Non vel leo. Sed fringilla porta ligula egestas tincidunt. Nullam risus magna, ornare vitae varius eget, scelerisque a libero. Morbi eu porttitor ipsum. Nullam lorem nisi, posuere quis volutpat eget, luctus nec massa. Pellentesque aliquam lacinia tellus sit amet bibendum. Ut posuere justo in enim pretium scelerisque. Etiam ornare vehicula euismod. Vestibulum at risus augue. Sed non semper dolor. Sed fringilla consequat velit a porta. Pellentesque sed lectus pharetra ipsum ultricies commodo non sit amet velit.

Suspendisse volutpat lobortis ipsum, in scelerisque nisi iaculis a. Duis pulvinar lacinia commodo. Integer in lorem id nibh luctus aliquam. Sed elementum, est ac sagittis porttitor, neque metus ultricies ante, in accumsan massa nisi non metus. Vivamus.

Sagittis quam a lacus dictum tempor. Nullam in semper ipsum. Cras a est id massa malesuada tincidunt. Etiam a urna tellus. Ut rutrum vehicula dui, eu cursus magna tincidunt pretium. Donec

Figure B-3: The Roots theme.

Smashing WordPress

Just another WordPress site

Home   Archives   Post a recipe for us   Sample Page   Submit a guest blog post

Lorem Ipsum

Posted on February 6, 2012

Lorem ipsum dolor sit amet, consectetur adipiscing elit. Nullam in dui mauris. Vivamus hendrerit arcu sed erat molestie vehicula. Sed auctor neque eu tellus rhoncus ut eleifend nibh porttitor. Ut in nulla enim. Phasellus molestie magna non est.

Bibendum non venenatis nisl tempor. Suspendisse dictum feugiat nisl ut dapibus. Mauris iaculis porttitor posuere. Praesent id metus massa, ut blandit odio. Proin quis tortor orci. Etiam at risus et justo dignissim congue. Donec congue lacinia dui, a porttitor lectus condimentum laoreet. Nunc eu ullamcorper orci. Quisque eget odio ac lectus vestibulum faucibus eget in metus. In pellentesque faucibus vestibulum. Nulla at nulla justo, eget luctus tortor. Nulla facilisi. Duis aliquet egestas purus in blandit. Curabitur vulputate, ligula lacinia scelerisque.

Tempor, lacus lacus ornare ante, ac egestas est urna sit amet arcu. Class aptent taciti sociosqu ad litora torquent per conubia nostra, per inceptos himenaeos. Sed molestie augue sit amet leo consequat posuere. Vestibulum ante ipsum.

Primis in faucibus orci luctus et ultrices posuere cubilia Curae; Proin vel ante a orci tempus eleifend ut et magna. Lorem ipsum dolor sit amet, consectetur adipiscing elit. Vivamus luctus urna sed urna ultricies ac tempor dui sagittis. In condimentum facilisis porta. Sed nec diam eu diam mattis viverra. Nulla fringilla, orci ac euismod semper, magna diam porttitor mauris, quis sollicitudin sapien justo.

In libero. Vestibulum mollis mauris enim. Morbi euismod magna ac lorem rutrum elementum. Donec viverra auctor lobortis. Pellentesque eu est a nulla placerat dignissim. Morbi a enim in magna semper bibendum. Etiam scelerisque, nunc ac egestas consequat, odio nibh euismod nulla, eget auctor orci nibh vel nisi. Aliquam erat volutpat. Mauris vel neque sit amet nunc gravida congue sed sit amet purus. Quisque lacus quam, egestas ac tincidunt a, lacinia vel velit. Aenean facilisis nulla vitae urna tincidunt congue.

Sed ut dui. Morbi malesuada nulla nec purus convallis consequat. Vivamus id mollis quam. Morbi ac commodo nulla. In condimentum orci id nisl volutpat bibendum.

Quisque commodo hendrerit lorem quis egestas. Maecenas quis tortor arcu. Vivamus rutrum nunc non neque consectetur quis placerat neque lobortis. Nam vestibulum, arcu sodales feugiat consectetur, nisl orci bibendum elit, eu euismod magna sapien ut nibh. Donec semper quam scelerisque tortor.

Dictum gravida. In hac habitasse platea dictumst. Nam pulvinar, odio sed rhoncus suscipit, sem diam ultrices mauris, eu consequat purus metus eu velit. Proin metus odio, aliquam eget molestie nec, gravida ut sapien. Phasellus quis est sed turpis sollicitudin venenatis sed eu odio. Praesent eget neque eu eros interdum malesuada.

Non vel leo. Sed fringilla porta ligula egestas tincidunt. Nullam risus magna, ornare vitae varius eget, scelerisque a libero. Morbi eu porttitor ipsum. Nullam lorem nisi, posuere quis volutpat eget, luctus nec massa. Pellentesque aliquam lacinia tellus sit amet bibendum. Ut posuere justo in enim pretium scelerisque. Etiam ornare vehicula euismod. Vestibulum at risus augue. Sed non semper dolor. Sed fringilla consequat velit a porta. Pellentesque sed lectus pharetra ipsum ultricies commodo non sit amet velit.

Suspendisse volutpat lobortis ipsum, in scelerisque nisi iaculis a. Duis pulvinar lacinia commodo. Integer in lorem id nibh luctus aliquam. Sed elementum, est ac sagittis porttitor, neque metus ultricies ante, in accumsan massa nisl non metus. Vivamus.

A text widget

This is a text widget, placed here just for the sake of having something to show off. Enjoy it!

Archives

- February 2012
- January 2012
- December 2011
- November 2011
- January 2011

Recent Posts

- Lorem Ipsum
- Image embed test
- Lorem ipsum review
- The product title
- No love

Figure B-4: The Toolbox theme is a great start.

CONSTELLATION

The Constellation Theme (http://constellationtheme.com) is a pretty simple HTML5 theme built using the HTML5 Boilerplate (see Figure B-5). The theme uses media queries to adapt to various resolutions, although not using a fully fluid layout. It is worth a look if you want to get a kick-start on a straightforward content project or just want to get more accustomed to media queries.

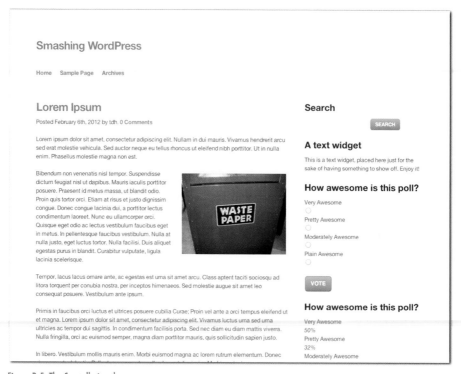

Figure B-5: The Constellation theme.

SPECTACULAR

Spectacular (http://bit.ly/hJQpjn) is a very visual theme included here more as an inspiration than as something you might want to use for your projects (see Figure B-6). It is a good example of how a theme can be extremely visual and more or less suited for smaller sites. The layout of the content is a good fit for smaller sites, and analyzing it could be useful for your future projects.

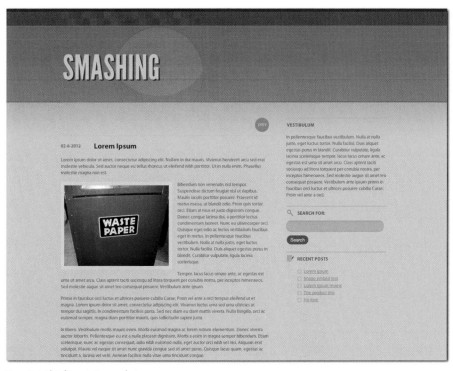

Figure B-6: This theme is Spectacular!

BONES

Bones (http://themble.com/bones) is an HTML5 theme available in both a simple standard (called *Classic*) version (see Figure B-7), as well as a Responsive fluid version. It can be both a nice starting point for building just about any website.

Figure B-7: The Bones theme is a Classic.

YOUR THEME, YOUR RULES

No matter what theme you choose, remember that although someone else might've done the bulk of the work, you're the one who is using it. Don't be afraid to change things, to make it your own, and to continue development. Give credit where credit is due, by all means, and if you have a fancy solution for something, do share it with the community if you will.

The themes listed in this appendix are by no means graphical or even particularly good-looking in their original form. The idea is for you to use them as a stepping stone, allowing you to save time on development and even get a head start consisting of great WordPress code. Sometimes it will be enough to just add CSS and visuals, styling the themes to look and feel the way you want. Other times, you'll fork them entirely, create your own theme, and take it from there. For example, the Swedish blog Nutopia (http://nutopia.se) uses a simple HTML5 core and is mostly CSS and visuals (see Figure B-8).

Figure B-8: The Swedish blog Nutopia.

No matter what you end up with, know that picking a starter theme can save you time and help you get started. Even if it means that you'll have to create the perfect starter theme yourself, they are a good idea all in all.

Now get building and publishing; that's what WordPress is there for!

INDEX

SMASHING
Web Design Series

Second Edition

Thord Daniel Hedengren

SMASHING
WordPress

BEYOND THE BLOG

978-1-119-99596-5

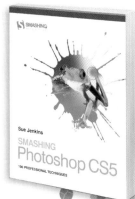

Sue Jenkins

SMASHING
Photoshop CS5

100 PROFESSIONAL TECHNIQUES

978-0-470-66153-6

Eric Meyer

SMASHING
CSS

PROFESSIONAL TECHNIQUES FOR MODERN LAYOUT

978-0-470-68416-0

Bill Sanders

SMASHING
HTML5

978-0-470-97727-9

Jake Rutter

SMASHING
jQuery

978-0-470-97723-1

Thord Daniel Hedengren

SMASHING
WordPress Themes

MAKING WORDPRESS BEAUTIFUL

978-0-470-66990-7

Jesmond Allen and James Chudley

SMASHING
UX DESIGN

FOUNDATIONS FOR DESIGNING ONLINE USER EXPERIENCES

978-0-470-66685-2

Gareth Hardy

SMASHING
Logo Design

THE ART OF CREATING VISUAL IDENTITIES

978-1-119-99332-2

Professional Web Design

THE BEST OF SMASHING MAGAZINE

978-1-119-99275-2

Successful Freelancing for Web Designers

THE BEST OF SMASHING MAGAZINE

978-1-119-99273-8

Cameron Chapman

The Smashing Idea Book

FROM INSPIRATION TO APPLICATION

978-1-119-97742-1

WILEY
Now you know.